MONTR

THE
ULTIMATE
GUIDE

MONTREAL

THE
ULTIMATE
GUIDE

Anne Smith and Brian Pel
with Louis Fortier

Chronicle Books ● San Francisco

Published in Canada by Douglas & McIntyre Ltd., Vancouver/Toronto.

Library of Congress Cataloging-in-Publication Data available.
ISBN: 0-8118-0145-4

Printed and bound in Canada
Production coordinator: Terri Wershler
Editor: Maja Grip
Photographs by Brian Pel (except where noted)
Maps by Fiona MacGregor
Cover design by RayMahDesign,Inc
Cover photo by Jurgen Vogt
Type by Vancouver Desktop Publishing Centre

10 9 8 7 6 5 4 3 2 1

Chronicle Books
275 Fifth Street
San Francisco, California 94103

For our parents and Andrew

ACKNOWLEDGEMENTS

Writing a guidebook is a lot of work and requires the assistance and encouragement of a great many people. We are particularly grateful to Maja Grip, our editor, and Terri Wershler of Douglas and McIntyre, who have made the experience enjoyable for us. We would like to thank the following individuals for helping us gather the information and illustrations in the book: Pierre Bellrose of the Office des Congrès et du Tourisme du Grand Montréal; Maurice Boucher, Phyllis Lambert and Daniela Renosto of the Canadian Centre for Architecture; René Cadieux; Normand Charbonneau of the Archives Nationales du Québec; Louis-Alain Ferron of the Communauté Urbaine de Montréal; Catherine Guex and Pierre Théberge of the Montreal Museum of Fine Arts; Normand Julien, Nicole Rodrigue and Ginnette Gauthier of the Ville de Montréal; Nicholas Kasirer and François Roy.

We would also like to express our appreciation to Louis Fortier, who, with the able assistance of Clodelle Rondeau, researched portions of the book and prepared the Transportation and Essential Information chapters. Thanks are also due to Miyako Tomita, who typed much of the manuscript in her usual efficient fashion, and to Robert White, who printed many of the photographs.

Finally, a special thanks to Maurice Forget, well-known Montreal corporate lawyer, *bon vivant* and man-about-town, for contributing the first-rate Restaurants chapter.

CONTENTS

LIST OF MAPS

ABOUT MONTREAL

AN INTERNATIONAL CITY

Montreal, Canada's second-largest urban centre, is a thriving cosmopolitan city that attracts more than five million visitors annually. Many come to see the excellent museums, world-famous Olympic Park and charming Old Montreal with its horse-drawn carriages, outdoor cafés and historic buildings. Jazz, comedy, film and even fireworks keep Montreal active on the international festival circuit. Grand Prix Formula 1 racing, the Expos baseball club and, of course, the Canadiens hockey team have all helped Montreal achieve international recognition in the field of sport. Shopping here is the envy of other Canadian cities, and there are more than 5000 restaurants offering everything from superb French cuisine to good old Montreal favourites like *poutine* and smoked meat sandwiches.

A recent American study ranked Montreal one of the three most live-able cities in the world. Montreal has less air pollution and fewer traffic jams than any other city in Canada. A healthy mix of residential and commercial development, parklands and bicycle paths has resulted in a series of vibrant neighbourhoods throughout the island. This means that you won't find many deserted streets on weekends, and you can enjoy a very Montreal pastime— people watching— from the comfortable vantage point of almost any café.

You will find English speakers nearly everywhere you go in Montreal, but your eyes will tell you that French is the official language of business and government. Francophone Québécois, who number 5.7 million, remain fearful of their future on a continent of 267 million English

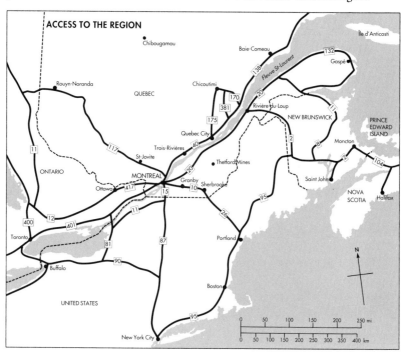

2

speakers. Two successive draconian French-only language laws, commonly referred to as Bills 101 and 178, were intended to protect francophones' cultural identity—but did so at the expense of anglophone and allophone (those whose first language is neither English nor French) minorities. These laws have had some bizarre effects on previously bilingual signage and have led to impassioned debates on the permissibility of words like "hotdog" on storefronts.

GETTING ORIENTED

Montreal is on an island in the St. Lawrence River, a major waterway that leads northeast to the Atlantic Ocean and southwest to the Great Lakes via the St. Lawrence Seaway. The city's most salient feature is unquestionably the mountain. One of the first things that every visitor should do is head to Mount Royal for a panoramic view of the city. Looking to the southeast, you will see the McGill University campus and the skyscrapers of the downtown core. Farther east, along the waterfront, are the narrow streets and low-rise buildings of Old Montreal. You will also be able to see the St. Lawrence and two small islands, Île Ste-Hélène and Île Notre-Dame, with their many fine sports and recreational facilities.

It's sometimes hard to remember that Mount Royal and most of the city of Montreal are on an island. This has a lot to do with its size. The island of Montreal is 50 km (31 mi.) long and 14 km (8½ mi.) wide and is linked to the north and south shores of the mainland by an efficient system of roads and bridges. Chances are, though, that you will spend much of

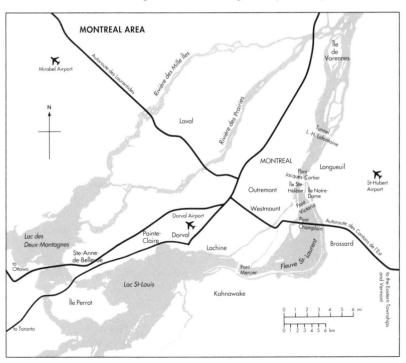

your time on the island as this is where you'll find most of the major sights.

Montreal is remarkably accessible to visitors. Given the proximity of many major attractions, a good deal of sightseeing can be comfortably done on foot. Public transit is also excellent and the cleanliness of the *métro* (subway) stations is a source of civic pride. Finding your way around Montreal is easy. Two of the principal east-west streets are Sherbrooke and Ste-Catherine. Several museums and art galleries are located on Sherbrooke ouest (west), while Ste-Catherine ouest is the place to go for serious shopping. To the east of St-Laurent, these streets change from "ouest" to "est" (east). In other words, St-Laurent (commonly referred to as the Main) serves as the divide between west and east. Other major east-west arteries downtown are de Maisonneuve, René-Lévesque and Notre-Dame; the other main north-south arteries are Atwater, Côte-des-Neiges, Guy, St-Denis and Berri.

Visitors to the city should be aware of the aggressive nature of Montreal's drivers. Picture New York's cabbies driving blindfolded, and you'll get the right idea. Be very, very careful and *never* assume that an approaching vehicle will stop—even if you have the right of way or are standing in a crosswalk.

When they are not behind the wheel of a car, Montrealers really know how to unwind. This will become especially obvious when you go out at night. Most bars and clubs stay open until 3 AM and are usually jam-packed on weekends. Even the long lineups outside the more popular watering holes don't seem to dampen the enthusiam of local *bons vivants*.

It is important to distinguish between the *city* of Montreal and the

COMMUNAUTÉ
URBAINE
DE MONTRÉAL

island of Montreal. The city is only one of the 29 municipalities on the island. The Montreal Urban Community (MUC) administers inter-municipal services for the member municipalities on the island of Montreal and several adjoining smaller islands. The MUC has jurisdiction over property assessment, air quality, food inspection, mass transit, and the like. The *metropolitan Montreal region* includes the municipalities to the north and south of the MUC, from the lower Laurentians to the Richelieu River.

MONTREAL'S PRINCIPAL DISTRICTS

It would be impossible to do justice to all of Montreal's fascinating neighbourhoods in just a few pages. As you tour the city on your own, you are sure to stumble across many charming side streets and interesting sights never mentioned in any tourist guide. The *quartiers* (districts) described here include the principal tourist areas (Old Montreal, downtown and the St-Denis Latin Quarter) and several neighbourhoods that, in our opinion, reflect the spirit of the city. When our friends come to visit us, this is where we take them.

OLD MONTREAL
A walk through Le Vieux-Montréal is always a big hit with tourists. With its

narrow streets, numerous historic buildings and monuments, many fine restaurants and lively cafés, Old Montreal's atmosphere is both delightful and very European in feel. Thirty years ago, the area wasn't nearly as attractive. Many of the handsome buildings that now bustle with activity either stood empty or were in disrepair. A number of notable buildings had already been demolished to make way for parking lots and high-rise office towers. Eventually a grassroots citizens' movement led to the establishment of the Viger Commission in 1962. The commission, named after Montreal's first mayor, had as its mandate the preservation and restoration of the entire *quartier*. One of its first successful acts was to persuade the provincial government to declare Old Montreal a designated historic area. Consequently, the demolition of additional buildings was arrested and any new construction or restoration, either exterior or interior, was closely scrutinized. More recently, extensive work has been done to the Vieux-Port (Old Port) area immediately south of Old Montreal. The long-term result has been the successful rejuvenation of one of Montreal's most interesting neighbourhoods. See Sightseeing (Attractions) for more on what to see in Old Montreal.

DOWNTOWN

Downtown Montreal is a sprawling area roughly bordered by Atwater to the west, St-Laurent to the east, des Pins to the north and St-Antoine to the south. Here you will find the major hotels and shopping areas, two of the city's best museums, the McGill University campus, Chinatown, hundreds of restaurants and bars, much of the financial district and the vast subterranean network known as the underground city.

In recent years, the focus of Montreal's downtown has shifted to the east; the construction of Place des Arts, Complexe Desjardins and the Palais des Congrès (Convention Centre) upset the notion that the intersection of Ste-Catherine and Peel was the true centre of the city. At the moment, that centre lies somewhere near the intersection of de Maisonneuve and University.

There are innumerable points of departure for tours of the downtown area. If you wish to begin at the centre, exit the *métro* at McGill. Head south two blocks on University, where you'll see a large cruciform building known as Place Ville-Marie, Montreal's first truly modern office/commercial development, opened in 1962. Below Place Ville-Marie you'll find a large shopping mall, which connects with a vast network of other malls, commercial towers, hotels, the train station and the métro. This is the famous underground city. While it's an interesting concept and an entirely practical solution to the ravages of Montreal's winter, we don't recommend that you spend much time there.

Principal streets in the downtown area include Sherbrooke, with its many art galleries, expensive boutiques, luxury hotels and *antiquaires*; Ste-Catherine, a shopping mecca with all the big department stores; and the trendy trio of Bishop, de la Montagne and Crescent streets. The latter are lined with handsome stone townhouses, which have been transformed into specialty shops, restaurants and numerous popular bars that come alive after dark. Montrealers are waiting to see if these charmers will survive a recent wave of questionable redevelopment in the area.

Downtown Montreal boasts a large number of opulent residences built by

The Montreal skyline at night, taken from Mount Royal.

the wealthy of previous generations. By the turn of the century, the area bordered by René-Lévesque (then named Dorchester), Guy, des Pins and University had become known as the Golden Square Mile, and it was estimated that the neighbourhood's prosperous residents controlled 70 per cent of Canada's wealth. The railway boom had fuelled a building frenzy on the area's steep slopes. Fabulous mansions were erected at close quarters in a wide variety of styles; Sherbrooke was suddenly the most desirable address. Sadly, the eventual expansion of Montreal's commercial district heralded the prestigious neighbourhood's decline. As wealthy residents gradually moved to Westmount and Outremont, many impressive houses fell to the wrecker's ball, particularly during the high-rise building craze of the 1960s and early '70s.

Almost every large Canadian city has a Chinatown, and Montreal is no exception. Most of the city's diminu-

tive Chinatown is located along de la Gauchetière between Jeanne-Mance and St-Laurent. The Chinese community here traces its roots to the late

"High tech" street cleaning.

19th century, when thousands of Chinese labourers came over to work on the Canadian Pacific Railway. The Chinese suffered miserable working conditions and low wages. They lived apart from the English and French communities where, at the time, they were not well accepted. Today's Chinatown is still home to a number of Chinese-Canadian families but the specialty shops and restaurants here also attract many who live outside the neighbourhood. Anyone who likes exotic shopping and good Chinese food will enjoy spending time in Chinatown. It's best to visit on Saturday or Sunday, when the neighbourhood is at its bustling best.

ST-DENIS
(THE LATIN QUARTER)

Since the 1920s, St-Denis has been the intellectual and cultural mecca of French Canada. This is a *très chic* area of cafés, restaurants and fashionable boutiques. While goods here tend to be almost as expensive as downtown, you will also find much less mass-produced merchandise. The neighbourhood is also part student ghetto (McGill and the University of Quebec at Montreal are not far away) and part bohemia. One of the best areas for nightlife, St-Denis caters to a young, trendy and mostly francophone crowd. Walking north from de Maisonneuve, you will soon find the lively spots. Watch for the handsome *carré* (square) St-Louis, a lovely park surrounded by charming Victorian houses, where you can skate in winter. At the western end of the park is Prince Arthur, a great street for restaurants and nightlife, as is Duluth (several blocks to the north). Many of the restaurants on these two streets permit patrons to bring their own wine with them, which makes for a cheap evening out.

Buildings of note in the St-Denis area include the 1898 Bruce Price-designed **Gare-Hôtel Viger** in Carré Viger, the 1916 **Théâtre St-Denis** (1594 St-Denis) where the legendary Sarah Bernhardt performed, and the 1914 **Bibliothèque Nationale du Québec** (1700 St-Denis).

BOULEVARD ST-LAURENT (THE MAIN)

This culturally diverse neighbourhood screams with personality. Don't expect to find anything too fancy. To the contrary, the Main is simply a slice of life, Montreal style. The area has lots of excellent and inexpensive restaurants and is home to several of the city's best bagel shops. Montrealers have lively divisions of opinion over which sells the city's best bagels. Is it Fairmount Bagel (74 Fairmount ouest) or the Bagel Shop (158 and 263 St-Viateur)? Even we can't agree on that one. Mordecai Richler fans will recognize Willensky's Restaurant (also on Fairmount) where the special (bologna on white) is a Montreal institution.

During the day, St-Laurent is a great place to do your grocery shopping, as there are a number of first-rate specialty food shops in the several blocks north of des Pins. At night, the street switches gear—trendy nightclubs and bars attract sleek, elegant types whose diets would never include bologna. Dress well, and leave your tourist maps at home.

PLATEAU MONT-ROYAL

This area just east of the mountain along Ave. Mont-Royal is commonly called the Plateau and is well known for its many distinct ethnic neighbourhoods (*petites patries*). The Plateau has the highest population density of

7

any area on the island, yet you won't find any large apartment buildings. The neighbourhood is a densely woven tapestry of tenants and shop-keepers who co-exist in crowded low-rises. Saturday morning ushers in a marvellous bustle of activity on the Plateau as Montrealers of various cultures run their errands in a multiplicity of languages. This is a wonderful area to visit for those who have an interest in successful urban planning.

WESTMOUNT

Westmount has one of Montreal's most beautiful parks (Westmount Park), one of its most compact and exclusive shopping areas (along Greene) and some of Montreal's most gorgeous (and expensive) houses. While you can simply head up the mountain anywhere in Westmount to see some of these palaces, we suggest that you make a point of seeing the **Hurtubise House** (563 Côte-St- Antoine), the only remaining 17th-century farmhouse in Westmount; **Braemar** (3219 The Boulevard), an 1830s house with a

two-storey veranda seemingly more suited to the Old South than Montreal; and the former **Timmins House** (55 and 65 Belvedere), a huge mansion that has literally been sawn into two.

OUTREMONT

Primarily residential, the neighbourhood of Outremont (its name means "beyond the mountain") also has three good shopping streets: densely populated Van Horne, home to a large Jewish community, has an excellent assortment of modern stores and old-fashioned family businesses; Bernard, with its popular repertory moviehouse, Cinéma Outremont, and several good restaurants, caters to the young crowd; Laurier has all the bourgeois inclinations of Paris's sixteenth *arrondissement. Bon chic, bon genre* residents trotting tense little pooches can even pop into a prized local outlet of Paris's Pâtisserie Lenôtre for sublime *petits-fours*.

The earliest European settlers to the area were British farmers. By the late 1800s, several wealthy

The Timmins House at 55/65 Belvedere was cut in two to create a second residence.

Montrealers had acquired property in Outremont, either for country residences or for real estate speculation. The expansion of the city of Montreal and the establishment of a railway yard in Outremont spurred rapid urbanization after 1900. Luckily, the politicians of the period had the foresight to set aside a considerable amount of parkland. They also decided to bury ugly telephone and electrical wires, and Outremont became the first Canadian city to light its streets using underground cables.

Buildings of note in Outremont include the 1915 beaux-arts **Académie Querbes** (215 Bloom-

Residential buildings on the fringes of Outremont.

field); the early 19th-century **Outremont City Hall**, thought to have been a Hudson's Bay trading post (543 Côte Ste-Catherine); and **Henri Bourassa House** (221-223 McDougall) home of the politician, journalist and founder of the Montreal daily *Le Devoir*.

HISTORY

NATIVE PEOPLE
What is now the island of Montreal was originally inhabited by various native peoples. Just before the first European contact, Hurons lived in the pallisaded village of Hochelaga.

EXPLORATION AND SETTLEMENT
Colonial Era, French Regime (1534-1760)

1535 French explorer Jacques Cartier visits the island and names the mountain Le Mont Royal in honour of the French king, Francis I. (By this time, Hochelaga had completely disappeared, the Hurons having been driven westward by the powerful first league of the Iroquois, the Five Nations, later the Six Nations. Champlain had assisted the Algonkin and Montagnais in their struggle against the Five Nations. In consequence, the Iroquois became bitter enemies of the French until their defeat by Frontenac in 1696. The descendants of the Six Nations converted to Christianity by French missionaries continue to inhabit reserves in the Montreal area.)

1611 Samuel de Champlain, French explorer and founder of Quebec City, visits the island and builds a small fort.

1642 Sent by the Compagnie des Cent Associés, Paul de Chomedey, Sieur de Maisonneuve, founds a colony named Ville-Marie de Montréal in honour of the Virgin Mary. The stated objective of the colony is to Christianize the native Indian population.

1643 The colony narrowly escapes the ravages of a major flood. To celebrate Ville-Marie's deliverance, Sieur

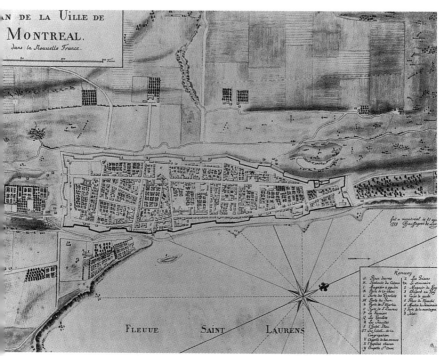

N DE LA UILLE DE
MONTREAL.
Dans la Nouvelle France.

FLEUVE   SAINT   LAURENS

One of the earliest maps of Montreal, executed by Chaussegros de Lévy in 1729.
(Archives nationales du Québec)

de Maisonneuve erects a wooden cross on Mount Royal.

1663 New France, with a population of about 10,000, officially becomes a French Crown colony. The religious order of the Messieurs de St-Sulpice is granted title to all the lands on the island of Montreal.

1672 The father superior of the Sulpicians, François Dollier de Casson, lays out and names the first streets.

1682 Montreal becomes the head office of the Compagnie du Nord, the main competitor of the Hudson's Bay Company.

1701 The governor of New France signs a peace treaty with the Iroquois Confederacy. Montreal prospers and becomes the commercial centre of New France.

1716-36 Construction of a wall around the city is begun by French engineer Gaspard-Joseph Chaussegros de Lévy. (The wall surrounded what is now the section of Old Montreal bounded by McGill, Berri, St-Jacques and the St. Lawrence River. It was demolished between 1803 and 1820.)

1756 Europe's Seven Years' War extends to the New World colonies.

1759 Battle of the Plains of Abraham near Quebec City. Forces led by British general James Wolfe defeat those of the Marquis de Montcalm. Both Wolfe and Montcalm die of wounds received in the battle.

1760 The governor general of New France, the Marquis de Vaudreuil-Cavagnal, signs a treaty with British general Jeffrey Amherst, ceding control of New France to England.

1760-63 The British military govern New France.

1763 The Seven Years' War ends with the signing of the Treaty of Paris, and New France officially becomes a British colony.

Colonial era, English regime

1774 Under the Quebec Act, French civil law is re-established and guarantees are given respecting freedom of the French language and the Roman Catholic religion.

1775-76 Occupation of Montreal by the revolutionary American Continental Army. Benjamin Franklin tries to persuade the local people to join the American cause.

1778 Montreal's first newspaper, the bilingual *La Gazette de commerce et littéraire*, is published by Benjamin Franklin and printed by Fleury de Mesplet. (The paper is now the daily *Gazette*.)

1791 Under the Constitutional Act of 1791, Canada is divided into Upper Canada (what is now the core of Ontario) and Lower Canada (now Quebec).

1792 Montreal is divided into eastern and western sectors by Boulevard St-Laurent.

1801 A waterworks is established to provide running water.

1821 McGill College receives its Royal Charter.

1824 Opening of the Lachine Canal.

1832 Royal assent given by William IV to a law incorporating the city of Montreal.

1833 Jacques Viger becomes the first mayor of Montreal.

1837 Revolt of the French-Canadian Patriotes, led by Louis-Joseph Papineau. A parallel rebellion is led in Upper Canada by William Lyon Mackenzie.

1841 Under the Act of Union, Upper and Lower Canada are reunited and become the Province of Canada.

1844 Montreal becomes the capital of the united Canada. (In 1849 the Parliament building is destroyed by fire, and Quebec City becomes the new capital a year later.)

1866 Adoption of the Civil Code of Lower Canada.

CONFEDERATION

1867 The British Parliament passes the British North America Act. The confederation of the Province of Canada (now Quebec and Ontario) with New Brunswick and Nova Scotia creates the Dominion of Canada.

1876 Branch of Université Laval of Quebec City established in Montreal.

1884 The French-language daily *La Presse* is founded.

1924 Beginning of the construction of St. Joseph's Oratory.

1931 Opening of the Montreal Botanical Garden.

1934 The Société des concerts symphoniques de Montreal is founded. (In 1953, it becomes the Montreal Symphony Orchestra.)

1943 Opening of the Université de Montréal building on Mount Royal.

Rush hour, circa 1937. (Archives nationales du Québec)

POST-WW II

1954 Jean Drapeau is elected mayor of Montreal. (He serves in this position for more than 20 years and has a seminal influence on the city's modern-day development.)

1959 Opening of the St. Lawrence Seaway.

1962 Opening of Place Ville-Marie, the first major office and commercial complex in Montreal.

1963 Opening of Place des Arts.

1966 Opening of the Montreal Métro.

1967 Canada's centennial. The city hosts Expo '67. Opening of Château Champlain Hotel.

1970 Robert Bourassa of the Liberal Party is elected premier of Quebec. The kidnapping of a British trade commissioner and murder of a provincial cabinet minister by the Front de libération du Québec (FLQ), an extremist Quebec separatist group, leads to the imposition

of martial law for a short time. Creation of the Montreal Urban Community.

1976 The Summer Games of the XXI Olympiad are held in Montreal. René Lévesque of the separatist Parti Québécois is elected premier of Quebec. The objective of the party is to make Quebec an independent state and French the only official language.

1977 Adoption of Bill 101. French becomes the official language of Quebec and particularly of education, commerce and business.

1980 In a provincial referendum, a majority of Quebeckers vote against leaving the Canadian confederation.

1982 Robert Bourassa is again elected premier of Quebec.

1983 Opening of the Palais des Congrès, Montreal's convention centre.

1986 Jean Doré of the Rassemblement des citoyens de Montréal is elected mayor of Montreal.

Market day in Place Jacques-Cartier, circa 1940. (Archives nationales du Québec)

1988 The Quebec government adopts Bill 178. Use of the English language on signs outside buildings is forbidden. English signs are allowed inside buildings, but French signs must predominate.

1989 Opening of the Canadian Centre for Architecture.

1992 350th anniversary of the founding of Montreal.

POPULATION

According to the 1986 census, the population of the city of Montreal is 1,015,000. The Montreal Urban Community has 1,734,150 residents, and the Montreal metropolitan region has 2,921,350.

The Montreal metropolitan region is the second-largest population centre in Canada. About 45 per cent of the population is between 20 and 44 years of age.

First Language of Residents of Montreal

	MUC	Metropolitan region
French	61.8%	71.7%
English	20.4%	15.7%
Italian	6.4%	4.2%
Greek	1.8%	1.4%
Other	9.6%	7.0%
Total	**100.0%**	**100.0%**

Source: Statistics Canada, 1986 census, and the MUC Economic Development Office

Useful French Words

In this book, street and other names are given in French, as you would see them on maps and signs, with translations wherever the French and English are very different. Some useful words to help you navigate bilingually:

accès interdit	do not enter
autoroute	highway
carré	square
centre-ville	downtown
chemin	road
dépanneur	convenience store
église	church
est	east
E.U. (États-Unis)	United States
fermé	closed
gratuit	free
île	island
lac	lake
libre-service	self-service
métro	subway
mont	mountain
non-fumeur	non-smoking
nord	north
ouest	west
ouvert	open
pont	bridge
premier étage	first floor
rang	concession road
rez-de-chaussée	ground floor
rue	street
sens unique	one way
sortie	exit
stationnement	parking
sud	south
urgence	emergency
vieux	old
voie	road

A victim of Quebec's language-law sign wars.

LANGUAGE

After Paris, Montreal is the second-largest francophone city in the world. French is the official language of Quebec and the primary language of education, commerce and business. Most Montrealers are fully bilingual. Although the French and the English communities are predominant, there are more than 30 other cultural communities in Montreal.

CLIMATE

Montreal has four distinct seasons, and what you choose to pack will definitely depend on the time of year. Winters are normally bitterly cold, so dress accordingly. A warm overcoat, hat and gloves are essential. Protective footwear is also a must, especially for those days when deep snowfalls melt into oceans of slush. If you insist on leather boots (many fashion-conscious Montrealers now wear vinyl look-alikes), make sure to waterproof them.

Temperatures start to drop below freezing some time in early November. The middle of March usually sees the first signs of spring. Spring weather is brisk, and you should expect some rainy days during April and May. June, July and August typically bring hot and frequently humid weather. Wear very light clothing and protect your skin from the sun. Between late September and mid-November the weather gets progressively colder. This is the season for tweeds and woollens.

Whatever the season, you should expect to enjoy at least a few bright sunny days. Montreal is farther south than most European capitals, and the dazzling days of winter come as a pleasant surprise. For winter driving, it's a good idea to have sunglasses.

COMMERCE AND INDUSTRY

Montreal is Quebec's economic capital and is a major industrial, business, commercial and financial centre. In fact, the MUC has often been called the economic motor of Quebec. Because of its position on the St. Lawrence Seaway, Montreal also serves as a major port even though it is 1,600 km (995 mi.) from the Atlantic Ocean.

The economy of Montreal is well diversified. In the Montreal metropolitan region, 72 per cent of the jobs are in the service sector, 22 per cent in manufacturing. Leading manufacturing sectors include textiles, fashion, food and beverages, transportation equipment, aerospace, electrical and electronic products, telecommunications, printing and publishing, and metal, chemical and pharmaceutical products.

Month	Average maximum temperature (°C)	Average minimum temperature (°C)	Total precipitation (mm)	Number of days with precipitation (days)	Bright sunshine (hours)
Jan	-5.7	-14.6	7.3	17	106
Feb	-4.4	-13.5	65.2	14	128
Mar	1.6	-6.7	73.6	13	155
Apr	10.6	0.8	74.1	12	186
May	18.5	7.4	65.6	12	241
Jun	23.6	12.9	82.2	12	249
Jul	26.1	15.6	90.0	12	274
Aug	24.8	14.3	91.9	12	239
Sep	19.9	9.6	88.4	12	168
Oct	13.3	4.1	75.5	13	136
Nov	5.4	-1.5	81.0	15	85
Dec	-3.0	-10.8	86.7	18	79

Employment in Metropolitan Montreal Area

	(000s)	(%)
Manufacturing industries	313.7	22.3
Construction	72.3	5.1
Transport and communications	127.0	9.0
Commerce	250.5	17.8
Finance, insurance, property	94.6	6.7
Other services	471.9	33.5
Public administration	70.6	5.0
Other	8.1	0.6
TOTAL	**1,408.7**	**100.0**

Source: Statistics Canada and the MUC Economic Development Office (1988)

ESSENTIAL INFORMATION

EMERGENCY PHONE NUMBERS

GENERAL

Bell Canada provides telephone services in the Montreal region. The area code for Montreal is 514. Directory Assistance can be reached by dialling 411. There are two bilingual telephone directories: the *White Pages* and the *Yellow Pages*. At the back of the *White Pages* is a section called the "Blue Pages," which lists the various departments of the federal, provincial and municipal governments. The *Yellow Pages* contains separate French and English sections and lists products and services alphabetically.

POLICE, FIRE, AMBULANCE

In Montreal, dial 911; outside Montreal, consult the *White Pages*.

DOCTOR

The Corporation professionnelle des médecins du Québec, the governing medical body, does not sponsor a doctor telephone referral service; however, the Information and Referral Centre of Greater Montreal may be able to put you in touch with the type of doctor you need. Call them at 527-1375, Mon to Fri 8:30-4:45. After hours and on weekends, call the out-patient department at the nearest hospital.

DENTIST

For information or a referral, call the Ordre des dentistes du Québec at 875-8511.

OPTICIAN

For information or a referral, call the Ordre des opticiens d'ordonnances du Québec at 288-7542. There are a number of centrally located opticians, including:

Barlow and Barlow
1525 Sherbrooke ouest near Simpson
932-1189

Henri Cohen Optician
1017 Ste-Catherine ouest at Peel
286-1241
1235 Ste-Catherine ouest at Drummond
286-9636

LEGAL ASSISTANCE

The Barreau du Québec (Quebec Bar Association) operates a lawyer-referral service. Call 954-3413 during business hours.

A bilingual computerized telephone service offering information on various legal topics can be reached at 845-0888.

QUEBEC POISON CONTROL CENTRE

Call toll free 1-800-463-5060.

SEXUAL ASSAULT LINE

Call 934-4504 for counselling and assistance.

DISTRESS AND SUICIDE

842-7557 (depression)
522-5777 (suicide prevention)

KIDS HELP PHONE

Call toll free 1-800-668-6868.

PARENTS ANONYMOUS

For parents in trouble. Call 288-5555.

SPOUSAL ABUSE

Call toll free 1-800-363-9010.

ALCOHOLICS ANONYMOUS

Call 376-9230.

NARCOTICS ANONYMOUS

Call 939-3092.

DIAL-A-FACT

Bilingual information on drug and alcohol problems, Mon to Fri 9- 5. Call 288-0800; outside of Montreal call toll free 1-800-361-4640.

INFORMATION AND REFERRAL CENTRE OF GREATER MONTREAL

Bilingual information on welfare, health and leisure, Mon to Fri 8:30-4:45. Call 527-1375.

VETERINARIAN

Côte-St-Luc Hospital for Animals, among others, maintains a 24-hour emergency service. Call 489-6845.

LOST OR STOLEN CREDIT CARDS

American Express 931-9311
MasterCard 877-8610
(Bank of Montreal)
VISA 289-0312
(Toronto Dominion Bank)
Toronto Dominion Bank and Bank of Montreal personnel will refer you to other bank MasterCard and VISA offices. See also Banking, this chapter.

MAJOR HOSPITALS

The following hospitals are in the downtown core or are easily accessible from downtown. All have emergency rooms. Consult the *Yellow Pages* for hospitals in outlying areas.

Royal Victoria Hospital
687 des Pins ouest at University
842-1231

Hôpital Hôtel-Dieu de Montréal
3840 St-Urbain near des Pins ouest
843-2611

Hôpital St-Luc
1058 St-Denis near de la

Gauchetière est
281-2121

Jewish General Hospital
3755 Côte Ste-Catherine near Légaré
340-8222

Montreal Children's Hospital
2300 Tupper at Clossé
934-4400

Montreal General Hospital
1650 Cedar
937-6011

Reddy Memorial Hospital
4039 Tupper
933-7511

AUTOMOBILES

See also Transportation (Automobile).

QUEBEC'S RULES OF THE ROAD

The Société de l'assurance automobile, the government automobile insurer, publishes the *Driver's Handbook* in English; it's available at most bookstores.

Speed limits and distances are posted in metric (to convert kilometres into miles, multiply by 6 and then divide by 10). The possession or use of radar detectors is illegal.

Seatbelts must be worn at all times, and infants and children up to 18 kg (40 lbs.) must be safely secured in approved car seats.

Right turns on red lights are *not* permitted (Quebec is the only Canadian province that imposes such a rule). A flashing green arrow or light permits you to turn left while oncoming traffic is stopped.

Drivers must stop at least five meters from a school bus with its lights flashing, and may pass (in either direction) only when the flashing lights are off. (Where traffic lanes are separated by a median or other divider, oncoming vehicles are not required to stop.)

The use of studded tires is permitted in Quebec between October 15 and May 1. The use of anti-skid devices likely to damage the road surface is illegal.

For a visitor, driving in Montreal can be challenging—written traffic signs are in French only. The city's drivers are known to be creative and at times aggressive. While pedestrians have right of way at crosswalks, this rule is ignored by most Montreal drivers. Do your best to uphold the law.

EMERGENCY ROAD SERVICE
The local chapter of the Canadian Automobile Association provides emergency road service to CAA members and those of the American Automobile Association.

CAA-Quebec
**1180 Drummond at
René-Lévesque ouest
861-7111 (Mon to Fri, 9-5)**
Call 861-1313 for emergency road service.

CAA/AAA members can obtain free maps of the Montreal region and a tourbook entitled *Atlantic Provinces and Quebec*, which has a section on Montreal. The CAA also operates a travel service, which can help CAA/AAA members book hotel rooms and plan trips outside the Montreal region.

LA SÛRETÉ DU QUÉBEC (QUEBEC POLICE FORCE)
The province's highways, including several that run through Montreal, are under the jurisdiction of the SQ. Con-

sult the *White Pages* under "Sûreté du Québec" or call the operator for the nearest SQ office. The main SQ number in Montreal is 598-4141.

VISITOR INFORMATION

INFORMATION CENTRES
In addition to booths in the Dorval and Mirabel airports, the Ministère du Tourisme du Québec (Tourism Quebec) maintains the following permanent offices in Montreal:

 Tourisme Québec

Centre Infotouriste
**1001 Square Dorchester at Metcalfe
873-2015**

Centre Infotouriste
**174 Notre-Dame ouest at Place
Jacques-Cartier
873-2015**

Seasonal offices:
Lacolle
**Autoroute 15 in Que. (Interstate
87 in N.Y. State)**

Rigaud
**Autoroute 40 in Que. (Hwy. 417 in
Ont.)**

Rivière-Baudette
**Autoroute 20 in Que. (Hwy. 401 in
Ont.)**

Dégelis
Route 185 in Que. (Rte. 2 in N.B.)

Stanstead
**Autoroute 55 in Que. (Interstate
91 in Vermont)**

Tourism Quebec has produced a series of first-rate guides for various regions of the province. The guide for Montreal was prepared in conjunction with the Office des Congrès et du Tourisme du Grand Montréal (Greater Montreal Tourism and Convention Bureau). Contact either organization or the Infotouriste offices and ask for free copies of the most recent edition of *Montreal Tourist Guide* and *Montreal Tourist Map*.

L'Office des Congrès et du Tourisme du Grand Montréal
Suite 600
1555 Peel at Ste-Catherine ouest
Montreal H3A 1X6
844-5400

Tourism Quebec
C.P. 20,000
Quebec City G1K 7X2
873-2015 (Montreal)
1-800-363-7777 (elsewhere in North America)
For information on other parts of Canada, call the Canadian Office of Tourism at (613) 954-3854, Mon to Fri 8:30-5.

TOURISM HOTLINE
Montréal aujourd'hui, a French-only hotline for visitors to the city, can be reached at 933-1424. It features a recorded daily tourist schedule that highlights events of all kinds as well as restaurants and nightclubs.

TOUR GUIDES
Tour guides are recognized as professionals in Montreal, and city by-laws require that they hold a permit. Permit-holders have completed an exhaustive 240-hour theoretical and practical course covering the historical, archeological, geological, economic and political aspects of the city

as well as the time-management and psychological aspects of touring. The course is administered by the Institut de touriste et d'hôtellerie du Québec, 282-5108.

L'Association Provincial des Guides Touristiques (APGT) has its own bylaws and a code of ethics and can recommend guides. To retain the services of tour guides fluent in languages other than French and English, contact the association at:

APGT
C.P. 982, succursale Place D'Armes
Montreal H2Y 3J4

WEATHER FORECASTS
If you're wondering if it might rain on your parade, call Environment Canada for the latest forecast: 636-3302 (French); 636-3026 (English).

The Météomédia television channel (cable 17) broadcasts reasonably up-to-date forecasts.

PUBLIC HOLIDAYS
New Year's Day, Jan 1
Good Friday, date varies
Easter Monday, Mon after Good Friday
Fête de Dollard (Victoria Day), fourth Mon in May
Fête Nationale (St-Jean-Baptiste Day), June 24
Canada Day, July 1
Labour Day, first Mon in Sept
Thanksgiving, second Mon in Oct
Remembrance Day, Nov 11
Christmas, Dec 25
Boxing Day, Dec 26

LOST AND FOUND

For items lost on buses and the *métro*:

MUC Transportation Commission
280-4637
The Lost and Found office is in Pie-IX *métro* station.

For items left in taxis:

Taxi Bureau
280-6600

For items lost elsewhere in Montreal:

MUC Police
280-4636

FOREIGN VISITORS

CONSULATES

Many countries maintain consulates in Montreal. A complete list can be found in the *Yellow Pages* under "Consulates and Other Foreign Representatives." The following are the more frequently visited consulates:

British Consulate General
1155 University near René-Lévesque ouest
866-5863

Consulate General of France
Place Bonaventure at University
878-4381

Consulate General of Japan
600 de la Gauchetière ouest at Beaver Hall Hill
866-3429

Consulate General of Switzerland
1572 Docteur-Penfield near

Simpson
932-7181

United States Consulate General
Complexe Desjardins
(Ste-Catherine ouest and Jeanne-Mance)
281-1886

INTERPRETER SERVICES

Because most people in central Montreal speak both English and French, few visitors will require interpretation services to make their basic needs known. Those that do need translation of another language into French or English should consult the *Yellow Pages* under "Translators and Interpreters."

CUSTOMS REGULATIONS FOR U.S. VISITORS

Every 30 days, U.S. citizens going home after 48 hours or more can take with them $400 (U.S.) worth of duty-free merchandise. If you are 21 or over, this may include 200 cigarettes, 100 cigars (not Cuban), 454 g (1 lb.) of smoking tobacco and 946 ml (32 oz.) of alcohol. After a visit of less than 48 hours, only $25 (U.S.) worth of merchandise may be taken back duty free. U.S.-manufactured goods purchased in Canada may be brought back duty free and are not included in the basic exemption.

For further information, call U.S. Customs in Montreal at 636-3875.

BANKING

For branches of Canadian and foreign banks in Montreal, see the *Yellow Pages* under "Banks." Hours vary, but most branches are open Mon to Fri 10-4 (some branches also offer Saturday banking). Many banks have automated tellers linked to the Interac and Plus

METRIC CONVERSION

Unit	Approximate equivalent
Length	
1 kilometre	0.62 mile
1 mile	1.61 kilometres
1 metre	1.09 yards
1 yard	0.91 metre
1 centimetre	0.39 inch
1 inch	2.54 centimetres
Area	
1 hectare	2.47 acres
1 acre	0.41 hectare
1 square mile	259 hectares
Capacity	
1 litre	1.06 U.S. quart
1 U.S. quart	0.95 litre
Weight	
1 kilogram	2.2 pounds
1 pound	0.45 kilogram

System networks. The Royal Bank of Canada has automated tellers in both airports.

CURRENCY EXCHANGES

Foreign visitors may exchange currency at all major banks and at foreign exchange dealers. There are no restrictions governing the amount of currency that may be converted into Canadian dollars. Some institutions that exchange currency:

Bank of America Canada
Foreign Currency Services
1230 Peel near Square Dorchester
396-1855
Also at Mirabel airport
466-3762

Maison de change Forexco
1210 Greene at de Maisonneuve ouest
Westmount
935-6929

National Commercial Foreign Exchange
2000 McGill College at de Maisonneuve ouest
844-8200, 879-1300

Thomas Cook Foreign Exchange
625 René-Lévesque ouest near Union
397-4029
Also at Dorval airport
636-3582

POSTAL SERVICES AND COURIERS

The main downtown post offices are:

Centre-ville
1025 St-Jacques near de la Cathédrale
283-2567
1250 University at Palace Lane
283-2576
1970 Ste-Catherine ouest near Bordeaux
283-5649

Desjardins
5 Complexe Desjardins
(Ste-Catherine ouest and Jeanne-Mance)
283-4980

Tour de la Bourse
800 Carré Victoria at St-Antoine
283-3901

The following couriers provide domestic and international service:

Federal Express
345-0130

Purolator
731-1000

United Parcel Service (UPS)
633-0010

LATE-NIGHT SERVICES

PHARMACIES

Pharmaprix
5122 Côte-des-Neiges at de la Reine-Marie
738-8464
Open 24 hours.
1500 Ste-Catherine ouest near Guy
933-4744
Open until midnight.

Pharmacie Jean-Coutu
1836 Ste-Catherine ouest near St-Mathieu
933-4221
Open until midnight.

RESTAURANTS
Most Montreal bars close at 3 AM, so there is usually little problem in getting a meal or snack late at night. After 3, try one of the restaurants below; both are open 24 hours.

Ben's
990 de Maisonneuve ouest at Metcalfe
844-1000
A Montreal institution, Ben's serves excellent breakfasts and deli food at reasonable prices.

Lux
5220 St-Laurent near Fairmount
271-9272
A combination restaurant and newsstand. A great place for insomniacs who like to make good use of their time.

BABYSITTING
Many major hotels can arrange babysitters for you if given adequate notice. See also With the Kids (Useful Information for Parents).

LIQUOR/WINE/BEER
The drinking age in Quebec is 18. Bars close at 3 AM. Drinking alcohol in public is permitted only with a permit. Liquor is sold exclusively at the Société des alcools du Québec (SAQ). Wine and beer are sold by the SAQ, grocery stores and convenience stores (*dépanneurs*). The SAQ has a number of branches that specialize in fine wines. Many Montreal restaurants permit patrons to bring their own wine; look for a sign in the restaurant window that reads "*Apportez votre vin*" ("Bring your own wine").

Centrally located stores are at:

SAQ
1500 Atwater near Ste-Catherine ouest
931-4178
3575 du Parc near Prince Arthur
288-3493
505 Président-Kennedy near Alymer
873-2274
1246 Ste-Catherine ouest at Beaudry
861-7908

TELEVISION

The downtown core of Montreal is serviced by two cable companies, CFCF Cable and Videotron Cable. In the list below, Videotron channels that differ from CFCF's are given in parentheses.

3 WCAX Burlington CBS
4 CBFT Montreal Radio-Canada
5 CFJP Montreal Quatre Saisons
7 CTFM Montreal TVA
8 CIVM Montreal Radio-Québec
11 CFCF Montreal CTV
13 CBMT Montreal CBC
14 (27) WCFE Plattsburgh PBS
15 TV5 (French TV)
16 WPTZ Plattsburgh NBC
17 Météomédia
18 (28) Youth TV
20 MusiquePlus
21 CJOH Cornwall CTV
22 WVNY Burlington ABC
25 The Sports Network (ESPN)
26 (36) CHLT Sherbrooke TVA
31 (29) Canal Famille
32 Super Écran (pay TV)
33 (31) First Choice (pay TV)
34 TSN

RADIO

AM STATIONS
600 CFCF (English)
690 CBF (French)
730 CKAC (French)
800 CJAD (English)
850 CKVL (French)
940 CBM (English)
990 CKIS (English)
1040 CFZZ (French)
1280 CJMS (French)
1410 CFMB (multilingual)
1570 CKLM (French)

FM STATIONS
90.3 CKUT (English), community radio
92.5 CFQR (English), easy listening
93.5 CBM (English), CBC, classical music
94.3 CKMF (French), dance music
95.9 CJFM (English), easy listening
96.9 CKOI (French), rock and dance music
97.7 CHOM (English), rock
98.5 CIEL (French), easy listening
99.5 CIME (French), easy listening
100.7 CBF (French), CBC
104.5 CIBL (French), community radio
105.7 CFGL (French), easy listening
107.3 CITE (French), easy listening

NEWSPAPERS

The Downtowner (English)
Free community-oriented weekly.

The Mirror (English)
Free weekly. Emphasis on entertainment, art and culture.

The Gazette (English)
With the demise of the *Montreal Star* in 1979, the *Gazette* is the only remaining English-language daily in Montreal. The paper recently began publishing a Sunday edition.

Journal de Montréal (French)
A daily tabloid with a wide readership. Good for sports scores.

La Presse (French)
The largest French daily in Montreal.

Le Devoir (French)
The daily newspaper of Quebec's French-speaking intelligentsia. An influential presence on the province's cultural and political scene, despite its chronic financial instability.

Voir (French)

Free weekly. Similar to the *Mirror* in content.

Foreign Newspapers/Magazines

Montreal has no shortage of specialized vendors of newspapers and magazines. One excellent source is the Multimags chain, with two shops downtown.

Multimags

1570 de Maisonneuve ouest near Mackay
935-7044
2197 Ste-Catherine ouest near Chomedey
937-0474

TIPPING

Waiters and taxi drivers expect 10 to 15 per cent of the bill or fare. Be careful not to tip on the combined provincial/federal sales tax component of the bill (15.6 per cent of the total). Some restaurants may add the tip to the bill (maximum 15 per cent). Porters usually expect $1 per suitcase. Coatchecks normally charge $1.

SALES TAXES

As of July 1, 1992, Quebec will impose an 8 per cent tax on virtually all goods and services purchased in the province. The province may rebate most of the provincial sales tax paid by non-residents of Canada who visit Quebec. No details have been announced, but it will likely be similar to the existing rebate for the 7 per cent federal Goods and Services tax (GST), which is already charged on nearly everything purchased in the province, from shoes to haircuts.

Visitors to Canada can claim a rebate of any GST they pay on short-term accommodation and on most consumer goods that they purchase to take home, as long as they are not residents here and their total claim is for at least $7 of GST. Goods qualify for the rebate if they were purchased *for use outside Canada* and are removed from Canada within 60 days of purchase. There is no rebate for GST paid on such services as dry cleaning and shoe repair, goods left in Canada, meals in restaurants, alcoholic beverages, tobacco products, automotive fuels and certain appreciating used goods such as coins, paintings and jewellery.

The rebate claim form will be available in most major Montreal hotels and stores. You can claim your rebate in one of two ways—take the completed form to a participating border duty-free shop for an immediate cash rebate of up to $500 (Cdn.) per day, or mail the form to Revenue Canada's Ottawa office. Rebate applications must include original bills of sale or itemized receipts. Accommodation receipts must show the number of nights of lodging supplied. (Original receipts and other supporting documentation will be returned.)

There is an absolute exemption from GST and provincial sales tax on goods purchased by a non-resident of Canada if the vendor ships the goods outside Canada directly. This is useful in the case of certain used goods for which no rebate may be claimed, such as paintings, jewellery, rare books and coins.

WHERE TO STAY

Montreal offers accommodation to suit every taste and budget. First-class hotels provide all the luxuries you would expect for standard rooms in that range. Budget-minded travellers can choose from less expensive hotels, bed-and-breakfasts, college dorms and campgrounds. Prices hit their peak during the high season from May to October, but special rates and discounts often apply throughout the year. Many hotels don't charge for children under 12 staying in their parents' room. Wherever you decide to stay, we strongly advise that you confirm the rates beforehand and book well in advance. Remember that foreign visitors can apply for a rebate of GST paid on short-term accommodation.

Only recommended hotels are listed. Most are located downtown for easy access to sightseeing, shopping and dining. Unless otherwise noted, prices quoted are based on standard double occupancy during high season in late 1991, exclusive of applicable taxes. Given the large number of available rooms in the city, though, visitors can often book rooms for much less. For further information on accommodation and rates, call the Montreal Tourist Office:

L'Office des Congrès et du Tourisme
C.P. 889
Montreal H5A 1E6
873-2015

DOWNTOWN ACCOMMODATION

1. Holiday Inn Crowne Plaza Metro Centre
2. Hôtel de l'Institut
3. Hôtel Le Meridien
4. Journey's End
5. Hôtel la Citadelle
6. Hôtel Inter-Continental
7. Holiday Inn Crowne Plaza
8. Montreal International Youth Hostel
9. McGill Student Apartments
10. Le Grand Hôtel
11. Le Reine Elizabeth/Queen Elizabeth
12. Bonaventure Hilton
13. Le Château Champlain
14. Le Shangrila
15. Le Quatre Saisons/Four Seasons
16. YMCA
17. Ritz-Carlton Hotel
18. Le Centre Sheraton
19. Le Vogue
20. Hôtel de la Montagne
21. YWCA
22. Manoir Lemoyne
23. Le Château Versailles
24. Le Nouvel Hôtel
25. Château Napoleon
26. Apartment-Hôtel Le Richebourg
■ subway station

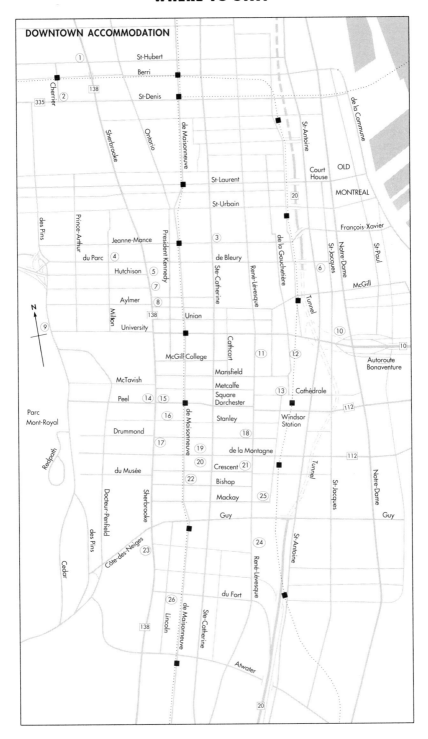

DOWNTOWN ACCOMMODATION

HOTELS

DOWNTOWN

Ritz-Carlton Hotel
1228 Sherbrooke ouest at Drummond
842-4212
1-800-363-0366
Fax: 842-3383

The Ritz-Carlton calmly presides over the corner of Sherbrooke and Drummond like a dowager queen. Its distinctive canopy and richly decorated façade command the attention of passers-by (the impressive entrance is a popular backdrop for tourist snapshots and feature films). As the doorman ushers you into the formal lobby, you'll begin to see why the service here is legendary.

When the Ritz first opened its doors in 1912, it immediately won the hearts of the local gentry. Built by a consortium of wealthy Montrealers, the classically elegant hotel became the preferred venue for lavish weddings, corporate balls and other gala events. The hotel's exquisite Oval Room continues to attract important bookings years in advance, and its restaurants are among the city's finest.

Guests at the Ritz have always included the rich and famous. The utterly discreet, superb service ensures an intensely loyal clientele. This is not to say that significant events go unnoticed. An official history commissioned and sold by the hotel reminds us, for example, that Elizabeth Taylor and Richard Burton were once married here.

The rooms at the Ritz are expensive for a hotel that offers no pool or health club. On the other hand, you will never be obliged to share an elevator with gregarious strangers in wet bathing suits. The Café de Paris restaurant offers *haute cuisine* and a more than respectable wine list. During the warmer months, afternoon tea can be savoured at the Garden Court while ducklings frolic sweetly in the pond. If you can resist the urge to eavesdrop on important business deals in the piano bar, venture outside to the exclusive shops, art galleries and restaurants of the downtown core, all at your doorstep. If it should happen to rain the Ritz will, of course, provide you with a handsome umbrella. Doubles $300-650.

Le Quatre Saisons/Four Seasons
1050 Sherbrooke ouest at Stanley
284-1110
1-800-268-6282 toll free (Canada)
1-800-332-3742 toll free (U.S.)
Fax: 284-1162

Also renowned for the quality of its service and luxurious accommodation, the modern Four Seasons is the Ritz-Carlton's arch-rival. Guests are thoroughly pampered here. Plush terry bathrobes, a built-in hair dryer, remote-control TV, at least two telephones, a mini-bar and a small safe are standard in even the least expensive rooms. What the hotel lacks in Old World charm it makes up for with state-of-the-art swimming and fitness facilities. There is a year-round heated outdoor pool, a whirlpool, a sauna and a fitness gym. The hotel's three restaurants, including the grand, white-pillared Le Restaurant, receive consistently high ratings. Near the Ritz, the Four Seasons is also a short walk from many excellent art galleries, boutiques and restaurants and only a block from the Peel *métro*. Valet parking available for a fee. Doubles $225-630.

Bonaventure Hilton
1 Place Bonaventure (de la Gauchetière ouest at University)
878-2332
1-800-268-9275 toll free (Canada)
1-800-455-8667 toll free (worldwide)
Fax: 878-3881

The excellent facilities of the Bonaventure attract a constant stream of conventions and trade shows. Its location across from Central Station in the heart of downtown also makes it a convenient luxury hotel for solo travellers. The lobby is always a hub of activity despite the fact that it is 17 floors above the ground. The adjacent 2½-acre roof garden has a duck pond, and the heavenly outdoor swimming pool remains open year-round. Also on the 17th floor are the Bonaventure's three fine restaurants, including the popular Le Castillon, and a lounge. The hotel's elevator provides direct access to the underground city with its several kilometres of connected underground shopping malls, the train station and the Bonaventure *métro* station. This means that during the coldest days of winter you can leave your heavy coat and boots behind. The modern, comfortable rooms at the Bonaventure offer garden or city views. Life at the top. Doubles $150-335.

Le Reine Elizabeth/Queen Elizabeth Hotel
900 René-Lévesque ouest at Mansfield
861-3511
1-800-268-9420 toll free (Canada)
1-800-828-7447 toll free (U.S.)
Fax: 954-2256

A perennial favourite of business travellers, the venerable Queen E is a tightly run ship, handling daily turnovers of more than a thousand executive rooms with professional ease.

A view of the Queen Elizabeth Hotel from René-Lévesque. Immediately in front of the Queen E is Mary, Queen of the World Cathedral. (Queen Elizabeth Hotel)

Don't be misled by the hustle and bustle of the main lobby. Originally built as a Canadian National Railway hotel directly above Central Station, the Queen Elizabeth has evolved into a convenient, handsome passageway for hordes of commuters heading to and from downtown office complexes. By contrast, the guest floors above are whisper-quiet and graceful. The conservatively decorated rooms are spotless and offer lots of perks like free shoeshines and sewing kits. The hotel's three restaurants include the flagship Beaver Club. If you don't have a chance to do lunch here with the corporate crowd, you can experience the restaurant's illustrious past through museum-like displays of memorabilia housed in the lobby. The hotel also has four lounges, a gift shop and an old-fashioned beauty shop that offers soothing steam baths and massages.

The Queen E is extremely well situated, and is connected to the underground city. As Montreal's largest hotel, it serves as a major terminus for airport buses and a variety of city tours. Doubles $240-999.

Le Château Champlain
1 Place du Canada (Peel and St-Antoine)
878-9000
1-800-268-9420 toll free (Canada)
1-800-828-7447 toll free (U.S.)
Fax: 878-9000

This 36-floor landmark with distinctive half-moon windows was built during the heady '60s by Canadian Pacific Hotels. At the time, the Château Champlain's stark architecture represented a significant departure from the romantic towers and turrets of CP's much-acclaimed storybook castles. Montreal's link in the hotel chain looks nothing at all like the Banff Springs, Victoria's Empress or Que-

The distinctive façade of the Château Champlain Hotel, referred to by Montrealers as the "cheese grater."

bec City's Château Frontenac. Some Montrealers still refer to the Champlain as "the cheese grater." Despite all the humbugs, the Château Champlain has firmly established itself as one of the city's premier hotels, a reputation it has smoothly maintained for more than 20 years. The hotel has five good restaurants, including the penthouse L'Escapade with its breathtaking views. There is an indoor pool, a health club with an exercise room, a whirlpool and saunas. Rooms are modern and most have mini-bars. The Château is only a short walk away from shopping, transportation and downtown sights either through the underground city or aboveground. If you get lost, the hotel is a cinch to spot from a distance. Doubles $225-270.

Hôtel La Citadelle
410 Sherbrooke ouest at Hutchison
844-8851
1-800-663-1144 toll free (Canada)
Fax: 844-0912

A smaller, 186-room hotel with a low-key but definitely European style. All rooms have cable TV, in-house movies, mini-bars and, unlike many major hotels, windows you can open. Fresh-air fiends will also appreciate the non-smoking floors. Some suites offer kitchenettes, but no utensils are provided. Facilities include an indoor pool, a gym with Nautilus machines, a Swedish sauna, a wet-steam bath, a full massage service and an esthetician. Included in the regular room rate is a free overnight shoeshine, a morning paper and continental breakfast in the C'est La Vie restaurant (which at night reverts to a popular piano bar). Children under 18 stay free in parents' rooms; other discounts are generally available to seniors and auto-club members. Doubles $150-190.

Le Centre Sheraton
1201 René-Lévesque ouest at Drummond
878-2000
1-800-325-3535 toll free (Canada and worldwide)
Fax: 878-3958

The Sheraton is a sleek midtown high-rise offering attractive modern facilities including a heated indoor pool, saunas, a whirlpool and an exercise room. The five-storey lobby atrium, filled with cascading tropical plants, is a refreshing place to linger at the end of the day. The three restaurants include Le Point de Vue with its panoramic views of the city and unusual reflecting ceiling. There are also five lounges and a night club to entertain the frequent convention crowds. Room decor is restrained and comfortable; service meets Sheraton's worldwide standards. Doubles $175-220.

Le Meridien
4 Complexe Desjardins (Ste-Cathérine ouest at Jeanne-Mance)
285-1450
1-800-361-8237 toll free (Que., Ont., the Maritimes)
1-800-543-4300 toll free (elsewhere in Canada and the U.S.)
Fax: 285-1243

A modern four-star hotel, the Air France-owned Meridien has 600 luxurious rooms including the exclusive Le Club Président suites, reserved for business travellers. Health-conscious guests can opt for the non-smoking floor. Whatever room you choose, you will be indulged with miniature toiletries by Hermès of Paris. Vacationers will appreciate the hotel's direct access to the upscale boutiques of Complexe Desjardins, the *métro*, Place des Arts and the underground city. Just riding the elevators is fun—they're glass-walled. One of the Meridien's biggest attractions is the heated indoor pool (perhaps the best hotel pool in town) and adjoining garden sundeck. For non-swimmers, there is an exercise room, a whirlpool, a sauna and a golf simulator. The hotel's most appealing restaurant is the plant-filled Café Fleuri, a good choice for Sunday brunch. And no, the food isn't served on airline trays. Doubles $225.

Delta Montreal
450 Sherbrooke ouest at Président-Kennedy
286-1986
1-800-268-1133 toll free (Canada)
1-800-877-1133 toll free (U.S.)
Fax: 284-4306

Finally, a hotel that understands parents' needs. The Delta offers not only four-star accommodation, a downtown location, good restaurants and great health facilities, but also a Children's Creative Centre with toys and crafts. If you and the kids need to burn off steam, there are indoor and outdoor pools, two squash courts, a games room, a sauna, a whirlpool and exercise rooms with aerobic instructors for a fee. The hotel also organizes special nursery weekends. The tastefully appointed rooms each have a small balcony. Doubles $170-175.

Hôtel Le Grand
Square Victoria, 777 University at St-Antoine
879-1370
1-800-361-8155 toll free (Canada)
Fax: 879-1761

The hotel's aptly named Tour de Ville is Montreal's only revolving rooftop restaurant. Originally part of the Hyatt group and now managed by a major Quebec chain, the Grand has that typical ultramodern glass palace look. There is an atrium-style lobby

The Hôtel Le Grand. (City of Montreal)

with glass-walled elevators that rise to a glassed-in pool. The hotel is a short walk south of the downtown core (this slight separation allows great views of the city skyline), but still conveniently situated for sightseers, on the fringe of Old Montreal and next to the Place Victoria *métro*. All rooms are finished to a luxury standard, and the bathrooms have flattering lighting and extra-thick towels. To help you relax, the spa facilities by the pool include a sauna and Nautilus gym. The *belle époque* Chez Antoine Bistrot-Grill serves aromatic steak and seafood dishes while the Bar Chez Antoine offers a musical feast of great jazz piano. Doubles $180-215.

Hôtel Inter-Continental
360 St-Antoine ouest at de Bleury
987-9900
1-800-361-3600 toll free (Canada)
1-800-327-0200 toll free
(worldwide)
Fax: 847-8550

This new, $78-million hotel, connected to Montreal's World Trade Centre, consists of two buildings: a new brick tower at the corner of St-Antoine and de Bleury, and the renovated, century-old Nordheimer Building fronting on St-Jacques. The new building is stylistically linked to the old through a harmonious mix of warm woods, granite and Celtic motifs. The hotel's 359 rooms and 23 suites are decorated in soft Victorian colours. Each room has several telephones with hookups for computers and fax machines, a large desk and a spacious four-piece bathroom. Four of the hotel's six bars and restaurants are in the Nordheimer, and three of these are housed in old vaults in the basement. The vaults, which clearly predate the Victorian age, are believed to have been used for ammunition storage when the site was part of the ramparts of Old Montreal. The hotel's main ballroom is named after legendary *fin de siècle* actress Sarah Bernhardt, who is believed to have once performed in the Nordheimer Company's theatre. Even if it isn't true, it's an adequate excuse for such opulence. Doubles $195-295.

Holiday Inn Crowne Plaza
420 Sherbrooke ouest at Hutchison
842-6111
1-800-465-4329 toll free
(Canada, U.S.)
Fax: 842-9381

This is the flagship of Holiday Inn's Montreal-area hotels. It adheres to the chain's well-established formula, offering predictably good rooms, service and facilities. There are 486 rooms (some of them at the luxury level), a heated indoor pool, a sauna, a whirlpool, an exercise room, a coin laundry and paid valet parking. Doubles $155-175.

A period façade incorporated into the new Hôtel Inter-Continental.

**Holiday Inn Crowne Plaza
Metro Centre**
505 Sherbrooke est near St-Denis
842-8581
1-800-465-4329 toll free
(Canada, U.S)
Fax: 842-8910
Near St-Denis and Prince Arthur, this
is the right place if you're planning to
spend a lot of time enjoying the local
nightlife. Back at the hotel, you will
find pleasant, recently renovated
rooms, an indoor pool, a restaurant
and a bar. Most rooms come with two
double beds, so this can be a good
choice for families. Children under 18
stay free in their parents' room. Free
covered parking. Doubles $159-175.

Hôtel de la Montagne
1430 de la Montagne near
Ste-Catherine ouest
288-5656
1-800-361-6262 toll free in
(Canada)
Fax: 288-9658
Don't be put off by the somewhat
kitschy art nouveau-inspired lobby with
its nymph, fountain and crystal chande-
lier. The rooms are mercifully plain,
spacious and comfortable. There is a
small outdoor pool on the 20th floor
with a superb view of the city, a gourmet
French restaurant and a popular dance
club. In the heart of the downtown
nightlife scene, this is a very European
hotel, perfect for night owls who want to
practise their French. Excellent Sunday
brunch. Doubles $210.

The Château Versailles Hotel. (Pierre Louis Mongeau)

Le Vogue
1425 de la Montagne near Ste-Catherine ouest
285-5555
Fax: 849-8903

Another hotel in the popular Crescent Street area is this spectacular new facility created from the former Texaco Building. A $40-million renovation has produced 150 stunning Empire-style rooms, most with cherry four-poster beds and down comforters. Bathrooms are *grand luxe*, with whirlpools and mini-TVs. There is a handsome restaurant and an outdoor pool. Paid parking. Doubles $290-725.

Le Shangrila
3407 Peel at Sherbrooke ouest
288-4141
1-800-361-7791
Fax: 288-3021

Looking for something a little different? This Asian-style Best Western hotel blends Chinese, Japanese, Korean and Indian themes. The rooms are not only unusual but also

among the largest of the downtown hotels. Guests have access to the Four Seasons' health club across the street for a nominal fee. Restaurants offer both Szechuan and continental dishes. Paid parking. Doubles $175.

Le Château Versailles
1659 Sherbrooke ouest at St-Mathieu
1-800-361-7199 toll free (Canada)
1-800-361-3664 toll free (U.S)
Fax: 933-7102

For years one of Montreal's best-kept secrets, the Château Versailles offers dignified accommodation right downtown for much less than you would pay at, say, the Ritz-Carlton. There are no five-star restaurants here, and no bars or exercise facilities. But the Versailles does have a certain *je ne sais quoi*. The hotel has been developed from four converted stately Edwardian stone townhouses. Many rooms are furnished with antiques and retain their original fireplaces and attractive architectural mouldings. All are equipped with private bath, TV and air conditioning. In keeping with the European style, the room rate includes a continental breakfast. Afternoon tea is available on request. Recently annexed to the original complex is the modern Tour Versailles. If you require a large desk, a small safe, fax and secretarial services, this may be the place for you. But if you prefer Old World elegance, stick to the Château. Pleasantly helpful staff. Close to all the downtown sights and the Guy *métro*. Doubles $86-139.

Journey's End
3440 du Parc near Milton
849-1413
1-800-668-4200 toll free (North America)
Fax: 849-1413

A brand-new hostelry with clean,

modern rooms at a fair price. Joggers will appreciate the hotel's proximity to Mount Royal. The hotel is a short walk from the many restaurants found on Prince Arthur and Duluth and a short cab ride away from several excellent Greek restaurants on du Parc. Free parking. Doubles $80.

Hôtel de l'Institut
3535 St-Denis near Malines
282-5120
1-800-361-5111 toll free (Que.)
Fax: 873-9893

Shhhh. Keep this one to yourself. The Institute may lack charm, but it offers excellent value for your dollar. This is actually a training academy for hotel and restaurant managers, owned and operated by the Quebec government. The staff tend to be exceptionally helpful (presumably they are keen to get good marks). Rooms can be somewhat dowdy, and there aren't any recreational facilities, but the restaurant is a find. Supervised student chefs prepare great meals at a very reasonable cost. Continental breakfast is normally included with the room. Book early as there are only 42 rooms. Doubles $100-110.

Le Nouvel Hôtel
1740 René-Lévesque ouest near Guy
931-8841
1-800-363-6063 toll free (Que., Ont., the Maritimes, New England)
Fax: 931-3233

This modest, functional hotel is housed within a new condominium complex. It's short on luxuries but provides pleasant studios and small apartments at a reasonable price. Facilities (shared with the condominiums) include an indoor pool, a health club, a restaurant, a live theatre supper club and a covered parking garage. Queen-

size beds are standard, and rates are the same for single or double occupancy. Doubles $120-275.

Château Napoléon
1030 Mackay near René-Lévesque ouest
861-1500
Fax: 861-5372

The modern, mostly beige rooms look nothing like the handsome lobby (which, as one would expect, is decorated in the ornate Empire style). It's just as well since this keeps the prices down. Next to the Lucien-l'Allier *métro* and a short walk from the downtown sights, the Napoléon has no recreational facilities but does have a pleasant little restaurant. Paid parking. Doubles $56-95.

NEAR THE AIRPORTS

DORVAL

Montreal Aéroport Hilton International
12505 Côte-de-Liesse
631-2411
1-800-268-9275 toll free (Canada)
1-800-445-8667 toll free (worldwide)
Fax: 631-0192

Is this a test? How do you enter the parking lot from the expressway? And then how do you find your room in the sprawling, spoke-shaped building? If you manage to check in to your room without calling off your honeymoon, rest assured that you can then unwind in comfort. The ravages of time are beginning to show, but on the whole this Hilton lives up to its name. Tastefully appointed rooms have well-stocked mini-bars, comfortable armchairs and bathrooms with handy built-in hair dryers. Hotel facilities include indoor and outdoor pools, saunas, a health club, restaurants and a lounge. For plane freaks, there are excellent panoramic views of the Dorval airport. Don't worry, though—the building is remarkably soundproof. A 20-minute drive from downtown. Doubles $200-235.

Holiday Inn Aéroport
6500 Côte-de-Liesse near Cavendish
739-3391
1-800-465-4329 toll free (Canada, U.S)
Fax: 739-6591

A convenient, updated hostelry down the road from the Hilton. Not quite as fancy, but the rooms are fine given the difference in price. There are indoor and outdoor pools, a sauna, a health club and a restaurant. Doubles $105-115.

Journey's End
340 Michel-Jasmin at Orly
636-3391
Fax: 674-3088
1-800-668-4200 toll free (North America)

Handy, straightforward motel rooms that are clean and modern. All rooms have either two doubles or one queen. No restaurant. No frills. Free parking. Doubles $69.

Journey's End Suites, Pointe Claire
6300 Trans-Canada Highway
426-5060
1-800-668-4200 toll free (North America)

The newest Journey's End hotel in Montreal's west end, the Suites offer a lot more comfort for a little more money. Each unit has a king-size bed, a separate living room, two TVs, a coffee-maker, a mini-bar and a spacious bathroom. No restaurant.

Free parking. Suites $96.

MIRABEL

Hôtel le Château de l'Aeroport
Montreal International Airport (Mirabel)
476-1611
1-800-268-9420 toll free (Canada)
1-800-828-7447 toll free (U.S.)
Fax: 476-0873

You couldn't possibly stay any closer to Mirabel airport. This modern facility has quiet, comfortable rooms perfect for recovering from jet lag. If you don't feel like sleeping, there's lots to do. Work out in the exercise room, have a sauna, and then head to the piano bar. Doubles $105-165.

ALTERNATIVE ACCOMMODATION

McGill Student Apartments
3935 University at des Pins
398-6367

From mid-May to mid-August, the dorms are rented out to summer students, small conference groups and tourists. Most of the approximately 1000 rooms have two single beds with shared bathrooms in the halls. The location is attractive and the setting rather pastoral. Access to McGill's athletic facilities for a fee. Students $23, non-students $32.

Auberge de Jeunesse International de Montréal/ Montreal International Youth Hostel
3541 Aylmer near Sherbrooke ouest
843-3317

Space here is extremely limited during the summer. At this price, no wonder. Most rooms are single-sex dormitories but there are a few rooms available for couples and families. Dorm $13 members, $16 non-members.

Résidence de l'Université de Montréal
2350 Edouard Montpetit
343-6531
Not nearly as convenient for sightseeing as McGill, the U of M is nevertheless handy to the *métro*. It's also a really cheap place to stay. Open May 1 to mid-Aug. Singles $19.95 students, $30 non-students.

Concordia University Student Residence
7141 Sherbrooke ouest at Belmore
848-4756
Similar accommodation to that offered by McGill but much less central. Singles $17 students, $23 non-students.

YMCA
1540 Stanley near Sherbrooke ouest
849-8393
As the song says, it's fun to stay here. It's cheap, friendly and close to everything. What a deal! They even accept credit cards. Men only. Singles from $33.

YWCA
1355 René-Lévesque ouest near Crescent
866-9941
A lot smaller than the YMCA, this is a safe, friendly place to stay for women travellers on a budget. Women only. Singles from $32.

Apartment-Hôtel Le Richebourg
2170 Lincoln near Atwater
935-9224
1-800-263-2593 toll free (Canada)
1-800-678-6323 toll free (U.S.)
Fax: 935-5049
Just two blocks from the Forum and a

short walk from downtown, the Richebourg attracts a steady business clientele with its excellent weekly rates. Some rooms are equipped with kitchenettes. Other features include 24-hour security, an indoor pool, sauna and paid parking. The weekly rate for a family of four sharing one room was as low as $320 during the summer of 1991, with an additional $35 for parking. Doubles $65-135.

Manoir Lemoyne
2100 de Maisonneuve ouest near du Fort
931-8861
1-800-361-7191 toll free (Canada)
Fax: 931-7726
A good choice for young families or long-term visitors on a budget, the 262 split-level suites each come with a fully equipped kitchenette complete with complimentary coffee and tea. There are saunas, a small health club and free in-room movies. Close to the Forum and the Atwater métro, this apartment hotel is an easy walk from Sherbrooke, Westmount or downtown. Weekly and monthly rates are available, with or without parking (covered or uncovered). Doubles $110-150. Special weekend rates.

BED AND BREAKFAST

Montreal Bed and Breakfast
Marian Kahn
4912 Victoria near Mira
738-9410
The oldest B&B agency in Montreal. Most of the houses are centrally located in Westmount, Outremont or downtown. Hosts are friendly, helpful types full of useful information and motherly advice. Doubles $35-55, discounts for seniors.

Montreal Bed and Breakfast Downtown Network
Bob Finkelstein
3458 Laval near Sherbrooke est
289-9749

A reputable, long-standing service offering central, hospitable accommodation. The network makes a special effort to place handicapped visitors in easy-access homes. A morning paper is usually provided with breakfast, and discounts are offered for some local tours and restaurants. Doubles $35-55.

Relais Montréal Hospitalité
3977 Laval near Napoléon
287-9635

Another bed and breakfast network that will place you in private homes in the city. Ask for Marthe Pearson. Doubles $40-65.

TRAILER PARKS/ CAMPGROUNDS

Ministère de Tourisme
Third floor
710 Place d'Youville
Quebec City G1R 4Y4
1-800-463-5009 toll free (Que.)

A comprehensive guide to licensed campgrounds throughout the province is free for the asking from the ministry and from tourist offices in Montreal. There are about 50 campgrounds within an hour's drive of Montreal. Many have organized sports programs and most have pools. We suggest that you stay near Mirabel, Carillon, Hudson, St-Jérôme or Ste-Agathe.

Fédération Québécoise de Camping et de Caravaning Inc.
4545 Pierre-de-Coubertin
C.P. 1000, Station M
Montreal H1V 3R2
252-3003

If you are planning an extended stay in Montreal or want to camp your way around the province, it might be worthwhile to take out a $38 membership. In return, the federation offers campground discounts, lower rates on gas and lubricants, lots of useful information and organized travel packages. Social events are also organized.

Camping Daoust
3861 Harwood
Vaudreuil
(514) 458-7301

Camping Daoust is a full-facility campground offering many sports and recreational activities. Open mid-June to Sept. Call ahead at other times of the year. Serviced sites $18 a night; unserviced sites from $14.50 (extra charge for more than four persons per site).

Camping KOA Montréal Sud
130 Monette
St-Philippe
(514) 659-8626

Another full-service campground, but more expensive than Camping Daoust.

RESTAURANTS

Montrealers take their food very seriously. Montreal's reputation as a restaurant city goes back to the 19th century and has much to do with the natural gregariousness and hospitality of the Québécois, the all-pervasive European influence (especially French) and, in recent decades, the vast numbers of immigrants Montreal has absorbed and made to feel at home.

Montrealers love to go out to eat, often in large groups, and tend to be faithful to a small selection of favourite places. All four Montreal daily newspapers have well-regarded restaurant critics, and a favourable review invariably brings an initial flurry of interest to any new restaurant, but only the exceptional survive and acquire a permanent place in the locals' affections.

Most of the restaurants we recommend here are in the city centre or close to *métro* stops. We have tried to provide a cross-section of everything that is available but have emphasized the tried and true.

The price scale is based on the average cost of dinner for two without wine and before tax: **$** = under $30; **$$** = $30-$50; **$$$** = $50-$70; **$$$$** = over $70. B = breakfast, L = lunch, D = dinner.

Unless indicated, all restaurants accept at least two major credit cards. Reservations are recommended (except where noted). Some restaurants close for extended holidays, usually in July or Aug; it is always wise to call ahead.

BARBECUED CHICKEN

Montrealers love barbecued chicken, which is grilled on a revolving spit and anointed with a distinctive, spicy sauce that each establishment claims as its secret. This manner of preparation was actually imported from Switzerland by the family that started what is now the Swiss Chalet chain, of which there are several branches in Montreal.

The menu of these barbecued chicken establishments is almost always the same: chicken served in quarters or halves, with French fries and coleslaw. Some have branched out into ribs, which are served alone or in combination with chicken. Chicken pot pie, chicken sandwiches and chicken salads are also usually available.

Bar-B Barn $$
**1201 Guy at Ste-Catherine ouest
931-3811**
Primarily known for ribs; also excellent chicken.

Chalet Bar-B-Q $
**5456 Sherbrooke ouest at Décarie
489-7235
6825 Décarie at Van Horne
739-3226**
These reliable and straightforward establishments are the ancestors of the Swiss Chalet chain (although not part of it).

Laurier Bar-B-Q $
**381 Laurier ouest at du Parc
273-3671**
This is the most "chic" of the group; also known for its mocha cake and house salad.

St-Hubert Bar-B-Q $
**2152 Ste-Catherine ouest at Closse
385-5555
862 Ste-Catherine est at
St-Timothée
385-5555
6355 St-Hubert at Beaubien
385-5555**
Branches of this chain are found throughout Quebec. Excellent take-out and delivery service.

BISTROS

A true phenomenon of the 1980s, the bistro is a happy combination of good food, informal yet elegant surroundings and a casual (if somewhat hectic) crowd. Most bistros are open late, and all are conducive to long and spirited discussions on politics and occasionally sports.

Alexandre $$
1454 Peel at de Maisonneuve ouest
288-5105

A hangout of the advertising crowd, this pub-restaurant (*brasserie*) serves food until 2 AM. Well-known for its imported beers (10 of them on tap). Efficient waiters serve typical bistro fare such as *steak frites*, *choucroute au champagne*, *moules marinière* and assorted sandwiches, salads and pastas. Good choice of desserts. L and D daily.

Bagatelle $$
4806 du Parc at Villeneuve
273-4088

Chef Pascal Gellé's menu features simple, inventive dishes and well-selected wines at extremely reasonable prices, with many items not usually thought of as bistro food served on a rotating, fresh-daily basis. The restaurant's furnishings, imported from Belgium, are beautiful, but the room is somewhat noisy. L Mon to Fri, D daily except Sun.

Boulevards $$
3435 St-Laurent at Sherbrooke
499-9944

This former tavern has been turned into one of Montreal's hottest bistro/bars. The owner and one of the waiters are refugees from L'Express, and they have attempted to reproduce that recipe for success here. Good,

nouvelle cuisine-inspired bistro food, served until very late. Contemporary decor, lots of noise, excellent people-watching and a good selection of wines by the glass. L and D daily.

Chez Gauthier $$
3487 du Parc at Milton
845-2992

Saved from coldness by an abundance of greenery, mirrors and a glassed-in terrace, this large bistro is always busy. A varied permanent menu, including steaks, pasta, sandwiches, salads and delicious desserts (from the adjoining pâtisserie), keeps them coming back. Reasonable prices; wines by the glass. L and D daily, B on Sat.

Crocodile $$
4238 St-Laurent at Rachel
848-0044
5414 Gatineau at Lacombe
733-2125
636 Cathcart at University
866-4979

Les Beaux Jeudis/Thursdays
1449 Crescent at de Maisonneuve ouest
288-5656

These restaurants, the creation of well-known Montreal restaurant impresario Bernard Ragueneau, elevate trendiness to a fine art. Ragueneau's restaurants—all large, noisy, excitingly decorated—appeal to the young crowd in search of the pleasure of each other's company. The food is what the French call *honnête* (honest): namely fresh, filling and well-prepared, if not extraordinarily inventive. But people-watching is fabulous, the kitchens are open late, and the decor is "worth the detour," as the Michelin guide would say. The Crocodile restaurants brew their own beer (which makes up for a somewhat uneven wine list). L and D daily, brunch on Sun.

L'Express $$

3927 St-Denis at Duluth
845-5333

Now 10 years old, L'Express is the grandfather of Montreal bistros, a common meeting ground for Montrealers of all backgrounds and language groups, who pack the place until the wee hours to see, to be seen, to eat and to drink. The well-thought-out menu is based on a relatively short permanent bill of fare, with a few daily specials. Although basic bistro, the food is well known for its quality (try the steak tartare, or the cold roast beef, both of which are served with heavenly French fries). The desserts, from the Pâtisserie de Gascogne, are sublime. The wine list features a great number of special imports, all at a modest mark-up over the prices set by the provincial liquor board. L Mon to Sat, D daily. Open until 3 AM (until midnight on Sun).

Le Sam $$

3715 St-Laurent at des Pins
842-0653

This is a must-see for fans of contemporary architecture and design. An extremely austere, sober interior, based on blond wood and steel, serves as a background for fundamentally good food, French bistro classics with a *nouvelle cuisine* touch. Reasonably priced wine list. Open till 1 AM. L and D daily except Sun.

Au Petit Extra $

1690 Ontario est at Papineau
527-5552

Inspired French cooking at reasonable prices. The substantial menu offers well-prepared meat and fowl dishes lightly spiced and sauced, often with fruit. The vegetables are always fresh, and the cheeses are excellent. The restaurant is furnished with a random assortment of wooden chairs and tables, placed rather close together. The menu is written out on a blackboard (two, actually; the restaurant is made up of two relatively large rooms), and the service is very friendly. L and D Mon to Fri.

Au Petit Resto $

4650 de Mentana at Mont-Royal est
598-7963

A charming neighbourhood restaurant offering well-prepared French food at extremely reasonable prices. The menu is well balanced between meat and fish; the fixed-price menu (about $10) includes an appetizer, main course and tea or coffee. Steak tartare with French fries is also a favourite. Good desserts will add a little to the check. Patrons must bring their own wine. D daily.

L'Entre-Pont $

4622 Hôtel-de-Ville at Villeneuve
845-1369

Rather lost on a residential street, this 15-table restaurant is an example of the sophisticated simplicity and tasty bistro food of the new generation. The food is well seasoned and spiced, the sauces are light and include unusual ingredients (try the *noisette de porc* with blueberries and pepper). Patrons must bring their own wine. D daily.

Le Grain de Sel $
2375 Ste-Catherine est at Fullum
522-5105

Chef Dominique Roquet, from the Lyon area of France, opened this restaurant about five years ago, near the headquarters of both Radio-Canada (the French broadcasting service of the CBC) and Radio-Québec. The mildly intellectual regulars clearly enjoy the fresh Lyonnaise cuisine listed daily on the blackboards (appetizer, main course and tea or coffee are available at several prices, but never more than $15, all-inclusive). The well-selected wine list includes some American, Australian and South American vintages. L Mon to Fri, D Tues to Fri.

BREAKFAST/BRUNCH

Bagel, Etc. $$
4320 St-Laurent at Mont-Royal
845-9462

This charming restaurant is difficult to classify. The decor is vaguely 1930s and the menu resembles that of a New York diner. It is open very late (until 3:30 AM on Sun, Tues and Wed nights; until 4:30 AM on Thurs night; until 6 AM on Fri and Sat nights). The restaurant serves a classic brunch, including caviar and champagne, on Sat and Sun from 9 AM onwards. Closed Mon (except on holiday weekends. Opens at 11 AM Tues to Fri.

Beauty's $
93 Mont-Royal ouest at St-Urbain
849-8883

Although this restaurant is open every day for breakfast and lunch (and very early dinner: it closes at 6 PM), it is known mainly for its weekend brunches. Excellent fresh orange juice, unlimited fresh coffee (regular or decaffeinated), blintzes, French toast, salads and omelettes, including the well-known *mishmash* (eggs, frankfurter, salami, green peppers and fried onions). Many regulars order the "Special," smoked salmon and cream cheese on a bagel. B, L and early D daily.

A Montreal landmark, Beauty's is a great place for Sunday brunch.

Dusty's $
4510 du Parc at Mont-Royal ouest
273-5431

While Beauty's tends to be slightly upscale, Dusty's is just as happy being downscale. Its claim to fame is that it serves brunch every day, all day: excellent orange juice, delicious bagels and 23 types of omelettes. The rest of the menu, which extends to sandwiches (including smoked meat), steaks and pizzas, is good but not remarkable. B, L and D daily.

COFFEE HOUSES AND TEA ROOMS

In addition to the ubiquitous Van Houtte chain, which serves excellent coffees, sandwiches and pastries at dozens of locations in Montreal, the following establishments are worth noting:

La Brûlerie St-Denis $
3967 St-Denis at Duluth
286-9158

Dozens of types of coffee beans from all corners of the world are imported by La Brûlerie and roasted on the premises. Needless to say, the aroma is wonderful. Although open for lunch and dinner daily, breakfast is the best time to visit for a cup of coffee and a croissant. Good sandwiches and excellent pastries. Outdoor terrace. The restaurant also operates a branch in the Ogilvy department store. Coffee (beans or ground) to take out. L and D daily, B Mon to Sat.

Café Santropol $
3990 St-Urbain at Duluth
842-3110

This original and unassuming establishment attracts a crowd of students and counter-culture types who come for the choice of espresso, Ovaltine, fruit juices, more than 60 different black and herbal teas and various ice-cream malts and sodas. The menu includes remarkable two- and three-layer sandwiches with any number of delicious fillings, served with fruits, vegetables and sprouts. The management donates one per cent of the amount of all meal checks to the United Nations. L Tues to Fri, D Tues to Sun, brunch on Sun.

Calories $
4114 Ste-Catherine ouest at Greene
933-8186

Although this establishment serves sandwiches and soups, the main reason for its appeal is the remarkable selection of desserts (including over 20 types of cheesecakes). Wide variety of herbal and other teas; good selection of coffees, including Irish, Spanish and cappuccino. Open at least until 1 AM (2 AM Fri, 3 AM Sat). L and D daily.

Le Daphné $
3803 St-Denis at Roy
849-3042

A classic tea room with lace curtains and small tables, Le Daphné serves excellent cakes, pastries and ice-cream dishes along with more than 30 types of tea and excellent coffee. Open late. L and D daily.

A garden café off Place Jacques-Cartier.

Franni $
5528 Monkland at Old Orchard
486-2033
Headquarters for cheesecake, to go or eat here. Excellent coffee. Also known for its Viennese tortes and chocolate mousse cake. L and D Tues to Sun.

Toman Pastry Shop $
1421 Mackay at Ste-Catherine ouest
844-1605
This second-floor walk-up has been around for over 20 years, serving homemade pastries and cakes based on old Czech family recipes. The strudels, cheesecakes, mousse cakes and Black Forest cake are all excellent. Sandwiches and salads are also served. Montreal hostesses enjoy receiving little gift boxes of the excellent chocolates made on the premises. L and D Mon to Sat (closed Mon in the summer).

CUISINE QUÉBÉCOISE

For a number of years, the Quebec Hotel and Restaurant Institute has been urging both its graduates and other Quebec restaurateurs to serve a *nouvelle cuisine* Québécoise based on locally available products and compatible with the lifestyles of contemporary Quebec. While many restaurants have heeded the call, others continue to serve traditional, hearty *habitant* cuisine favoured by visitors and (occasionally) by Montrealers.

La Binerie Mont-Royal $
367 Mont-Royal est at St-Denis
285-9078
More than 50 years old, this proletarian establishment serves up traditional Quebec cooking, centred on *fèves au lard* (pork and beans), which simmer all day in large pots and are served either plain or with ketchup, molasses,

brown sugar or maple syrup. The rest of the menu gives a good idea of what well-fed woodsmen and trappers eat: pig's knuckle stew, ham or cold roast pork and split-pea soup are favourites. Try the "Canadian plate," which includes beans, a portion of *tourtière* (meat pie) and meatballs in brown sauce. Also known for its Quebec-style desserts, such as *tarte à farlouche* (pie with raisins and molasses); *pouding chômeur* (literally "unemployment pudding"), which is white cake cooked with brown sugar and water; and *bagatelle*, a similar cake with jam, blancmange and maple syrup. The restaurant opens at 6 AM and serves large and inexpensive breakfasts. It is hard to spend more than $10 per person at any time. As you may have suspected, no credit cards or reservations. B and L Mon to Sat, D Mon to Fri.

Auberge Le Vieux St-Gabriel $$
426 St-Gabriel at Notre-Dame est
878-3561
This large and ancient inn (the oldest in North America) contains many artifacts from French Canada's colonial period. The restaurant is a must for the decor alone, although the Québécois dishes, including split-pea and onion soups, *tourtière*, Oka cheese fondue and the smoked trout, are all worth trying. Unfortunately, the desserts are not up to the same standard. L and D daily.

Les Filles du Roy $$
415 Bonsecours at St-Paul est
849-3535
This standby, opened in 1965 on one of the busiest corners in old Montreal, is still owned by the Trottier family. From time to time, it has sunk into little more than a tourist trap, but it now serves a creditable cuisine that highlights traditional Quebec cooking.

Although the dishes are rather heavy, it is worthwhile to taste, at least once, authentic French-Canadian split-pea soup, *tourtière*, meatball stew, ham in maple syrup and Lac Saint-Jean *cipaille* (another type of meat pie). Excellent service by waitresses in 18th-century costumes. Many authentic antiques are incorporated into the decor. Reasonable wine list. L and D daily.

Hélène de Champlain $$$
Île Ste-Hélène
395-2424

During Expo 1967, this restaurant served as the Pavillon d'honneur, where foreign heads of state were received. Now operated by a local restaurateur, Pierre Marcotte, it continues to be one of the city's most beautiful: in an impressive stone building, overlooking the water and surrounded by greenery—just the place for a special celebration. The feel is baronial, the menu and wine list suitably impressive (so is the service). While the food does not reach the same heights, it is almost always satisfactory, and the atmosphere more than makes up for any deficiency. L and D daily.

DELICATESSENS

Montreal has a large Jewish population, and émigrés from Romania are responsible for one of the city's culinary treasures, smoked meat. The secret in preparing this brisket of beef, which is not unlike pastrami, lies in the marinating process and in the skilfully blended spices employed. Smoked meat is best eaten with French fries, a dill pickle and a cola or ginger ale (never with milk!).

Schwartz's/Montreal $
Hebrew Delicatessen
3895 St-Laurent at Marie-Anne
842-4813
This Montreal institution has been open for over 50 years. The smoked meat and the steaks are what draw the crowds, rather than the tawdry decor (highlighted by a long counter on the right, long communal tables on the left, all-over linoleum and bright fluorescent lighting). The rather brusque service is also part of the charm. There are almost always lineups. A must-see. No reservations or credit cards. B, L and D daily.

Other reliable establishments serving smoked meat are **Ben's** (990 de Maisonneuve ouest at Metcalfe, 844-1000), **Dunn's** (892 Ste-Catherine ouest at Mansfield, 866-4377) and the **Briskets** chain (several locations, including 2055 Bishop at de Maisonneuve ouest, 843-3650, and 1073 Beaver Hall Hill at René-Lévesque ouest, 878-3641; see also Hamburgers and Hotdogs).

Wilensky's Light Lunch $
34 Fairmount ouest at Clark
271-0247
This establishment, while not a full-fledged delicatessen in the strict sense, was "created" by Moe Wilensky in 1932, and was originally a barber shop as well as a tobacconist and lunch counter. The atmosphere has remained unchanged, and the cross-cultural clientele would not have it any other way. Most of the faithful order the "Special," which is a sandwich composed of beef, bologna and salami with mustard on special toasted bread. Hotdogs, sandwiches, dill pickles, *karnatzel* (smoked sausage) and fountain soft drinks complete the bill of fare. Popular for take-out. L daily (open 9-4). No credit cards, no reservations.

DEPARTMENT-STORE HAVENS

Eaton $
Ninth floor
677 Ste-Catherine ouest at University
284-8421

Combine an architectural experience with a pleasant luncheon: the 9th-floor restaurant in the Eaton store was designed by a master of the French art-deco style and is one of Montreal's truly great rooms. The food (from the menu or buffet) is simple, fresh and well prepared. L Mon to Sat, D Thurs and Fri.

Tartan Room at Ogilvy $
1307 Ste-Catherine ouest at de la Montagne
842-7711 ext. 232

A favourite with Montreal's shopping elite, recommended mainly for its afternoon tea, a charming throwback to a bygone age. For more serious food in the same store, the **Café Sifon** in the basement is recommended. L Mon to Fri, D Thurs and Fri, tea served Mon to Sat 3-5 PM.

HAMBURGERS AND HOTDOGS

Il Était Une Fois $
600 Place d'Youville at McGill
842-6783

In the former station of the Montreal and Southern Counties Railway, this establishment is decorated with vintage signs and memorabilia. The excellent half-pound hamburgers are served in a dozen different styles, in baskets with large-cut French fries, and are best accompanied by old-fashioned fountain drinks and beer. Good hotdogs, too. L and D daily.

La Paryse $
302 Ontario est at St-Denis
842-2040

Named for owner Paryse Taillefer, this rabbit's-warren of little rooms serves up high-quality hamburgers, which look and taste like they were made at home. Delicious hand-cut French fries. Ask for a "Regular," which is served with mozzarella cheese, pickle, onions, tomatoes and mayonnaise, or a "Special," which includes bacon and cream cheese. Soft drinks are served in the bottle with straws. Excellent chocolate and carrot cakes. L and D daily. No credit cards.

Montreal Pool Room $
1200 St-Laurent at Ste-Catherine
861-1397

More than 75 years old and in a class of its own, this counter-style operation serves the best hotdogs in town. For less than a dollar, you get a hotdog dressed with onions, coleslaw and mustard, accompanied by very creditable French fries. Service is fast, but the decor and ambience leave something to be desired. Located in Montreal's (not very dangerous) "tenderloin" district, and open until 3 AM. Colourful crowd. L and D daily. No reservations, no credit cards.

For other good hotdogs, try the **Valentine** chain (numerous locations, including 1101 de Maisonneuve est at Amherst and 405 Sherbrooke est at St-Denis). Adventurous visitors are urged to try a relatively new Quebec specialty known as *poutine*, a rather decadent dish of French fries, cheese curds and brown gravy served in a cup, usually available wherever hotdogs and hamburgers are served.

RESTAURANTS

HOTEL DINING

The Beaver Club $$$$
Queen Elizabeth Hotel
900 René-Lévesque ouest at
Mansfield
861-3511

This restaurant is the stuff of legends, a favourite for special occasions. The original Beaver Club was an association of fur traders in the 18th century, known for its good times. This restaurant has attracted the moguls of the business community since it opened in the 1950s. Several business leaders have their own reserved tables at lunch, and to be recognized by maitre d' Charles is regarded as a sign of status. The excellent food is based on fine meats and seafood. The cooking is original, the accompaniments always fresh, and the desserts wonderful. Try the banana bread (included in the bread basket). Chocolates made on the premises come with the coffee. L Mon to Fri, D daily.

Société Café $$$
Hôtel Vogue
1415 de la Montagne at
Ste-Catherine ouest
987-8168

A stunning restaurant in Montreal's newest luxury hotel, the Société Café was a hit from the first day. The striking salmon and royal-blue decor speaks of up-to-date comfort; the menu, while basically modern French, has many international accents and flavours. Management calls the cooking "Eurasian;" you will have to decide. In fine weather, you can sit outside and watch the elegant passers-by. B, L and D daily, brunch on Sun.

Le Café de Paris $$$$
Ritz-Carlton Hotel
1228 Sherbrooke ouest at
Drummond
842-4212

A restaurant fully in tune with its surroundings. The sumptuous dining room has service and prices to match. The food is classic French, the crowd international. Excellent smoked and fresh salmon, sole and all the traditional meat dishes, served with style. This room opens onto the greenery and duck pond of the famous Ritz Garden. B, L and D daily, brunch on Sun.

Le Castillon $$$
Bonaventure Hilton
1 Place Bonaventure at Mansfield
878-2332

A magnificent room in country château style, with waiters in 18th-century garb. There is a wonderful terrace for summer dining outdoors. Popular with business types, the restaurant offers a special 55-minute lunch. Le Castillon is just as enjoyable in the evening at a more leisurely pace. The cuisine is modern French: novel fare prepared with a light touch. Good seafood and a remarkable Caesar salad. Good wine list, with an experienced sommelier to give advice. L and D daily, brunch on Sun.

Le Cercle $$$
Four Seasons Hotel
1050 Sherbrooke ouest at Peel
284-1110, ext. 6452

The decor here is extraordinary: the large circular room is highlighted by a central white-columned rotunda, surrounded by art-deco railings and lamp standards. Various intimate nooks have been created with mirrored columns and glass bead curtains. The food is Californian in inspiration, with touches of French, Italian, Asian and other cuisines, all based on the freshest of ingredients. Well-known sommelier Don Jean Léandri is a charming guide to the appropriate wine. Impeccable service. B, L and D daily.

Other notable hotel rooms are **Le Neufchatel** (in the Château Champlain Hotel), **Le Lutétia** (in the Hôtel de la Montagne).

LATE NIGHT

Montreal's bars stay open until 3 AM, so finding a late-night snack usually isn't a problem. But if the urge for bacon and eggs hits at 5 AM, this restaurant's for you:

Lux $
5220 St-Laurent at Laurier
271-9272
This extraordinary place combines a well-stocked international newsstand, tobacconist, restaurant and bar and is open 24 hours a day, seven days a week. The building, once a clothing factory, is remarkable for its dramatic central stairwell, surrounded by numerous green and grey balconies on which all of the action takes place. The restaurant offerings are of the fast-food variety (but creditable nonetheless), and breakfast is served around the clock. Good desserts. Prices are somewhat high, but reasonable given the convenience factor. B, L and D daily. No reservations.

PIZZA

In addition to the **Donini** (take-out number 383-6000) and **Mike's** (take-out number 731-3030) chains, each of which has many eat-in branches, several Montreal pizzerias rank head and shoulders above the others. Two are:

Da Pizzettaro $
1121 Anderson at René-Lévesque ouest
861-7076
This restaurant serves up *nouvelle* pizza, cooked in wood-burning ovens. The selection is excellent and unusual: try in particular the *Quattro Stagioni* (Four Seasons), a pizza divided into four sections, each with different toppings. Charming outdoor terrace in the summer. Under the same ownership as the Latini restaurant next door. L and D daily.

La Pizzaiolle $
1446-A Crescent at de Maisonneuve ouest
845-4158
5100 Hutchison at Laurier ouest
274-9349
Another upscale pizzeria with wood-burning ovens; excellent choice of very fresh toppings. Frequented by a young cosmopolitan crowd. L and D daily.

PUB FOOD

Peel Pub $
1106 de Maisonneuve ouest at Peel
845-9002
1107 Ste-Catherine ouest at Peel
844-6769
3461 du Parc at Milton
843-7993
The ultimate college crowd hangout. Serves hundreds simultaneously with cheap (but high-quality) food and (most importantly) inexpensive beer. The staff is friendly, and the atmosphere reminds one of a perpetual party. A must for visitors of the right age group. Open until 3 AM on Fri and Sat nights. L and D daily. No credit cards, no reservations.

SEAFOOD

Although Montreal is a port city and has always had fine seafood restaurants, the appreciation of fresh seafood varieties—outside the "fish on Friday" syndrome—is a relatively recent phenomenon. Montreal's best seafood restaurants tend to be French, Greek or, for their wonderful way with mussels, Belgian.

Chez Delmo $$$
211 Notre-Dame ouest at St-Laurent
849-4061
A restaurant that dates back to Victorian times, Delmo's is wonderfully atmospheric. The first room has two long bars on either side, facing walls of mirror and ceramic tiles. In the back is a small but warm country room, preferable for groups larger than two and the only facility open in the evening. Fish is prepared simply and traditionally here. Famous cream of tomato soup and good oysters in season. L Mon to Fri, D Mon to Sat.

Desjardins $$$
1175 Mackay at René-Lévesque ouest
866-9741
One of Montreal's oldest seafood restaurants, this establishment has recently changed hands. The dining room is comfortable and beautifully appointed, the seafood fresh. Try the Gaspé salmon or the lobster. Good vegetables, properly cooked, accompany the classic dishes. L and D daily.

La Marée $$$$
404 Place Jacques-Cartier at St-Paul est
861-9794
Now 15 years old, La Marée is in a magnificent 18th-century house at the very centre of Old Montreal. The standards are high, and the cooking is classical French. There are meat dishes for those less enthusiastic about fish. Memorable meals. The tables are well separated, the service attentive and polished. L Mon to Fri, D daily.

Les Mauvais Garçons $$$
4466 Marquette at Simard
524-7989
The kitschy mirrored decor here is aimed at a yuppie clientele, with shrimp specialties the bait. The shrimp is prepared in many novel ways; one is sure to please. Other seafood and meat dishes are also available from the original and inventive menu. D Tues to Sat.

STEAK HOUSES

Gibby's $$$
298 Place d'Youville at St-Pierre
282-1837
Despite its location in one of the most charming buildings in old Montreal, Gibby's has managed to take on a rather American flavour and a clientele of out-of-town businessmen. No matter, because the steaks at Gibby's are magnificent, with quality cuts prepared exactly as requested. The accompaniments are simple and the portions huge. Each meal comes with a large salad tossed in a pewter bowl, which

does away with the need for a starter. Desserts are similarly generous but most diners are too overwhelmed to care. Attractive antique Québécois decor; large terrace for summer dining. Good service and adequate wine list. L and D daily.

Moishe's Steak House $$$
3961 St-Laurent at Duluth
845-3509

This well-known restaurant was founded in 1937 by Moishe Lighter, whose sons carry on the tradition. Steak and the trimmings is the *raison d'être* here, but the veal and chicken dishes are not to be ignored. Excellent breads, coleslaw and pickles are standard accompaniments; the *karnatzel* (smoked sausage), chopped chicken liver, onion rings and French fries are all exceptional. Fresh pastries made daily, huge portions, short but appropriate wine list. L and D daily.

Café-bar on Place Jacques-Cartier.

TAVERNS

Until 10 years ago, this kind of place was peculiar to Quebec: a men-only, beer-only drinking parlour where suds, sports on television and companionship were the primary concern and food, if available, was secondary. Certain taverns, such as Chez Magnan and the now-defunct Le Gobelet, distinguished themselves by offering better food. Today, taverns admit women, serve wine and are, for the most part, called *brasseries*. Chez Magnan retains some of the atmosphere of the old-style Quebec tavern and is well worth a visit.

Chez Magnan $
2602 St-Patrick at Charlevoix
935-9647

This remarkable establishment, in the blue-collar area of Pointe St-Charles, is the best-known tavern in Montreal. It specializes in roast beef and steaks

(available in four sizes, from six to 22 ounces), and regular festivals of lobster and shrimp add to its fame. Traditional Québécois fare is also served. Upstairs the atmosphere is still very much that of a traditional, sudsy tavern with a principally male crowd (males predominate at lunch); downstairs is a large and comfortable dining room, complete with salad bar. Low-priced wine list. Excellent, friendly service. L Mon to Fri, D Tues to Sun.

VEGETARIAN

Le Commensal   **$**
680 Ste-Catherine ouest at
University
871-1480
2115 St-Denis at Sherbrooke
845-2627
3715 de la Reine-Marie at
Côte-des-Neiges
733-9755
This chain presents an intelligent, businesslike approach to healthy eating. The decor is modern and clean with no counter-culture touches; the fully vegetarian menu features dishes that taste like homemade. Excellent desserts, a wide choice of teas, both black and herbal, and coffees. L and D daily at all locations; B at the St-Denis outlet.

WITH A VIEW

Le Tour de Ville   **$$$**
Le Grand Hôtel
777 University at St-Jacques
879-1370
Montreal has only one revolving restaurant. Fortunately, the "Tour" of its name does not stand for "tourist trap" but is the French word for "turn"; in fact, the food is excellent if somewhat

pricey. Try the tartare of fresh salmon, the rack of lamb and the various lobster dishes. Wonderful desserts (the *tarte tatin*, French apple pie, in particular). A short but appropriate wine list. D daily.

BY NATIONALITY

Visitors with adventurous tastes may wish to wander farther afield, into the cuisines of other European nations or of even more exotic lands. In either case, Montreal is endowed with a wealth of establishments of all types, awaiting your pleasure.

BELGIAN

L'Actuel   **$$**
1194 Peel at Cypress
866-1537
The specialty of this restaurant, which has a magnificent view over Square Dorchester, is mussels prepared 13 different ways, with or without their shells. Wonderful Belgian French fries are served with mayonnaise. The steaks and desserts are also notable. Good choice of imported beers and appropriate wines. L Tues to Fri, D Tues to Sat.

Witloof   **$$**
3619 St-Denis at Cherrier
281-0100
Founded by a couple who once owned a notable restaurant in Brussels, this Montreal bistro was an immediate success. Along with mussels and French fries, it also serves *witloof au gratin* (endive with melted cheese and ham), rabbit in a beer and cream sauce, *waterzooi à la gantoise* (chicken in cream sauce) and other Belgian specialties. Charming, lively turn-of-the-century bistro decor and reasonable prices. L Mon to Fri, D daily.

BRAZILIAN

Nega Fulo $
1257 Amherst near René-Lévesque est
522-1554

Nega Fulo presents a mixture of Brazilian, Mexican and Cajun cuisines, served up by charming chef and proprietress Norma Hernandez. All the classic Brazilian dishes are here: *feijoada, caipirinha, bobo, vatapa*, turtle stew and alligator steak. The decor is eclectic, informal and suggestive of a trip down the Amazon. L Mon to Fri, D daily.

CAJUN

La Maison Cajun $$$
1219 Mackay at Ste-Catherine ouest
871-3898

Although there are obvious historical connections between French Canada and the Louisiana Cajuns, the cooking of our southern brethren has been slow to penetrate the eating habits of Montrealers. The fact that this relatively small restaurant is almost always jammed speaks to the fact that the cultural connection has now been made. This restaurant serves up excellent gumbo (thick soup-stew based on pork and sausages), jambalaya (a stew of duck, chicken and shrimp) and other dishes done in the original and usually spicy Cajun style. Good pecan pie. The wine list includes several American selections. L Tues to Fri, D daily.

CHINESE

Until 1970 or so, every Chinese restaurant in Montreal served Cantonese food. Now, you are just as likely to find western Chinese cuisines such as Szechuan and Hunan or dishes from Shanghai or Canton. Also popular is the intriguing Chinese circulating buffet, *dim sum*.

Abacus $$$
2144 Mackay at Sherbrooke ouest
933-8444

Classic and grand Szechuan and Hunan cooking, served in an elegant townhouse. The piano bar downstairs is popular for cocktails or after-dinner drinks. L Mon to Fri, D daily.

Chinese Tea House $$
1424 Bishop at Ste-Catherine ouest
845-7441

A mix of Cantonese and Szechuan in a sophisticated atmosphere. L Mon to Sat, D daily.

Le Chrysanthème $$$
1208 Crescent at Ste-Catherine ouest
397-1408

A favourite with Montrealers. Peking and Szechuan cuisines are served in this comfortable and stylish restaurant with minimalist decor. Hot dishes are indicated by asterisks on the menu (even these have been tamed somewhat to accommodate local tastes). L Mon to Fri, D daily.

Élysée Mandarin $$$
1221 Mackay at Ste-Catherine ouest
866-5975

Top-quality Szechuan cooking in a sophisticated, comfortable environment. The somewhat French style comes from the fact that this is a branch of a Chinese restaurant in Paris. L Mon to Fri, D Mon to Sat.

Hunan $$

Second floor
1092 St-Laurent at de la
Gauchetière ouest
866-8108

A very large restaurant in Chinatown. Szechuan and Hunan dishes at reasonable prices. L and D daily.

Kam Fung $$

Second floor
1006 Clark at de la Gauchetière
ouest
866-4016

Dim sum served daily at lunch in a gymnasium-size room. Waiters circulate with carts offering a large selection of delicacies, mainly steamed. Diners choose at will and run a tab—a delicious and exciting adventure that can be habit-forming. There is sometimes a long wait on Sun. L and D daily.

Mei, Le Café Chinois $$

5309 St-Laurent at Laurier
271-5945

A moderately priced and quite exciting restaurant owned by an Iranian business consultant. The restaurant is large, bright and modern; the open kitchen allows the diners to watch the interesting goings-on between courses. Dishes from all regions of China are offered, along with a good selection of imported beers. L and D daily.

Le Piment Rouge $$$

1170 Peel at Cypress
866-7816

A remarkable restaurant in what was once the Windsor Hotel. Serves the cuisine of the western provinces of Szechuan and Hunan, which owners Chuck and Hazel Mah were the first to introduce to Montreal. L and D daily.

South Seas $

6690 St-Jacques, west of
Cavendish
489-3897

This is a place for nostalgia: the menu offers everyone's Cantonese favourites, plus such very special dishes as stuffed chicken South Seas and garland of shrimp. A family restaurant in a nondescript motel row. L and D daily.

FRENCH

Because Montreal is a French-speaking city in a French-speaking province, we use the designation "French" here with some hesitation—it could also be applied to virtually any restaurant that does not adopt another "ethnic" category.

Chez La Mère Michel $$$

1209 Guy between René-Lévesque
and Ste-Catherine
934-0473

Owner Micheline Delbuguet has run this classic establishment since 1965. Fresh ingredients and careful preparation mean classical French country cuisine in a warm, relaxed setting. Excellent wine list. L and D daily Mon to Sat.

Le Caveau $$

2063 Victoria between
Sherbrooke ouest and President
Kennedy
844-1624

Slightly difficult to find (roughly between the McCord Museum and the Eaton department store), this traditional restaurant is in a small house, reminiscent of a country inn, nestled among the office towers. *Cuisine bourgeoise* (plain cooking) is served in the intimate but rather dark lower room and in the airy, brighter rooms on the two floors above. Serves excellent French country breakfasts every morning from 7:30. B, L and D daily.

Les Halles $$$$
**1450 Crescent at de Maisonneuve ouest
844-2328**

This restaurant has a worldwide reputation as a temple of gastronomy. Meticulous cooking and presentation; service beyond reproach. The decor evokes the old food markets in Paris. Try the mousse of quail, the fish soup *en feuilleté*, the rack of lamb and, for dessert, the *tarte tatin* (exceptional apple pie). L Tues to Sat, D daily except Sun.

Les Mignardises $$$$
**2035-37 St-Denis at Ontario est
842-1151**

A jewel of the Montreal restaurant scene, this relatively new (1987) restaurant has quickly made it to the top. Owned and operated by veterans of Les Halles. Inventive dishes, admirably served under silver cloches in an elegantly decorated room one floor up from street level. Widely separated tables; courteous and knowledgeable service. Fabulous wine list. L and D Tues to Sat.

Le Paris $$
**1812 Ste-Catherine ouest at St-Mathieu
937-4898**

This restaurant, with its somewhat outdated (but comfortable) decor, seems impervious to change. For more than 40 years, it has been serving exactly the same food in the same traditional way. Such classics as poached salmon, veal liver, *blanquette de veau* and *boeuf bourguignon* keep serious diners coming back. Service by efficient, experienced waitresses. Reasonable all-French wine list. L and D Mon to Sat.

Le St-Amable $$$$
**188 St-Amable at Place Jacques-Cartier
866-3471**

Founded in the 1960s, this elegant restaurant, which specializes in game dishes, fish and seafood, has acquired an enviable reputation for consistency and excellence. Warm and characterful dining rooms on the ground floor. Those who like old stone walls and beams should ask to be seated in the basement. Located in the heart of old Montreal, Le St-Amable has a large and faithful following. L Mon to Fri, D daily.

Le Bonaparte $$$
**443 St-François-Xavier at
St-Sacrement
844-4368**

With a wonderful location in Old Montreal (try for a seat in the windows or in the lovely and surprising greenhouse room at the rear), this restaurant offers an inventive, light and exciting menu, served with panache by a corps of attentive waiters. The menu, which is based on always-fresh ingredients, will appeal to dieters. The adjoining pastry shop, L'Impératrice, is under the same management and is known for its wonderful desserts. L Mon to Fri, D daily.

Laloux $$
**250 des Pins at Laval
287-9127**

Although the decor is bistro-like, the atmosphere and food tell you that eating is taken seriously here. The menu emphasizes classic dishes such as *bavette* (a cut of steak), chicken dishes, pasta and salads, inventively prepared and seasoned, from a short but ever-changing menu. Good choice of wines by the glass. L Mon to Fri, D daily.

Le St-Honoré $$
**1616 Ste-Catherine ouest at Guy
932-5550**

Tucked in behind the large and popular Faubourg Ste-Catherine shopping centre and food fair, and located in an historic house that previously belonged to the Grey Nuns, this restaurant and its chef, Philippe Mollé, propose a fresh and inventive approach to several traditional French dishes. Wonderful dishes of beef and lamb are served with interesting vegetables and *faubourg* potatoes (baked with olive oil and sea salt and seasoned with curry). As befits a restaurant operated by a former disciple of Lenôtre in Paris, desserts are set out on a separate

menu and worth saving room for. Reasonably priced wine list. The ground-floor grill offers a simpler menu and a salad bar. L Mon to Fri, D daily.

Le Parchemin $$$
**1333 University at de
Maisonneuve ouest
844-1619**

A new and very chic restaurant is located in the former vestry of Christ Church Cathedral. The slightly solemn decor is a wonderful complement to the classic French cuisine; the six-course *menu dégustation* or the four-course *table d'hôte* are good choices. Very long and complete wine list. L Mon to Fri, D daily.

La Picholette $$$
**1020 St-Denis at Viger est
843-8502**

Two blocks south of the St-Denis restaurant row, in an elegant stone house, chef Ginette Van der Berg creates fresh and exciting variants on traditional French cuisine, elaborately presented and elegantly served. L and D Mon to Sat.

Le Tricolore $$
**2065 Bishop at de Maisonneuve
ouest
843-7745**

In a relaxed decor made up of found objects, this restaurant successfully combines informality with professionalism. The menu is well composed around wonderful roasts and very ably prepared fish dishes. Le Tricolore is not known for its desserts, but that does not appear to disturb its many followers. L and D daily.

Vent Vert $$
2105 de la Montagne at de Maisonneuve ouest
842-2482

Choose a table in the glassed-in front portion or one of the more intimate inner alcoves. Chefs Denis Généro and Patrick Vesnok offer a wonderful and elegant cuisine with a tinge of *nouvelle*. Excellent dessert selection and limited but well-chosen wine list. L Mon to Sat, D daily.

L'Escale Bretonne $
4007 St-Denis at Cherrier
843-6354

Although less popular than when introduced 20 years ago, the typical crêperie of Brittany continues to be a feature of the Montreal restaurant scene. L'Escale Bretonne offers a long list of fillings for the paper-thin sweet or savoury crêpes. Excellent onion soup is also available, and a dessert crêpe is a popular way to complete a meal. L and D daily.

La Ferrandière $
1652 Ontario est at Papineau
522-9897

La Ferrandière offers classic Lyonnaise cuisine, including chicken in the Brest style, *foie-gras*, sausages and a remarkable dish called *matefaim* ("triumph over hunger")—a filling crêpe based on beer, cheese and a meat or seafood filling. Simple decor and friendly service. A remarkable bargain. L Thurs and Fri, D Tues to Sat.

Le Mas des Oliviers $$
1216 Bishop at Ste-Catherine ouest
861-6733

This is an old standby for *cuisine bourgeoise* well prepared under the watchful eye of owner Jacques Muller. Specialties from the south of France include onion soup; a fish soup (*pescadou*) served with *rouille* (a peppery paste), croutons, mayonnaise, garlic, saffron and cheese; rack of lamb; good fish preparations; and excellent desserts. The decor is rustic and the service friendly. Lots of regular patrons. L Mon to Fri, D daily.

La Rapière $$$
1490 Stanley at de Maisonneuve ouest
844-8920

Opened almost 20 years ago by owner Louis Nault, this warm and friendly basement restaurant offers the vigorous and generous cooking of the Pyrenees. Excellent cheeses and an appropriate selection of wines. The atmosphere here is rather masculine, and the clients are mostly regulars. Close to many hotels. L and D Mon to Fri.

Citron Lime $$
4669 St-Denis at St-Joseph
284-3130

Just below ground level, the room is stark black and white, with touches of colour coming from a smattering of lemons which appear to be encased in glass behind the service bar. The overall effect is fresh, clean and inviting. The primary culinary influence here is Asian; the cooking is light, the ingredients fresh and the seasonings exotic. Good choice of reasonably priced wines. D Tues to Sun.

Champs Élysées $$$
1808 Sherbrooke ouest at St-Mathieu
939-1212

This relatively new restaurant is the creation of chef Christian Lévêque, formerly of the Café de Paris at the Ritz-Carlton Hotel. He dreamed of opening his own place and, to judge by the decor, the menu and the service, that dream has been realized. The restaurant reinterprets classic French dishes, with fresh ingredients and light sauces. Well-constructed wine list. On the ground floor of the Tour Versailles Hotel (although not part of it). Valet parking. L and D daily.

Claude Postel $$$
443 St-Vincent at Notre-Dame
875-5067

Monsieur Postel, previously the chef of Le Bonaparte, opened his restaurant about 18 months ago next to Montreal's courthouse (it's a regular haunt for Montreal's legal gourmets). The restaurant serves French provincial *cuisine bourgeoise* with remarkable *charcuterie*, well-seasoned soups, grilled and stewed meats and carefully prepared fish. Desserts are one of M. Postel's specialties, and they do not disappoint. L Mon to Fri, D daily.

Le Fadeau $$$
423 St-Claude at St-Paul est
878-3959

Several years ago, chef Henri Wojick took over what was a Portuguese restaurant, gallicized the name and went on to create an extremely personal little restaurant. The cooking is based on recipes of the great classic French chefs, reconstituted with present-day ingredients of the highest quality. The service is impeccable, and the decor, although a little cold, conveys a sense of occasion. One of the best wine cellars in Montreal, including many half-bottles. D Mon to Sat.

GERMAN

Chez Better $
160 Notre-Dame est at St-Laurent ouest
861-2617
1430 Stanley at Ste-Catherine ouest
848-9859
4382 St-Laurent at Mont-Royal
845-4554

This chain (there are even more branches than those listed above) has based its success on sausages; German, Czech and other wursts, served up with beer, French fries and sauerkraut, make for a most satisfying meal. Strudel and other desserts available. L and D daily.

GREEK

Montreal has more than a hundred Greek restaurants, many of them so-called *brochetteries*, which specialize in skewers (*brochettes*) of beef, chicken, scallops and shrimps, along with other Greek fare. These inexpensive restaurants are found everywhere and are particularly concentrated along Prince Arthur and Duluth streets. Many allow patrons to bring their own wine. The restaurants listed below are more authentic and serious in their approach to cookery than others.

Costas $$$
1236 Mackay at Ste-Catherine ouest
933-4565

Fresh, fresh, fresh fish is the mainstay at this *psarotaverna* (fish tavern). The offerings, selected by the chef from an assortment on a bed of ice, are grilled in the most simple manner. The restaurant also has a variety of excellent Greek hors d'oeuvres and salads. L Mon to Fri, D daily.

Milos $$$$
5357 du Parc at Fairmount ouest
272-3522

Owned by Costas Spiliadis, Milos excels in many ways. To start with, the fish and shellfish are always impeccably fresh, chosen to meet the exacting standards of the fussy owner. Then the broadly based clientele of regulars pays lavishly for the privilege of eating here: the place is always packed, despite being one of the most expensive restaurants of any type in Montreal. Finally, despite its "harbour rustic" style, the restaurant is nonetheless luxurious and comfortable. The washrooms, in particular, are incomparably grand and are definitely worth a visit. L Sun to Fri, D daily.

Symposium $$
4293 St-Denis at Marie-Anne
842-0867

The fare at this restaurant is similar to that at the ones listed above, but less expensive. L Mon to Fri, D daily.

INDIAN

Golden Curry House $
5210 St-Laurent at Laurier
270-2561

An extraordinarily narrow restaurant providing excellent southern Indian cuisine, well executed and spiced and served by a helpful and friendly staff. L Mon to Sat, D daily.

Pique-Assiette $
2051 Ste-Catherine ouest at St-Marc
932-7141

Northern Indian cuisine is featured at this restaurant, part of the Bombay Palace chain. The buffet at noon is an exceptional bargain. Excellent service by waitresses who are anxious to explain the spicing of each dish. Bass and Tartan beers on tap; hamburgers and steak available for those who do not like Indian cooking. Delightful curries. L and D daily, brunch buffet on Sun.

Le Taj $
2077 Stanley at Ste-Catherine ouest
845-9015

A buffet is available daily at this relatively new restaurant. Tandoori dishes are a specialty. L Sun to Fri, D daily.

ITALIAN

L'Altro $$$
205 Viger ouest at Jeanne-Mance
393-3456

This exceptional new restaurant, owned and operated by the same people as Latini, combines excellent Italian dishes with Japanese sushi. This pairing, while not obvious, is very pleasing and has attracted good crowds. Located in a building attached to the Convention Centre. There is a food store and wine bar on the ground floor; upstairs is a more luxurious room with a large open kitchen. Several types of *risotto* are always available, as is a wide variety of meat dishes. The exceptional wine list includes many unusual selections available by the glass. L and D daily.

Baci $$$
2095 McGill College at Sherbrooke ouest
288-7901

The architecture is almost as interesting as the food here. On the lower levels of a major office complex, Baci opens onto a greenery-filled atrium. The bar on the upper level leads to a series of staggered terraces with tables and ends in a relatively intimate dining room on the lowest level. Excellent pasta and *risotto*; splendid meat, fish and prepared vegetables. Homemade desserts. L Mon to Fri, D Mon to Sat.

Bocca D'Oro $$$
1448 St-Mathieu at de Maisonneuve ouest
933-8414

A luxuriously appointed restaurant in a townhouse, just west of the downtown core. Pasta made on the premises, excellent soups and other examples of classical Italian cuisine are served by extremely professional waiters who cater to the diners' every whim. L and D Mon to Sat.

Latini $$$
1130 Jeanne-Mance at René-Lévesque ouest
861-3166

This restaurant has been around for about 10 years. From a modest start, it was rebuilt entirely in 1990 and became one of the most lavish restaurants in the city. One feature that has been retained is the wonderful terrace overlooking René-Lévesque. The staff has a warm welcome for everyone. The pastas are perfect, the main dishes avoid the clichés of Italian cuisine. Fabulous wine list. L Mon to Fri, D Mon to Sat.

Da Marcello $$$$
825 Laurier est near St-Hubert
276-1580

Several blocks east of the fashionable section of Laurier, this small but serious restaurant attracts *cognoscenti* from around the city for the best Tuscan cooking in Montreal. The menu, in Italian only, gives poetic descriptions

of each dish, none of which will provoke a sense of *déjà vu*. A complimentary bowl of nuts is presented at the end of the meal. Well-selected wines complement the food. L Mon to Fri, D Mon to Sat.

Oggi $$$
108 Laurier ouest at St-Urbain
272-9122

As chic as its location, the cooking is a patchwork of various regional cuisines, perfectly served and prepared. Warm, friendly service and appropriately selected wines, reasonable in price. D daily.

One of several well-hidden courtyard restaurants to be discovered in Old Montreal.

L'Oleandro $$$
1637 Van Horne at Rockland
270-5057

This sophisticated restaurant, on the ground floor of a row house in residential Outremont, offers refined cuisine to a clientele that returns because of the personalized service. Exceptional antipasto, fresh pasta *al dente*, well-prepared (if not always generous) servings of meat and fowl and a good selection of cheese and wine.

Le Piémontais $$

**1145-A de Bullion at René-Lévesque est
861-8122**

Owner Remo Pompeo has been in Montreal for about 15 years, having arrived rather obliquely by way of the mining town of Sept-Îles on the north shore of the St. Lawrence River, where he ran a successful restaurant. Perhaps this explains why this basement eatery, expanded several times over the years, is such a warm and comforting refuge. There is invariably a wait for a table, even with a reservation, but the staff make diners feel at home and serve cocktails and chicken wings to render the delay more palatable. All of the Italian classics are on the menu, and the clientele is never less than satisfied. Remo keeps a very sophisticated wine cellar—many rare vintages not seen elsewhere in the city are available for the asking. L Mon to Fri, D Mon to Sat.

Prego $$$

**5142 St-Laurent at Laurier
271-3234**

This restaurant practises *nuova cucina italiana*, which has the same good qualities and faults as *nouvelle cuisine française*. The portions, although always admirably presented, are sometimes a bit meagre, and the wait between dishes is sometimes long. But the food is inventive, the preparation meticulous, and the service otherwise exemplary. The owner and his staff, masters at remembering clients' names, have fostered great loyalty among a sophisticated crowd. D daily.

JAPANESE

Le Jardin Sakura $$

**2114 de la Montagne at Sherbrooke ouest
288-9122**

A large conventional dining room, a sushi bar with aquarium and several little private tatami rooms. Connoisseurs come here for the tempura: they know that the test of good tempura is the lightness of the batter, and it is here that Sakura excels. This restaurant has been pleasing Montrealers since 1974. L Mon to Sat, D daily.

Katsura $$$

**2170 de la Montagne at Sherbrooke ouest
849-1172**

On the same street as Le Jardin Sakura, this restaurant is distinguished by the overall excellence of its food. The layout is similar to that of Sakura, but much more luxurious, and the prices are therefore higher. This establishment pioneered sushi in Montreal and it remains the highlight, although the teriyaki dishes, the tempura and the sashimi are also good bets. Operated by a large Japanese-owned chain. L Mon to Sat, D daily.

LEBANESE

Daou $$

**519 Faillon est at Lajeunesse
276-8310**

Montreal has a large Lebanese population, and Daou is its official dining room. The decor of this large room is nothing special (even mundane), and the appointments are far from luxurious. Nonetheless, it is always packed with eager diners, most of whom seem to know someone, either on the staff or in the room. The best way to approach this cuisine is through a *mezza*, a sort of hors d'oeuvre buffet in a plate, which may include meat and spinach pies, vine leaves, *hummus* (chick-pea puree with garlic and lemon), and *baba ganouj* (eggplant "caviar" with a smoky taste). Add to this a *kebe* or *kibbeh* (pronounced "kibby") a sort of steak tartare made of lamb, cracked wheat, onion and spices. The salads, including the wonderful *tabbouleh*, with parsley, cracked wheat, onion, tomato and lemon, and the *fatouche*, with cucumber, lettuce, mint and broiled pieces of pita bread, should not be overlooked. For dessert, try the cream of rice with orange water. L and D daily.

Olive $$$
4275 St-Denis at Mont-Royal
286-2922

This restaurant serves essentially the same dishes as Daou but the surroundings are far more luxurious. The interior has the feel of a Mediterranean inn, with plants and large terra cotta jars placed against sunny yellow walls. The building itself is a remarkable conversion of typical St-Denis residential flats into a very exciting restaurant and retail combination. Try the wonderful garlic chicken or the excellent shish kebab made with the finest cubed filet mignon. The pleasant and busy terrace outside the front of the restaurant attracts a trendy crowd. L and D daily.

MALAYSIAN

Le Singapour $
1452 St-Mathieu at de
Maisonneuve ouest
938-8228

The proprietors, a husband and wife team from Malaysia, serve up unusual dishes from their country as well as from China and Hong Kong. Among

the excellent choices are a beef *satay*, with peanut sauce and the *mee goreng*, which is a stir-fry of shrimp, bamboo shoots, Chinese noodles, chicken, peppers and onions. Coriander and coconut are the most prevalent seasonings. As an opener, the imperial rolls are a good bet. This restaurant, although not luxurious, is modern, well appointed and offers excellent value. L and D daily. No credit cards.

MALAGASY

L'Exotic $$$
3788 Laval at Roy
843-4741

The island of Madagascar off the coast of Africa is known for its harmonious mixture of races and cultures. Its cuisine reflects the influences of China, equatorial Africa, the Middle East and France. One of the most interesting features here is do-it-yourself cooking by the customers on a special stone that is heated in the kitchen and used at the table to cook chicken, shrimp or beef in the most healthy manner (oil-free: only a little salt is used to keep the food from sticking). Unusual fresh fruits and vegetables and complimentary vegetable fritters accompany the dishes. The common spices are ginger, saffron and curry, and three sauces (green pepper, chili mayonnaise and tamarind) are available as accents. L Mon to Fri, D daily.

MOROCCAN

La Medina $$
3464 St-Denis at Carré St-Louis
282-0359

This relatively luxurious restaurant is a good place to spend a relaxing evening. The atmosphere is that of a tent; the tables are of copper trays on wrought-iron bases. The specialty is *couscous*, which is a sort of stew based on vegetables and semolina grain, with or without meat, lamb or spicy sausages called *merguez*. In addition, meat casseroles called *tajines* are popular with the regulars. The owner-chef, Jalal Chachir, a Moroccan by birth, was trained in Switzerland, and his restaurant reflects the high standards of that hospitable nation. Belly dancing shows on Fri and Sat nights. D daily.

Rites Berbères $
4697 de Bullion at Villeneuve
844-7863
Much simpler (and cheaper) than La Medina, this neighbourhood restaurant is a great favourite of many Montrealers, including the conductor of the Montreal Symphony Orchestra, Charles Dutoit. Diners bring their own wine. In addition to excellent *couscous*, this restaurant serves a delicious *tajine* of chicken with olives and, with advance notice, *mechoui*, which is a whole roasted lamb served for seven or more. An open kitchen and a friendly staff make dining here a very pleasant experience. D Tues to Sun.

POLISH

La Petite Pologne $$
4475 St-Denis at Mont-Royal
845-6043
This charming little restaurant is below street level, within warm old stone walls. One recommended dish is the "Polish Plate," which includes a sampling of various items on the menu, including stuffed cabbage, *pierogis* (dumplings stuffed with cheese or meat), beef *rouladen* stuffed with vegetables and other delicacies. Start with a well-prepared *borscht* (beet soup) and complete your meal with one of the wonderful desserts, includ-

ing the *nalesniki*, crêpes stuffed with cheese and covered with a hot sour-cream-based sauce. The wine list is a bit short. L Mon to Fri, D daily.

Stash's Café Bazaar $
461 St-Sulpice at Place d'Armes
861-2915
A mainstay in Old Montreal, this warm and friendly establishment rests its reputation on its *pierogis* and *plakis* (potato pancakes), stuffed cabbage and *krokietys* (meat-stuffed crêpes) and its wonderful desserts (homemade and always fresh). The café on the ground floor and the dining room one floor up are always teeming with tourists and locals. L and D daily.

PORTUGUESE

Étoile d'Océan $$
101 Rachel est at Colonial
844-4588
A simple and satisfying restaurant with wooden beams, hand-painted blue tiles, domestic items typical of a modest Portuguese house and beautiful handicrafts. Delicious fish and seafood are served, including remarkable grilled *calamari*, accompanied by excellent Portuguese bread. Diners in the know ask for mussels, swordfish and the highly regarded clam and pork *alentejana*, a stew of little cubes of pork and clams served in their shells in a small crock of tomato and garlic bouillon. L and D daily.

RUSSIAN

Troika $$$$
2171 Crescent at Sherbrooke
849-9333
Restaurants come and go, but Troika lasts and lasts. The ambience is that of a

czar's hideaway, all red velvet curtains and glistening samovars. The menu proposes a wide variety of Russian specialties, including caviar (a Canadian variety is available for those on a budget) along with chicken Kiev, beef Stroganoff and filet mignon done in a goose-liver sauce. Start with a Zakuska plate, which includes a variety of Russian hors d'oeuvres. The iced vodka is an excellent palate cleanser, and it is a treat to select among the unusual Russian wines on the extensive wine list (the Russian rosé is surprisingly good). Musical entertainment nightly. D daily.

SPANISH

La Bodega $$
3456 Park at Milton
849-2030

Sancho Panza $$
3458 Park at Milton
844-0558

Although under different ownership, these restaurants are located next door to each other and cater to complementary moods: La Bodega is for large, gregarious groups in a friendly, table-hopping mood; Sancho Panzo is for a more subdued dinner, either *en tête-à-tête* or *à quatre*. Both serve delicious *paellas* and *zarzuelas* with seafood along with classic roasted meat dishes and have appropriate wine lists. Proximity to McGill University ensures good value at relatively modest prices. L and D daily at both; Sancho Panza is closed on Sun.

Fiesta Tapas $$
879 St-Alexis at Notre-Dame ouest
287-7482

As anyone who has visited Spain knows, *tapas* are the wonderful trick that allows a Spaniard to make it through the 10-hour stretch from

lunch to dinner. Served on small individual plates, a selection of these hors d'oeuvres makes quite a creditable meal and is a particularly good idea before the theatre or a concert in Old Montreal, where this warm and friendly basement restaurant is located. Shrimp and other shellfish, sardines, spicy *chorizo* sausages, salads and *albóndigas* (meatballs) are typical offerings. L Tues to Fri, D Tues to Sun, brunch on Sun.

SWISS

William Tell $$
2055 Stanley at Sherbrooke
288-0139

A take-out pastry shop shares the ground floor with a café; diners at the latter can pick and choose from the daily offerings at the former, including a delicious quiche and wonderful pastries. Special complete meals, different every day, are always tasty, and the selections seem to please just about everyone. The large multilevel upstairs room, done up in a folkloric motif (including the inevitable cowbells), has long been a favourite of Montrealers. The extensive menu covers the gamut of Swiss cooking, from fondue and *raclette* through excellent veal dishes and wonderful *rösti* potatoes, to a conclusion of rich desserts. L and D Mon to Sat.

THAI

Chao Phraya $$
50 Laurier ouest at St-Urbain
272-5339

This restaurant, named for a river running through the heart of Bangkok, serves up truly authentic Thai food. The restaurant itself shows signs of previous ownership (Greek) but is large and bright. The service is very friendly and informative. Symbols on the menu (little peppers) indicate how hot each dish is, although virtually all dishes have been toned down to the tolerance levels of North American palates. Try the *mou satay* (small skewers of pork in a peanut and coconut sauce), the *kung plik khing* (large shrimps in a garlic, pepper, coriander and ginger sauce on a bed of green beans) or many other dishes based on chicken and shellfish, often with peanut flavouring. The wine list is poor, but beer is the better accompaniment in any event. D daily.

Other recommended Thai restaurants are **Pattaya** (1235 Guy at Ste-Catherine ouest, 933-9949) and **Le Palais de Bangkok** (1242 Mackay at Ste-Catherine ouest, 939-2817). L and D; Pattaya is closed on Mon; Palais de Bangkok is closed at lunch on Sat and Sun.

VIETNAMESE

Escale à Saigon $$
107 Laurier ouest at St-Urbain
272-3456
Over the last 15 years or so, Montreal has witnessed a large influx of Vietnamese, to wonderful effect on the low-priced end of the restaurant scene. Among the more than 100 Vietnamese restaurants some particularly stand out, and Escale à Saigon is especially notable for the authenticity of its cooking and the refinement of its presentation. Try the crackling duck on a bed of soybean sprouts or one of the numerous exotically spiced fish dishes. Excellent noodles often replace rice in these dishes. The lime sherbet is a refreshing close to a wonderful meal. L Mon to Fri, D daily.

La Famille Vietnamienne $
4051 St-André at Duluth
524-5771
This Vietnamese favourite, tucked among the Greek restaurants on Duluth, offers a refreshing change of pace. The cooking is light and well spiced. The menu might be called "Montreal Vietnamese Standard," but everything is so well prepared that "standard" here refers not to uniformity but to the level of excellence to which others can only aspire. Try the imperial rolls, skewers of chicken, beef and shrimp, garlic chicken, sesame beef and, for desert, banana fritters with honey. L Tues to Fri, D daily.

OTHER

Citrus $$$
5282 St-Laurent at Laurier
276-2353
This chic restaurant attracts celebrities to its fresh and elegant black, yellow and white decor. California is the model for the light and inventive cooking, which is based on seasonal ingredients such as citrus fruits, herbs and the freshest of vegetables. The wine list is remarkable. L Mon to Fri, D daily.

Passiflore $$$
872 Querbes near Van Horne
Outremont
272-0540
This midtown restaurant is in a cul-de-sac in a residential area. A charming (and surprising) terrace beyond the restaurant creates a convincing Californian environment. The specialties are light meats and fish, prepared with such ingredients as citrus fruits and honey, with very fresh vegetables and appropriate California wines. Desserts are creative and memorable. D Tues to Sun, brunch on Sun.

BY LOCATION

DOWNTOWN

Abacus, see Chinese
L'Actuel, see Belgian
Alexandre, see Bistros
L'Altro, see Italian
Baci, see Italian
Bar-B Barn, see Barbecued Chicken
Les Beaux Jeudis/Thursdays,
  see Bistros
Beaver Club, see Hotel Dining
Ben's, see Delicatessens
Bocca D'Oro, see Italian
La Bodega, see Spanish
Boulevards, see Bistros
Briskets, see Hamburgers and Hotdogs
Café Santropol, see Coffee Houses
  and Tea Rooms
Calories, see Coffee Houses and
  Tea Rooms
Le Café de Paris, see Hotel Dining
Le Castillon, see Hotel Dining
Le Caveau, see French
Le Cercle, see Hotel Dining
Champs Élysées, see French
Chez La Mère Michel, see French
Chez Better, see German
Chez Gauthier, see Bistros
Chez Magnan, see Taverns
Chinese Tea House, see Chinese
Le Chrysanthème, see Chinese
Le Commensal, see Vegetarian
Costas, see Greek
Crocodile, see Bistros
Desjardins, see Seafood
Dunn's, see Delicatessens
Eaton, see Department-Store Havens
Elysée Mandarin, see Chinese
Les Halles, see French
Hunan, see Chinese
Le Jardin Sakura, see Japanese
Kam Fung, see Chinese
Katsura, see Japanese
Latini, see Italian
Le Lutétia, see Hotel Dining
La Maison Cajun, see Cajun

Le Mas des Oliviers, see French
Le Neufchatel, see Hotel Dining
Le Palais de Bangkok, see Thai
Le Parchemin, see French
Le Paris, see French
Pattaya, see Thai
Peel Pub, see Pub Food
Le Piment Rouge, see Chinese
Pique-Assiette, see Indian
La Pizzaiolle, see Pizza
Da Pizzettaro, see Pizza
La Rapière, see French
Le St-Honoré, see French
St-Hubert Bar-B-Q, see
  Barbecued Chicken
Sancho Panza, see Spanish
Le Singapour, see Malaysian
Société Café, see Hotel Dining
Le Taj, see Indian
Tartan Room at Ogilvy, see
  Department-Store Havens
Toman Pastry Shop, see
  Coffee Houses and Tea Rooms
Le Tour de Ville, see With a View
Le Tricolore, see French
Troika, see Russian
Vent Vert, see French
William Tell, see Swiss

EAST MONTREAL

Au Petit Extra, see Bistros
Daou, see Lebanese
L'Exotic, see Malagasy
La Famille Vietnamienne, see
  Vietnamese
La Ferrandière, see French
Le Grain de Sel, see Bistro
Les Mauvais Garçons, see Seafood
Nega Fulo, see Brazilian
La Paryse, see Hamburgers and
  Hotdogs
Le Piémontais, see French
Rites Berbères, see Moroccan
St-Hubert Bar-B-Q, see Barbecued
  Chicken

ÎLE STE-HÉLÈNE

Hélène de Champlain, see Cuisine
Québécoise

PLATEAU MONT-ROYAL

Au Petit Resto, see Bistro
Bagatelle, see Bistro
Bagel, Etc., see Brunch
Beauty's, see Brunch
Chao Phraya, see Thai
Dusty's, see Brunch
L'Entre-Pont, see Bistro
Escale à Saigon, see Vietnamese
Laurier Bar-B-Q, see Barbecued
   Chicken
Lux, see Late Night
Da Marcello, see Italian
Milos, see Greek
Montreal Pool Room, see
   Hamburgers and Hotdogs
Oggi, see Italian
L'Oleandro, see Italian
La Pizzaiolle, see Pizza
Passiflore, see By Nationality (Other)
Prego, see Italian
Wilensky's Light Lunch, see
   Delicatessens

OLD MONTREAL

Auberge Le Vieux Saint-Gabriel, see
   Cuisine Québécoise
Le Bonaparte, see French
Chez Better, see German
Chez Delmo, see Seafood
Claude Postel, see French
Le Fadeau, see French
Fiesta Tapas, see Spanish
Les Filles du Roy, see Cuisine
   Québécoise
Gibby's, see Steak Houses
Il Était Une Fois, see Hamburgers
   and Hotdogs
La Marée, see Seafood
Le St-Amable, see French
Stash's Café Bazaar, see Polish

ST-DENIS

La Binerie Mont-Royal, see Cuisine
   Québécoise
La Brûlerie St-Denis, see Coffee
   Houses and Tea Rooms
Citron Lime, see French
Le Commensal, see Vegetarian
Le Daphné, see Coffee Houses and
   Tea Rooms
L'Escale Bretonne, see French
L'Express, see Bistro
La Medina, see Moroccan
Les Mignardises, see French
Olive, see Lebanese
La Petite Pologne, see Polish
Le Picholette, see French
Symposium, see Greek
Valentine, see Hamburgers
   and Hotdogs
Witloof, see Belgian

ST-LAURENT

Chez Better, see German
Citrus, see By Nationality (Other)
Crocodile, see Bistros
Étoile d'Océan, see Portuguese
Golden Curry House, see Indian
Laloux, see French
Mei, Le Café Chinois, see Chinese
Moishe's Steak House, see Steak
   Houses
Le Sam, see Bistro
Schwartz's/Montreal Hebrew
   Delicatessen, see Delicatessens

WEST MONTREAL

Chalet Bar-B-Q, see
   Barbecued Chicken
South Seas, see Chinese
Franni, see Coffee Houses and
   Tea Rooms

TRANSPORTATION

AUTOMOBILE

PARKING

Most major downtown office buildings, shopping complexes and hotels
have underground parking lots. There
are also municipal and private parking
lots. Rates vary. There is metered
street parking in major commercial
areas. A parking permit is often
required in residential areas.

Montreal strictly enforces parking
bylaws, especially during the winter
when commando-style attacks are
made on snow that has fallen on the
city's streets. Parking tickets run from
$30 to $35 ($55 for double parking).
Towing costs $35 on top of the park-
ing-ticket price. Call the Montreal
Urban Community Police at 280-
4636 if you think your car has been
towed.

INSURANCE

The Quebec no-fault automobile
insurance plan compensates residents
for bodily injury sustained in automobile accidents, whether or not they are
responsible. Legal proceedings to
recover damages caused by automobile
accidents are no longer possible.

Under certain conditions, visitors
may also be covered. Non-residents
who own, drive or are passengers in a
vehicle registered in Quebec receive

the same coverage as residents if
they're injured in a traffic accident in
Quebec. Other non-residents,
including pedestrians, cyclists, drivers
or passengers in an automobile not
registered in Quebec are compensated
to the extent that they are not at fault.

All vehicle owners travelling in
Quebec, residents or non-
residents, must carry minimum property liability insurance of $50,000.
Make sure your automobile insurance
provides you with adequate coverage.

For more information concerning
the protection extended to non-residents, call:

Société de l'Assurance Automobile du Québec
In Quebec City
(418) 643-7620
In Montreal
873-7620
Elsewhere in Quebec
1-800-361-7620 toll free

Or write to:

Direction de l'indemnisation
Société de l'assurance automobile
du Québec
**C.P. 2500, Terminus postal
Quebec City G1K 8A2**

ROAD CONDITIONS

Ministère des Transports du Québec
Road conditions in Quebec
873-4121 (24 hours)
Road works in Quebec
873-4040 (24 hours)

Travel USA
Road conditions in the U.S.
861-5036
Mon to Fri 9:30-11:30 AM and 2-3:30
PM.

Distances from Montreal (in kilometres)

Boston	512
Buffalo	620
New York	608
Ottawa	210
Philadelphia	737
Pittsburgh	945
Portland	410
Quebec City	253
Toronto	546

CAR RENTALS

In addition to those listed below, most car rental companies have numerous other locations in the Montreal area.

Avis
1225 Metcalfe at Square Dorchester
866-7906, 1-800-879-2847

Budget
Central Station
895 de la Gauchetière ouest at University
866-7675

Hertz
1475 Aylmer at de Maisonneuve ouest
842-8537, 1-800-263-0678

Tilden
1200 Stanley near René-Lévesque ouest
878-2771, 1-800-361-5334

PLANE

There are two airports in Montreal. Dorval handles flights from within

Canada and from the U.S.; Mirabel handles all other international flights. Transport Canada has prepared a comprehensive 48-page bilingual brochure entitled "Montreal Airports—Dorval/Mirabel User Guide," which includes a road map, floor plans, information on parking and ground transportation, and a directory of services (such as assistance for handicapped passengers) available at both airports.

DORVAL AIRPORT

Be at the airport 1 to $1\frac{1}{2}$ hours before your scheduled departure to allow time for check-in and security screening. Distance from downtown Montreal is 22 km (14 mi.). Travelling time is 20 to 30 minutes.

Taxi fare from Dorval to downtown Montreal is about $23; Dorval to Mirabel is about $55 (tax included).

Dorval has one covered carpark connected by two covered walkways to the first floor of the terminal and one outdoor lot adjoining the carpark for long-term parking. Visa, MasterCard and American Express accepted.

The local transit commission operates a regular bus route serving Dorval airport.

Bus service counters are located on the ground floor of the terminal.

Voyageur
842-2281
Bus service between downtown Montreal and Dorval. Stops at the Queen Elizabeth, Château Champlain and Centre Sheraton hotels. Departures every half-hour 5:05 AM-7:05 PM; every hour 7:05-11:05 PM. Fare: $12.

Aerocar Inc.
397-9999
Daily bus service from the Queen Elizabeth Hotel between 5:25 AM and 7:25 PM. Departures every 20 minutes

on weekdays (every 30 minutes on weekends). One way $8.50, return $15 (tax included), free for children 5 years and under.

Aeroplus
633-1100, 476-1100

A shuttle bus between Dorval and Mirabel is available. Distance between Dorval and Mirabel is 47 km (29 mi.). Travelling time is about 35 minutes.

Daily bus service 9:20 AM-11:20 PM; departure times vary. One way $10.25 (tax included), free for children 5 years and under and for in-transit passengers with less than seven hours between connections.

Mont-Royal
738-5466

Limousine service from Dorval to downtown Montreal. One way is $31.50; Dorval to Mirabel is $55 (plus tax).

Dorval Information Service
633-3105

This computerized telephone service offers 24-hour information on Dorval Airport.

MIRABEL AIRPORT

Passengers should arrive 2 to 3 hours before scheduled departure to allow time for check-in and security screening. Distance from downtown Montreal is 55 km (34 mi.). Travelling time is about 45 minutes.

Taxi fare between Mirabel and Dorval runs about $53; between Mirabel and downtown Montreal the fare is about $56 (tax included).

Mirabel has one covered carpark connected to the terminal and four outdoor carparks. Visa, MasterCard and Amex accepted.

Bus service counters are located on the main level of the terminal in the arrivals area.

Voyageur
842-2281

Bus service between downtown Montreal and Mirabel with stops at Central Station (corner of de la Gauchetière ouest and University) and the Voyageur Terminal at 505 de Maisonneuve est.

Aeroplus
476-1100, 633-1100

Daily bus service, schedule varies. One way $12.25 (tax included), free for children 5 years and under.

See Dorval entry for information on shuttle service between Mirabel and Dorval. Aeroplus also provides service between Mirabel and Ottawa. The distance between Mirabel and Ottawa is 139 km (86 mi.). Travelling time is about two hours.

Limousines GTV Inc.
333-5466

Fares for Mirabel-Dorval and Mirabel-downtown Montreal are $60 (plus tax).

Mirabel Information Service
476-3010

This computerized telephone service has 24-hour information on Mirabel Airport.

TRAIN

Central Station (Canadian National/Via Rail), corner of René-Lévesque and Mansfield, handles both regional and commuter trains. Both train stations in Montreal are linked to the Bonaventure *métro* station.

Via Rail (Canada)
871-1331

Amtrak (U.S.)
1-800-426-8725

Windsor Station
1170 de la Gauchetière ouest at Peel
395-7492
Commuter trains only.

BUS

Voyageur Terminal
505 de Maisonneuve est at Berri
842-2281
All regional buses pass through the Voyageur Terminal, which is also linked to the Berri-UQAM *métro* station. There are suburban terminals in Laval, Longueuil and at Kirkland.

PUBLIC TRANSIT

BUS, SUBWAY AND COMMUTER TRAINS
Montreal has a clean, safe and efficient public transportation system. The Société de transport de la Communauté urbaine de Montreal/Montreal Urban Community Transit Corporation provides bus, *métro* (subway) and commuter train service throughout the MUC.

There are 65 *métro* stations on four different lines. Each line is distinguished by number and colour.

The MUCTC offers 142 bus routes with some 7,800 stops; 118 of the routes stop at *métro* stations. An express service (Métrobus), serving a limited number of marked bus stops, runs on certain routes during rush hours. There are 27 night bus routes, which are identified as such on bus-stop signs.

Line	Colour	Terminus	Rush hours*	Regular hours
1	Green	Honoré-Beaugrand Angrignon	3 min.	7 min.
2	Orange	Henri-Bourassa Côte-Vertu	3 min.	7 min.
4	Yellow	Berri-UQUAM	5 min.	10 min.
5	Blue	Saint-Michel Snowdon	3 min.	7 min.

* 7:30 to 8:45 AM and from 3:30 to 5:30 PM

FARES
Fares are posted in all buses, ticket collection booths and *métro* stations. Passengers can use tickets, cash, or a monthly pass. Exact change is required on buses and commuter trains. Tickets and passes are sold at *métro* ticket booths and by about 700 independent ticket agents throughout the island of Montréal. You can buy a monthly pass (called CAM, or *carte d'abonnement mensuel*) at the ticket collection booths up to 10 days before the month for which it's valid.

Tickets: adults $1.50 each, $6 for a strip of six, $38 for a monthly local pass; students (under 18) and seniors (over 65) with card from the MUCTC 75¢ each, $2.50 for a strip of six, $14.50 for a monthly pass.

Transfer tickets are valid in any direction for 90 minutes.

HOURS
The *métro* is open Sun to Fri 5:30 AM-12:42 AM, Sat 5:30 AM-1:12 AM.

Last departure from Berri-UQAM station is at 12:58 AM (1:28 AM on Sat).

TRANSIT INFORMATION
288-6287 (A-U-T-O-B-U-S)
Mon to Fri 7-11, weekends and holidays 8-10.

SUBWAY AND COMMUTER TRAINS

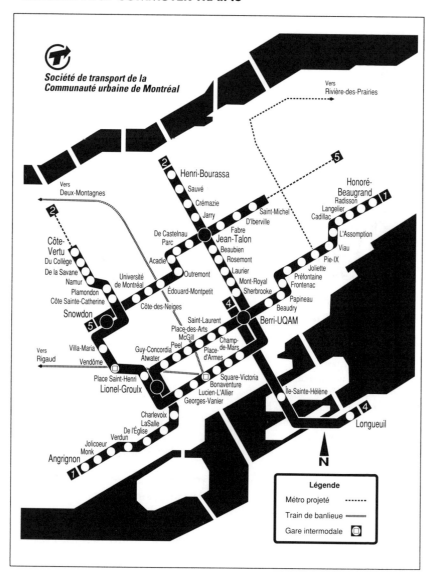

Touring Old Montreal by *calèche*.

PASSENGER'S COMMENTS AND COMPLAINTS
280-5653
Mon to Fri 8:30-4:30

LOST AND FOUND
280-4637
The MUCTC lost and found office is in the Pie-IX métro station.

TRANSPORTATION FOR THE HANDICAPPED
280-5341, 8:30-4:30
Transportation for the handicapped is provided in mini-buses and taxis, seven days a week.

TRANSIT GUIDES
Visitors can ask at ticket collection booths in *métro* stations for the following free material:
♦ *Guide Métro*, a pocket-size colour map of the *métro* system
♦ *Carte du centre-ville*, a pocket-size colour map of downtown Montreal
♦ *Carte réseau*, a full-size folded bilingual colour map of the public transit network
♦ *Service de nuit*, a full-size folded bilingual colour map of the public transit network night service
♦ commuter train schedules

This material is also available from the MUCTC public relations department. Call 280-5666, Mon to Fri 8:30-4:30.

COMMUTER TRAIN SERVICE
Two commuter train lines extend beyond the borders of the MUC.

The 64.4-km (40-mi.) Montreal/Dorion-Rigaud line running to the west connects downtown Montreal with the municipalities of Dorion and Rigaud. It stops at the Vendôme and Bonaventure *métro* stations.

The 26.9-km (17 mi.) Montreal/Deux Montagnes line running to the northwest connects downtown Montreal with the municipality of

Deux Montagnes. It stops at the Bonaventure *métro* station.

TAXI

Montreal actually has *too many* taxis, so it's generally easy to hail one. The Taxi Bureau of the MUC issues and regulates taxi licences. On the rear-door window of every taxi cab you'll find a four-digit ID number and posted rates (fixed by the Commission des transports du Québec); rates include GST.

Call the Taxi Bureau at 280-6600 to lodge complaints or to recover lost belongings.

Taxi Vétéran
273-6351

Taxi Diamond
273-6331

Taxi La Salle
277-2552

Taxi Co-op
725-9885

SIGHTSEEING

ATTRACTIONS

Old Montreal

Old Montreal is best explored by bicycle or on foot. The area's general boundaries are St-Jacques to the north, the Old Port to the south, Mc-Gill to the west and Berri to the east.

You may want to begin your tour in **Place Jacques-Cartier**, a short walk south of the Champs-de-Mars *métro* station. The square is popularly considered to be the heart of old Montreal and is an especially lively spot during warmer months. You can pick up free information at the Infotouriste centre at the corner of Place Jacques-Cartier and Notre-Dame.

The Montreal History Centre in Place d'Youville in Old Montreal. (MUC)

Another logical starting point is Place d'Youville, just east of McGill and south of the Place Victoria *métro*. The **Montreal History Centre** is lodged here within a 1903 fire station (see also Museums). The centre's exhibits provide an informative introduction to the history and development of Old Montreal to help you get your bearings (even restless children should find the audio-visual exhibits entertaining).

While the streets of Old Montreal are steeped in history, it does require imagination to picture the early days of settlement. You can walk by **Pointe-à-Callière**, where Montreal's founder, Paul de Chomedey, Sieur de Maisonneuve, landed in 1642, but don't expect to find his house. Instead, nearby in Place Royale you will find an obelisk that bears the names of the first 53 French settlers of Ville-Marie.

A restored period building in Place Jacques-Cartier.

The monument was erected in 1892 to commemorate Montreal's 250th anniversary.

Unfortunately, little original architecture has survived. Many early wooden structures were destroyed by fire. Rough stone buildings that might otherwise have weathered the centuries were demolished or refaced with more fashionable limestone during the prosperous late 18th and early 19th centuries. The 1716-36 stone fortifications, 4 ft. (1.2 m) thick and 18 ft. (5.5 m) wide, were also dismantled early in the 19th century, no longer considered useful. Sections of the wall still show up from time to time during construction excavations.

Of the few remaining 17th-century buildings, the best preserved is the **Sulpician Seminary** on the south side of Place d'Armes. The clock above the main doorway is thought to be the oldest public timepiece in North America. The seminary was built in 1685 and continues to be occupied by members of the order.

The Sulpicians played a seminal role in the city's development. The order was granted a feudal proprietorship to the entire island in 1663 (virtually every property in Montreal can be traced back to a lease tying it to a Sulpician), and the Sulpicians continued on as the city's seigneurs until the mid-19th century. Many of the streets and

This clock, at the Sulpician Seminary on the south side of Place d'Armes, is thought to be the oldest public timepiece in North America.

squares of Old Montreal were planned and named by them.

Another notable 17th-century building is the central part of **Grey Nuns' Hospital** on Normand. The order was founded by the devout pioneer Mère Marie-Marguerite

The Top 10 Sights

There's lots to see and do in Montreal. In no particular order, here are our choices for the top 10 sights:

Olympic Park
Place Jacques-Cartier and Old
   Montreal
Mount Royal Park

St. Joseph's Oratory
Montreal Botanical Garden
Square Dorchester and the Sun
   Life Building
Château Ramezay Museum
Île Notre-Dame
Montreal Museum of Fine Arts
Notre-Dame Basilica

d'Youville, for whom Place d'Youville is named. The Old Market, now called **Place Royale**, is the oldest public meeting place in the city.

Eighteenth-century buildings in Old Montreal are also relatively rare. One popular example is **du Calvet House** (401 Bonsecours est, 845-4596). Built in 1725 for a prosperous Huguenot merchant, du Calvet House was a typical residence for the well-to-do of the period. Note the steep metal roof, designed to prevent snow accumulation. The thick fieldstone walls and the fireplaces at each end of the house helped keep the family warm during the bitterly cold winters. The S-shaped metal bars that grace the façade are a typical adornment of the period (they're actually the ends of bars used to reinforce the house's thick wooden beams). Acquired by the Ogilvy family in 1963, the house and its interior have been carefully restored. The du Calvet House is now administered by the Montreal Museum of Fine Arts. The house, with its fine collection of early Quebec furniture, is open to the public.

Other notable 18th-century buildings include the 1705 **Château Ramezay** (280-290 Notre-Dame est; see also Museums) and **Notre-Dame-de-Bonsecours Church** (400 St-Paul est). Unfortunately, 19th-century renovations have radically altered the latter's appearance.

Notre-Dame-de-Bonsecours is also known as "the sailors' church." Be sure to step inside to view its numerous wooden carvings, many of which were donated by devout seamen in gratitude for having reached safe harbour. There is also a small museum dedicated to the life of the Canadian saint Marguerite Bourgeoys, a devout pioneer whose journals have provided historians

OLD MONTREAL

1. Royal Bank Building
2. Place d'Youville
3. Grey Nuns' Hospital
4. Montreal History Centre
5. D'Youville Stables
6. Point-à-Callière
7. Old Stock Exchange
8. Sulpician Seminary
9. Place d'Armes
10. Bank of Montreal Building
11. Aldred Building
12. Notre-Dame Basilica
13. Old Customs House
14. Place Royale
15. McTavish House
16. Old Port
17. Beaudoin House
18. Viger House
19. Del Vecchio House
20. Old Courthouse
21. Infotouriste Centre
22. Place Jacques-Cartier
23. Hôtel de Ville (City Hall)
24. Château Ramezay
25. Hotel Rasco
26. Beaujeu House
27. Papineau House
28. Bonsecours Market
29. Du Calvet House
30. Notre-Dame-de-Bonsecours Church
31. Brossard House
32. George-Étienne Cartier Museum
33. Dumas House
34. Clock Tower, Quai Victoria

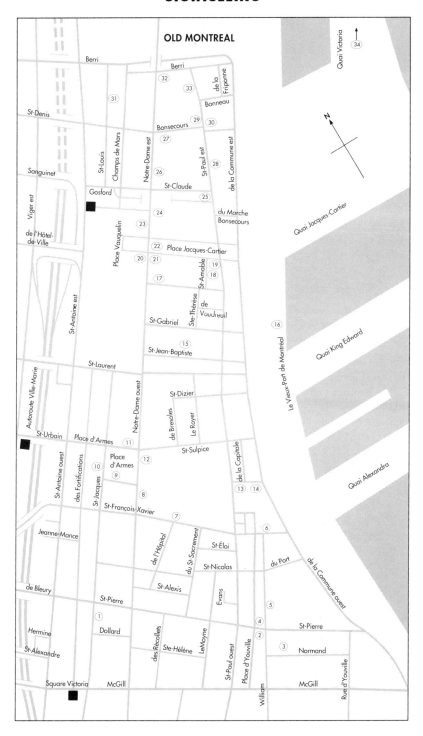

OLD MONTREAL

The main altar of Notre-Dame-de-Bonsecours Church in Old Montreal. (MUC)

(440 Bonsecours) houses also date from the 18th century.

The last two may be the most interesting. The Papineau House deserves special mention for several reasons. To begin with, it was home to six generations of Papineaus, the most famous of which was Louis-Joseph, a politician, lawyer and fiery leader of the Lower Canada Rebellion of 1837. Look carefully at the "cut stone" of the façade and you will find that it is actually a clever wooden imitation. The Papineau House was in particularly sad shape when Viger Commission member Eric McLean decided to buy it in 1961. Showing the courage of his convictions, McLean moved into the largely abandoned neighbourhood and undertook the building's painstaking restoration. The house was recently acquired by Parks Canada.

with rare and vivid accounts of colonial hardship and privation.

The **Beaujeu** (320 Notre-Dame est), **McTavish** (411 St-Jean-Baptiste), **Beaudoin** (427 St-Vincent), **Viger** (188 St-Amable) and **Papineau**

Examples of 19th-century architecture abound in Old Montreal and most commonly take the form of the five- and six-storey office buildings and warehouses that are found throughout the *quartier*. Visitors often ignore these buildings, but they merit closer inspec-

The Papineau House on Bonsecours. (MUC)

tion. Some display fanciful stone carvings and resemble Venetian *palazzi*. Many are excellent examples of what is called "stone-skeleton" architecture, a functional structural design characterized by no-nonsense beams and pillars, a stone-skeleton façade and large windows. The Royal Engineers who designed these first low-rise structures apparently made no pretense of following a distinct architectural style; their approach seems to have been entirely pragmatic.

These straightforward buildings resemble other commercial buildings of the period that sprang up in many east-coast American cities. They are excellent examples of nascent North American industrial design and are the forerunners of today's modern skyscrapers as popularized by the Chicago School and Le Corbusier. One of the most interesting is at 417 des Recollets. Note the building's powerful simplicity (marred by today's requisite fire escape). The obvious interior use of pillars and beams and the absence of partition walls were, at the time, somewhat revolutionary responses to the very practical need for light and ventilation. Other noteworthy examples of stone-skeleton architecture can be seen at 410 St-Vincent, 120 St-Paul ouest and 438-442 Place Jacques-Cartier. For commercial architecture *à l'italienne*, see the Renaissance-inspired **Bell-Rinfret Building** (366-68 Notre-Dame ouest).

Other fine 19th-century buildings include the neo-classical **Bonsecours Market** (330 St-Paul est), the **Old Customs House** (Place Royale), the classic revival style **Old Courthouse** (155 Notre-Dame est), the many haughty temples of finance that line St-Jacques (once known as Canada's Wall Street) and **Notre-Dame Basilica** in Place d'Armes (see also Muse-

The **Bell-Rinfret Building** at 368 Notre-Dame ouest, an excellent example of early stone-skeleton architecture. (MUC)

ums), one of the first Gothic revival churches in Canada. English Lit. fans may also want to stop by the former **Hôtel Rasco** (281-295 St-Paul est), a hostelry once frequented by artists and writers, including, in 1842, a most unimpressed Charles Dickens.

Nineteenth-century buildings of more modest proportions include the **Dumas** (445-447 St-Paul est), **Del Vecchio** (400-406 Place Jacques-Cartier) and **Brossard** (454 St-Louis) houses. You may also wish to visit **Sir George-Étienne Cartier House** at 458 Notre-Dame est (see also Other Principal Attractions).

In case you are wondering, Montreal's impressive **Hôtel de Ville (City Hall)** isn't technically a 19th-century building. Rather, it's a fairly

The Marché de Bonsecours in Old Montreal. (MUC)

faithful reconstruction of the original 1872 design. The earlier building was replaced in 1926 after a disastrous fire. It was on the balcony of this building in 1967 that then French president Charles de Gaulle uttered his inflammatory rallying cry to Quebec's separatists: *"Vive le Québec! Vive le Québec libre!"* ("Long live free Quebec!").

Twentieth-century buildings of merit in Old Montreal include the stunning art-deco **Aldred Building** (see Great Buildings) at 501-507 Place d'Armes, the **Royal Bank Building** (360 St-Jacques), the beaux-arts **Old Stock Exchange** building (453 St-François-Xavier) which now serves as the home of the Centaur Theatre, the fire station in Place d'Youville and the 1921 **clock tower** at Quai Victoria. The clock tower is used to display historical exhibits during the summer months and offers good views of the Old Port.

It would be unthinkable to describe Old Montreal without mentioning its public monuments. Visitors should see the impressive Louis-Phillipe Hébert sculpture of Paul de Chomedey, Sieur de Maisonneuve, in Place d'Armes. At Pointe-à-Callière is an often-missed statue of an important local merchant, John Young, also executed by Hébert. An English entrepreneur who came to Canada in 1826 at the age of 15, Young is recognized for his enormous contribution to the development of Montreal's railway and port infrastructure. By the end of the 19th century, due in no small part to his efforts, Montreal's port was second only to that of New York on the eastern seaboard.

Another important monument is Nelson's Column in Place Jacques-Cartier. News of Lord Nelson's great victory over the French at Trafalgar reached Montreal several months after the event, but Montreal's largely anglophone merchant class lost no time in erecting the world's first memorial in his honour.

Exploring Old Montreal really means wandering through a fascinating hodgepodge of four centuries of building. While each street has its own particular appeal, some are decidedly livelier than others. The public squares attract entertaining buskers and street vendors, especially during the summer, while St-Amable off Place Jacques-Cartier is a popular corridor for the inevitable street artists with their (somewhat tedious) souvenir sketches.

The recent revitalization of the Old Port, directly south of Place Jacques-Cartier, has vastly increased the number of visitors to Old Montreal, but the area's many excellent restaurants are more than able to handle the traffic. And what better way to conclude a tour of Old Montreal than by sampling the local cuisine? Even some of the restaurants have historical connections; see Restaurants for details.

LE VIEUX-PORT DE MONTRÉAL

GOLDEN SQUARE MILE

History buffs can still admire some vestiges of the Golden Square Mile area downtown, which at the turn of the century boasted an incredible concentration of fine houses and mansions. While a few of the remaining mansions are open to the public, the rest should be admired from a polite distance. Touring the area on foot takes about an hour, with at least half the time spent walking up steep slopes. Here are some notable properties:

Mount Stephen Club
**1440 Drummond near
Ste-Catherine ouest**
Open to the public on a limited basis

One of Montreal's best examples of art-deco architecture, the Aldred Building in Place d'Armes. (MUC)

during the summer. See George Stephen House under Great Buildings, this chapter.

Ritz-Carlton Hotel
**1228 Sherbrooke ouest at
Drummond**
See Where to Stay (Hotels) for a detailed description.

Atholstan House
**Southwest corner of Sherbrooke
ouest and Stanley**
Built in 1884 of cut stone for Hugh Graham (later Lord Atholstan), founder of the *Montreal Star*, an English-language daily that ceased publication in 1979. The carefully restored building is now part of the Aluminium

Company of Canada's corporate headquarters.

Labatt House
3418 Drummond north of Sherbrooke ouest
This red sandstone house was once home to Theodore Labatt of the well-known Canadian brewing family.

Birks House
3448 Stanley north of Sherbrooke ouest
This recently renovated 1887 house was originally the home of jeweller Massey Birks.

The Ross Houses
3644 and 3647 Peel north of Docteur-Penfield
These neighbouring houses, designed by the same architectural firm but in very different styles, were originally the homes of James Ross, an engineer for the transcontinental railway, and

The Meredith House at the corner of des Pins and Peel.

his son, John. The house at 3644 Peel is now the home of McGill's Faculty of Law.

Meredith House
Southwest corner of des Pins and Peel
This 1892 house, built by a successful financier, shows architectural eclecticism at its best. Note the pleasing blend of several styles. Designed by the same architects as the Ross Houses.

Ravenscrag
1025 des Pins near Peel
Ravenscrag was probably the most lavish of the Golden Square Mile estates and has been compared to Queen Victoria's Italian Renaissance summer residence on the Isle of Wight. Built for Sir Hugh Allan, a shipbuilder, railroad financier and founder of the Merchants' Bank of Canada, it now houses the Allan Memorial Institute, a medical research facility affiliated with McGill University.

OTHER PRINCIPAL ATTRACTIONS

McGill University
McGill College at Sherbrooke ouest
McGill's rolling 32-ha (80-acre) property on the slopes of Mount Royal houses internationally respected faculties of neurology, geology and physics, among others. The university was chartered in 1821 after a generous bequest by fur trade magnate James McGill. It is one of North America's oldest universities. McGill also operates two of Montreal's best museums, the McCord and the Redpath (see Museums). Free walking tours of the campus. A self-guiding pamphlet is available on request. Call the McGill Welcome Centre at 398-6555.

Lachine Canal Interpretation Centre
Monk Pavilion
7th Ave. at St-Joseph
Lachine

A permanent exhibition illustrating the canal's building, history and importance to the early prosperity of Montreal. You can combine this with a trip on the Lachine Canal cycle path and a visit to the Lachine Fur Trade Museum. Admission is free. Open mid-May to Labour Day, Tues to Sun 10 AM-noon and 1-6 PM; Mon 1-6 PM.

Abbaye cistercienne de Notre-Dame-du-Lac
1600 Oka
Oka
(514) 479-8361

The Cistercian Abbey, about a 45-minute drive from downtown Montreal, is famous for its Oka cheese. This Trappist monastery sold its cheese production facility several years ago, but you can still buy cheese here from monks robed in traditional white. Combine your visit with a short ferry trip across Lac des Deux Montagnes to the popular Saturday antique and flea market at Hudson.

SOS Labyrinthe
King Edward Pier
Vieux-Port (immediately south of Place Jacques-Cartier)
982-9660

A giant maze constructed in the shape of a ship with some 2 km of corridors. A great way to divert yourself on a rainy afternoon or to lose the kids for a few hours. Daily and seasonal prizes are awarded to those who can conquer the maze the quickest. Admission: adults $7; discounts for families, seniors and students; children under 5 free.

Jacques Cartier Flea Market
Vieux-Port (immediately south of Place Jacques-Cartier)
843-5949

More than 100 vendors. A good place to find old furniture, crockery, jewellery, handicrafts, leather wear and inexpensive children's clothing.

Expotec—IMAX Theatre
Vieux-Port (immediately south of Place Jacques-Cartier)
496-4629

A permanent exhibit space with audioguide-based shows that change every summer. The emphasis is on science and technology. A recent show took viewers back to the origins of man, highlighting some of the great Canadian paleontological finds. An Expotec ticket also lets you into the IMAX theatre to view spectacular images on a seven-storey-high screen. Admission: adults $11, discounts for students, seniors and groups, children under 4 free. Expotec is open daily June to Aug, Wed to Sun in Sept. The IMAX Theatre is open year-round.

Dow Planetarium
1000 St-Jacques at de la Cathédrale
872-4656

The Dow utilizes 220 projectors, including a 2½-tonne Zeiss Model V, to reproduce the heavens on the 20-metre (66-foot) dome-shaped screen in its Theatre of the Stars. Since its opening in 1966, the planetarium has created about 150 original productions. Shows are given in both French and English and are changed every few months. Call for times.

Images of the Future
Vieux-Port (immediately south of Place Jacques-Cartier)
849-1612

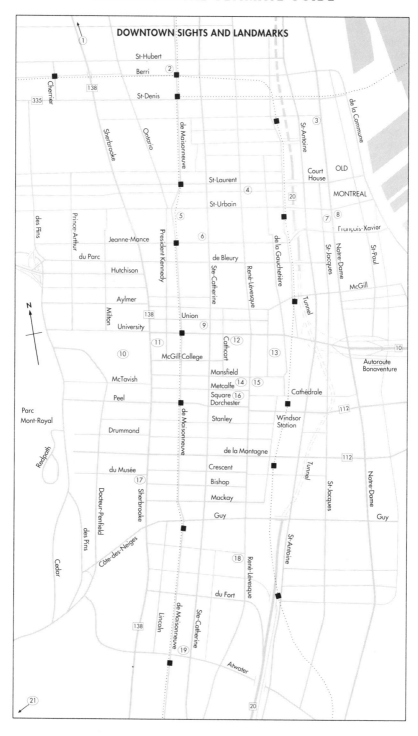

DOWNTOWN SIGHTS AND LANDMARKS

DOWNTOWN SIGHTS AND LANDMARKS

1. To Olympic Park, Biodome, Montreal Botanical Garden and Insectarium

2. Bus Terminal

3. City Hall (Hôtel de Ville)

4. Chinatown

5. Place des Arts

6. Museum of Contemporary Art

7. Place d'Armes

8. Notre-Dame Basilica

9. Christ Church Cathedral

10. McGill University

11. McCord Museum

12. Place Ville-Marie

13. Central Station

14. Sun Life Building

15. Mary, Queen of the World Cathedral

16. Infotouriste Centre

17. Montreal Museum of Fine Arts

18. Canadian Centre for Architecture

19. The Forum

20. St. Joseph's Oratory

■ subway station

An exhibition devoted to applied technology in the arts, such as computer imaging, holography, laser projection, digital music, video and telematics. Displays include magnetic landscapes that move in time to music, an empty cage that fills with howling animals as you approach and a video baby in a carriage. For an extra fee you can produce your own hologram in the laboratory (a reservation is required). Admission: adults $9, discounts for groups, families, seniors and students, children under 6 free.

Olympic Park
4141 Pierre-de-Coubertin at Pie IX
252-8687

The site of the 1976 Summer Games comprises a number of buildings including the Olympic Stadium and Aquatic Centre. Montrealers are still paying for the extravagant (and leaky) pre-fabricated concrete stadium designed by Frenchman Roger Taillibert (the average cost per seat has worked out to $11,500) with a special levy. The latest multimillion-dollar expense incurred for the Big O (or the "Big Owe" as it is also known) was for a fabric roof—which ripped shortly after installation. Municipal folly at its finest.

Visitors can take a cable car up the stadium mast (said to be the world's tallest inclined tower) to an observation deck for a spectacular panorama of Montreal and the surrounding region. Guided tours of the entire Olympic facility are available. Free shuttle bus service to the nearby botanical garden. You can swim in the park's five-pool Aquatic Centre for a small additional fee. See also Sports/Recreation (Swimming).

The park is open all year. Cost of a combined adult ticket is about $10, with discounts for children under 17.

Montreal's Olympic Stadium. (Régie des installations olympiques)

La Ronde
Île Ste-Hélène
872-6222

An amusement park originally created as part of Expo '67, La Ronde is open June to Labour Day. The 55-ha (135-acre) park boasts lots of great rides, including the highest dual-track roller coaster in the world, an enchanted children's village called Chnougui-Ville and the 21-slide Aqua-Parc, which also features a large heated pool.

Combined admission to both facilities: adults $24, discounts for children. Admission to the Aqua-Park only: adults $16, discounts for children and after 3 PM. Open Sun to Thur 11-11, Fri and Sat 11-midnight.

St-Leonard Caves
5200 Lavoisier
St-Leonard
328-8580

First discovered in 1811 and open to the public since 1981, the caves,

though not large, are particularly interesting to children. The largest cave is approximately 40 m (130 feet) long with heavily striated walls. Combine your visit here with a picnic in Pie-XII park, which lies above the caves. Reservations are required. The tour includes an explanatory slide show. Open early June to mid-Aug. Admission is $2.

St. Joseph's Oratory
3800 de la Reine-Marie near
Côte-des-Neiges
733-8211

One of the most heavily visited sites in the city, the oratory was built in the Italian Renaissance style between 1924 and 1955. Often compared to Montmartre's Sacré Coeur and Florence's Duomo, it's a monument to the tenacity and devotion of Brother André, of the Congregation of Ste. Croix, who was beatified in 1982 in recognition of the many miraculous cures attributed to him. It is not unusual to see pilgrims, including the sick and infirm, crawling up the steps to the basilica on their hands and knees in hope of divine intervention.

The oratory is also home to a museum of valuable religious works and a carillon of bells originally designed for the Eiffel Tower (they could not be installed there for technical reasons). Carillon as well as organ concerts are given throughout the year.

The oratory's observatory, the highest point in the city, provides excellent views.

The oratory's sanctuary includes the original chapel built by Brother André in 1904, together with his tomb and a votive chapel. Upon his death, Brother André's heart was preserved as a religious relic. It reposed in a jar on the oratory's main altar until it was stolen in 1973. Happily, the relic was recovered a year later.

Free admission. The oratory is open daily 6:30-9:30. Museum hours are 10-5 daily.

Fur Trade Museum
1255 St-Joseph near 12th
Lachine
637-7433

Montreal's early prosperity was closely linked to the fur trade. In the main warehouse (built in 1803) of the North West Company, one of the early major fur-trading companies, this museum chronicles the history of the Canadian fur trade. Admission is free. Open late Feb to early Dec. From mid-May to the end of Aug, the museum is open daily (except Mon morning) 10 AM-12:30 PM and 1-6 PM.

Sir George-Étienne Cartier House
458 Notre-Dame est at Bonsecours
283-2282

The home of one of Canada's Fathers of Confederation. A portion of the complex has been restored and illustrates daily life of the upper classes as it was in mid-Victorian times. Admission is free. Open 9-5 daily mid-

St. Joseph's Oratory. (City of Montreal)

May to Sept 3, Wed to Sun 10-5 from Sept 4 to mid-May.

Kahnawake Indian Reserve
Mercier Bridge, Route 138 ouest
Kahnawake
632-7500

Kahnawake makes an interesting half-day trip. With some 6,000 inhabitants, it is one of Canada's largest Mohawk communities. The Fort St. Louis Mission museum contains many interesting religious and ethnographic objects that trace the history of the reserve and the Mohawk people. The mission also contains the tomb of Kateri Tekakwitha, a Mohawk princess who was beatified in 1980. Kahnawake is home to the Kanien Kahaka Roatitahkwa resource and documentation centre, which keeps about 3,000 reference documents relating to the history of the Iroquois confederacy, the League of Six Nations. The reserve's St-François-Xavier Mission, founded in 1719, features a mass sung in Mohawk on Sundays at 11 AM.

The Kahnawake Mohawks are widely recognized off the reserve for their remarkable abilities in high steel construction. They also made headlines during 1990 when a territorial dispute involving the Mohawks at Oka evoked a strong show of solidarity. For several weeks, there was a great deal of tension between the Kahnawake people and the provincial government, most notably manifested by the Mohawks' barricade of the Mercier Bridge. The crisis has since been diffused, though a number of issues—mostly over land claims—remain unresolved. It is fully expected that the Mohawks will continue to welcome tourists in the same friendly way as they have in the past. Nevertheless, it would be wise to check on the current situation before you go.

Fort Chambly
2 Richelieu
Chambly
(514) 658-1585

A national historic site a half-hour drive from downtown Montreal, the fort is constructed in the French style of the 1750s, and the exhibits reflect the lifestyles of French settlers and soldiers of that period. Excellent access for the handicapped. Free admission. Hours: from the end of June to Labour Day, Mon 1-6, Tues to Sun 10-6; call for times during the rest of the year.

Pointe-du-Moulin Historical Park
2500 Don Quichote
Île Perrot
453-5936

The park, a short road trip to the west of Montreal, features a restored windmill and miller's house. An interpretive centre tells you how flour was made at the mill. Guided tours available. The park also contains a playground and picnic area, making it an ideal destination for a family outing. Free admission. Open daily mid-May to Labour Day 9-sunset; noon-6 on weekends thereafter until early Nov.

SPECIAL INTEREST TOURS

Montreal Stock Exchange
800 Square Victoria
871-2424

After a hiatus of several years, Canada's second-largest stock exchange is again offering 1-hour tours for summer visitors. The guides are usually quite knowledgeable and will likely be able to tell you all you need to know to begin trading citrus futures in short order. The French-language tour is at 9:30 AM; the English tour begins at 1:30 PM. Open July to Labour Day. Admission:

adults $5, discounts for students and seniors, children under 12 free.

Hydro-Quebec Rivière-des-Prairies Power Station
3400 Bariage
Laval
842-7861, ext. 4311
Free guided tours of this 45,000-kW facility are available mid-May to Labour Day. Hours: mid-May to June 30 9-3, July 1 to Labour Day 10-4. Call ahead to reserve a guide for groups of 10 or more.

GREAT BUILDINGS

A number of Montreal's more notable buildings are mentioned in the sections above on Old Montreal and the Golden Square Mile. The buildings and interiors here are some of our other favourites. Unless indicated, most are closed to the public; please admire them from a discreet distance. For those interested in a detailed survey of Montreal's architectural heritage, we recommend the books *Discover Montreal* by Joshua Wolfe and Cecile Grenier (Éditions Libre Expression, 1983) and *Montreal in Evolution* by Jean-Claude Marsan (McGill-Queen's University Press, 1981).

George Stephen House
1440 Drummond near
Ste-Catherine ouest
848-7338
A Renaissance-style mansion built in the 1880s for George Stephen (later Baron Mount Stephen), an early president of the Bank of Montreal and a founder of the Canadian Pacific Railway. A fine reflection of the Victorian era, Stephen House was renowned in its day as one of Montreal's most lavishly elegant private residences. It now serves as a private dining club for the city's business elite.

The 15 oversize rooms are rich in Old World atmosphere, craftsmanship and appointments. The satinwood, oak, walnut, mahogany, onyx and marble found throughout were imported from England, Europe, the Orient and Cuba. Many of the magnificent stained-glass windows, imported from Austria, are 300 years old.

Admission is free. Open July and Aug only, noon-4. Guided tours in groups of 10.

Bank of Montreal
119 St-Jacques at Place d'Armes
An excellent example of Palladian architecture, designed by John Wells. Still the head office of the Bank of Montreal, Canada's oldest chartered bank, this 1845 building has undergone significant remodelling over the years. The original dome was eliminated in 1859, then rebuilt during a 1905 restoration supervised by well-

The interior of the Bank of Montreal Building in Place d'Armes. (MUC)

known New York architect Stanford White. The main banking hall, supported by majestic columns of green nephrite, is well worth a look (and it won't cost you a penny). Open to the public during banking hours.

Sun Life Building
Square Dorchester
This grey, somewhat cake-shaped monolith was once the most massive building in Canada and remains an impressive sight to all but the most jaded. First constructed in 1914 as the head office of the Sun Life Assurance Company of Canada, the building had wings added to its north and east sides in the 1920s.

The interior of Mary, Queen of the World Cathedral on René-Lévesque. (MUC)

Mary, Queen of the World Cathedral
René-Lévesque ouest at Square Dorchester
Originally named after St. James, the cathedral dates from 1875 and is a quarter-scale reproduction of St. Peter's in the Vatican. The statues overlooking the imposing façade, often mistaken for Jesus' apostles, are of the patron saints of various local parishes.

The interior is richly decorated with murals by artist Georges Delfosse. The fresco on the canopy under the dome, painted in 1900 by Victor Vincent, is a faithful reproduction of Bernini's masterwork in St. Peter's. The cathedral also serves as the final resting place of Montreal's bishops.

Basilique Notre-Dame/ Notre-Dame Basilica
Place d'Armes
One of the finest examples of Gothic revival architecture in Canada, the exterior of the basilica was constructed between 1829 and 1842. Lack of funds delayed the completion of the church's magnificent wooden interior (designed by Victor Bourgeau) until the 1870s. One of the largest bells in North America, affectionately called "Jean- Baptiste," hangs in the west tower. This 12-tonne bell is now electrically operated; before, it took a dozen or so men to ring it. The church also boasts one of the largest organs ever made by the well-known Quebec firm Cassavant Frères. Notre-Dame is a popular concert venue because of its fine acoustics. It's an absolute pleasure to hear intricate works such as Handel's *Messiah* performed here.

Habitat
Cité du Havre

This unusual housing complex was designed by architect Moshe Safdie as a showpiece for Expo '67. An irregular assemblage of cubes and rectangular boxes, Habitat's style is perhaps best described as "residential Lego." Nevertheless, it has stood the test of time and remains one of the city's most unique buildings.

Westmount Square
1 Westmount Square at Ste-Catherine ouest

Two black steel-and-glass I-beam towers instantly recognizable as the work of American modernist Mies van der Rohe. Stark but beautiful. A smaller-scale version of a similar complex in downtown Toronto.

Aldred Building
501-507 Place d'Armes

This 24-storey building, completed in 1930, was considered very avant-garde in its time. Take a peek at the outstanding art deco foyer.

Eaton Cafeteria
Ninth floor
Eaton Building
677 Ste-Catherine ouest near University
284-8421

The interior of this department-store cafeteria is truly extraordinary, modelled on the art deco main dining room of one of Mrs. Eaton's favourite ocean liners, *L'Île-de-France*. This eccentricity, which dates from the late 1920s, boasts 9-m (30-foot) pink-and-grey marble columns, imposing murals and sweeping metal grillwork. Enjoy a bygone era while treating yourself to an inexpensive meal.

Windsor Station
Square Dorchester

Designed late in the last century by U.S. architect Bruce Price as the main station and head office of the Canadian Pacific Railway, Windsor Station is of considerable historical and architectural importance. As the primary gateway to the city for most of a century, Windsor Station welcomed many new immigrants through its portals. The main concourse dates from about 1914 and its roof makes extensive use of glass. Attempts by the CPR in the 1970s to redevelop the site were met with concerted, and ultimately successful, resistance by Montreal's citizenry.

The interior of Notre-Dame Basilica in Place d'Armes. (MUC)

10 Architectural Bests
Phyllis Lambert, Director, Canadian Centre for Architecture

1. **Milton-Parc neighbourhood** and **Hôtel Dieu**. Milton-Parc is a typical downtown neighbourhood of greystone vernacular buildings renovated without gentrification, re-establishing community living. The Hôtel Dieu, on whose land the neighbourhood was built, dates from the late 19th century and is a particularly fine example of institutional architecture.
2. **Grey Nuns' Convent**, René-Levesque ouest at Guy.
3. **Suplician Seminary**, Sherbrooke ouest at Atwater.
4. **Royal Bank Building**, St-Jacques near Place d'Armes, Old Montreal.
5. **Christ Church Cathedral**, Ste-Catherine ouest at Union.
6. **Alcan Building complex**, Sherbrooke ouest at Stanley.
7. **Congregation Notre-Dame** (now CEGEP Dawson), Sherbrooke ouest at Atwater.
8. **Marché Bonsecours**, St-Paul at de Bonsecours, Old Montreal.
9. **Ernest Cormier's Pavilion**, Université de Montréal.
10. The neighbourhoods of Maisonneuve, St-Henri, Plateau Mont-Royal and their institutional buildings.

Le Windsor
1170 Peel in Square Dorchester
393-9293

Now an expensive office complex complete with atrium, Le Windsor is all that remains of the once-proud Windsor Hotel. Fortunately, the owners saw fit to preserve the hotel's spectacular main-floor reception rooms. The rooms are often rented out for functions but can be viewed by the public most days.

Maison Alcan
1188 Sherbrooke ouest at Stanley
848-8000

The new head office of the Aluminium Company of Canada, Maison Alcan is an award-winning harmony of old and new. Its main entrance employs three arches from the former Berkeley Hotel doorway. Entering from Sherbrooke, visitors will find a stunning skylit atrium enclosed by the walls of adjoining restored buildings. Guided tours are available on request.

LOOKOUTS AND PANORAMIC VIEWS

Montreal has a number of excellent vantage points from which to view the city and surrounding region. We recommend the following:

Main Chalet
Mount Royal Park

The chalet's terrace provides an exceptional view of downtown, the St. Lawrence River and Montreal's south shore.

East Side Lookout
Mount Royal Park via Voie Camillien-Houde

A good view of eastern Montreal and in particular the Olympic Park.

Westmount Lookout
Belvedere near Côte-des-Neiges

The terrace of this small park affords excellent views of Westmount and the south end of the city.

Notre-Dame-de-Bonsecours Church Lookout
400 St-Paul est at Bonsecours
A good view of the city's harbour from the observatory. Free access with the purchase of a ticket to the chapel's museum.

St. Joseph's Oratory
3800 de la Reine-Marie near Côte-des-Neiges
This religious shrine is the highest point in Montreal, and its observatory provides excellent views of northwest Montreal and Lac St-Louis.

TOURING MONTREAL

IN THE AIR

Delco Aviation
335 Lévesque
Pont-Viau, Laval
663-4311
Seaplane tours of Montreal and the Laurentian Mountains from $21 and $86 per person, respectively, based on groups of five. Delco also offers whale-watching flights over the St. Lawrence and fly-in hunting and fishing trips in northern Quebec.

Air Panorama
St. Hubert Airport
286-9889
Flights in single-engine Cessnas or Pipers for up to three persons. A 45-minute tour of Montreal's principal sights costs $65 per person based on two or more, including all taxes and transportation to and from your hotel. Other itineraries can be arranged. Reservations required; call one day ahead.

L'Aérotour de Montreal
354-3897
A charter service offering 30- to 40-minute flights over the city for groups of two or three. A 30-minute tour for two costs $50 per person; a 40-minute flight for three costs $45 per person. Call for reservations and more information.

ON THE WATER

Amphi Tour
386-1298
A mixed water/land tour in an amphibious bus that takes you past some of Montreal's principal sights, including Place Royale, the Château Ramezay and the Lachine Canal. Tours depart from Place Jacques-Cartier every 90 minutes 9 AM-midnight during the summer. Tickets: adults $24, discounts for seniors and children. Reservations required.

Lachine Rapids Tours
Quai Victoria
284-9607
A chance for adventurous types to shoot the Lachine Rapids in a specially constructed jet boat. Trips run daily every 2 hours 10-6, May to Sept. Rainsuits are provided, but participants are advised to wear wool sweaters and bring a change of clothes. Waterproof bags are available for cameras. Reservations required. Adults $35, discounts for students and children under 12.

Montreal Harbour Cruises
Quai Victoria
842-3871
Modern multilevel ferries take you on a 90-minute, 25-kilometre cruise around Montreal. Daily from the last week in June to Sept. Departs 12:30 PM. Tickets: adults $13, discounts for seniors and children. MHC also offers twice-daily tours of the various islands around Montreal (which can be com-

bined with a Gray Line bus tour), an all-day cruise along the St. Lawrence River to Sorel and a 3½-hour evening dance cruise.

Le Maxim
7 de la Commune ouest near St-Dizier
849-4804
Billed as Montreal's newest and most luxurious cruise ship, the 200-ft. (61-m) three-deck *Le Maxim* offers a variety of early morning, lunchtime, afternoon, sunset and evening cruises on the St. Lawrence around Montreal. The ship has a theatre, a discothèque, a cocktail lounge and a 160-seat restaurant and can accommodate up to 800 passengers. From time to time, the ship has special "whodunit" evening cruises. Adults $25, discounts for se-

niors and students. Tickets can be purchased at the address above, most major hotels and the ship's mooring at the Alexandra Pier in the Iberville Passenger Terminal.

Montreal-Longueuil Ferry
842-1053
This ferry service between Quai de Horloge in Montreal's Old Port (Vieux-Port) and the south shore community of Longueuil's Port de Plaisance (next to Marie-Victorin Park) runs mid-May to mid Oct and is a cheap alternative to commercial ferry tours. The ferry also stops at La Ronde amusement park on Île Ste-Hélène. Frequency varies; during July and Aug it runs every hour each way 10 AM-1 AM. Cost: $2 one way. Boarding priority is given to passengers with return tickets. Bicycles welcome.

BY BUS

Murray Hill Bus Tours
875-TOUR, 937-5311
The company offers a five-hour tour that includes stops at Olympic Park, the Botanical Garden and St. Joseph's Oratory, as well as a special tour that emphasizes Montreal's maritime heritage. A general 3-hour city tour (including a 30-minute guided tour of Notre-Dame Basilica) costs about $20 for adults; discounts for children under 12. Departures from the Infotourist centre in Dorchester Square daily during the summer (beginning in late June) on the hour between 9 and 4.

Gray Line Bus Tours
934-1222
Gray Line runs city tours similar to those offered by Murray Hill, including a standard 3-hour tour that takes passengers to such principal sites as Place Jacques-Cartier in Old Mon-

Horse-drawn *calèches* lined up in front of City Hall.

treal, Olympic Park and St. Joseph's Oratory. Departures six times daily from late June to Oct. Gray Line also offers an extended 4½-hour tour of the city, a 3½-hour tour of the St. Lawrence Seaway, Île Ste-Hélène and Fort Chambly; and an all-day tour of Montreal and the seaway.

Tickets for the all-day tour: adults about $30, discounts for children. Gray Line picks up passengers at 20 of the city's larger hotels; tours begin at the Infotourist centre in Square Dorchester.

Voyageur Bus Tours
Voyageur Terminal (de Maisonneuve and Berri)
842-2281

Voyageur runs a number of one-day bus tours to Quebec City and Ste-Anne-de-Beaupré, site of the famous Roman Catholic shrine. The latter includes a brief visit to Quebec City.

BY CARRIAGE

Horse-drawn carriages (*calèches*) abound in Old Montreal and can be a relaxing way to see the major sites if you can stand the cars whizzing by. Good places to pick up a hack: in front of City Hall at Place Jacques-Cartier, and at the south end of Place d'Armes. Fare is about $30 per half-hour.

ON FOOT

Les Montréalistes Inc.
744-3009

Personalized 2-hour walking tours of the city. Call 3 hours in advance for reservations. Minimum group size of 10 persons. Pick-up can be arranged at any *métro* stop or hotel. The company also offers a 2-hour tour that departs the Infotourist centre in Dorchester Square at 10 AM daily during the peak tourist season. Cost: adults $12, dis-

counts for seniors and children between 8 and 16 accompanied by an adult.

Save Montreal Walking Tours
282-2069

Save Montreal, an organization devoted to preserving downtown Montreal's architectural heritage, sponsors occasional walking tours during the summer months. Call for details. Free (donations welcomed).

Old Montreal Heritage Network
282-2232

A clever new concept that allows you to stroll through Old Montreal and to listen to historical messages broadcast via short-range FM transmitters at 30 recognized heritage sites. All you need is an FM radio and a Heritage Network map. Maps can be purchased at various locations, including in the lobby of the *Gazette* (245 St-Jacques), for $3.95 plus tax. The *Gazette* also sells and rents radios. Frequencies: English commentary 89.5 FM; French commentary 88.5 FM. Operates 24 hours per day.

Calendar of Events

Late Jan: Fête des Neiges, Montreal's annual winter carnival, is run at various sites in the city, 872-6093.

Mid-May: Theatre of the Americas Festival, an annual showcase for visiting American and European theatre companies, 842-0704.

Late May: Benson & Hedges International Fireworks Competition, the world's largest and most spectacular fireworks contest, with participants from around the world (takes place over several weeks), 872-6222.

Early June: Le Tour de l'Île de Montreal, the world's largest popular cycling event, takes place in the streets of Montreal, 847-8687.

Molson Grand Prix, annual Formula 1 race on Île Notre-Dame.

Late June: Montreal International Jazz Festival, currently the world's largest, takes place over 10 days at various locations throughout downtown Montreal (many free outdoor concerts), 288-5363.

Early July: Carifête, an annual festival of Caribbean music and culture.

Mid-July: Just for Laughs Comedy Festival brings some of the world's best comics, and many up-and-comers to Montreal for non-stop laughs over a 10-day period, 845-3155.

Player's International Tennis Tournament, top professional tennis at Jarry Park, 273-1515.

Late Aug: Montreal World Film Festival, one of North America's better cinematic showcases, 933-9699.

Early Sept: Montreal International Marathon, 879-1027.

Early Oct: Grand Prix Cycliste des Ameriques, major international cycling race in the streets of Montreal, 879-1881.

Late Oct: International Festival of New Cinema and Video. Showcases the weird alternative stuff you never get to see on cable, 843-4725.

PARKS/GARDENS

MAJOR PARKS

Parc du Mont-Royal/Mount Royal Park
Voie Camillien-Houde
872-1415, 844-4928

The extinct volcano from which Montreal takes its name has been part of the city's history since 1535, when explorer Jacques Cartier dubbed it Le Mont Royal in honour of the French king. The 30-metre (98-foot) steel cross on its eastern side stands on the site where Paul de Chomedey, Sieur de Maisonneuve, placed a wooden cross in thanks to God for sparing the village from a flood in 1643. Many famous Montrealers are buried in the two large cemeteries that flank the mountain's slopes.

Today, the mountain is a 200-ha (494-acre) park, enormously popular with residents and tourists year-round. Designed by celebrated American landscape architect Frederick Law Olmsted (who also designed New York's Central Park), the grounds were developed following the land's natural topography, with a view to bringing man spiritually closer to nature. Naturalists should head to the chalet for a guide to the park's flora and fauna from the interpretation centre (844-4928). In winter, there's skating at man-made Lac des Castors (Beaver Lake), a beginner's ski run and several kilometres of good cross-country ski trails. Horse-drawn *calèches* tour the park in summer alongside joggers and Montreal's mounted police (you can visit the police stables; see With the Kids). Above all, Mount Royal provides some of the best panoramic views of the city.

Westmount Park
Sherbrooke ouest between
Lansdowne and Melville

This is probably Montreal's loveliest park, meticulously maintained by the City of Westmount. Large playing fields, tennis courts, a great children's playground, a wading pool and an artificial duck pond add to its charms. The Romanesque 1899 Westmount Public Library and the Westmount Conservatory are also located in the park. The conservatory, a fine example of a 19th-century greenhouse, is normally open daily from 9-3. In summer, look for the delightful floral clock on the lawn at the corner of Sherbrooke and Lansdowne.

The conservatory in Westmount Park.

Olympic Park
4141 Pierre-de-Coubertin between Pie IX and Viau
252-4141 or 252-4400
The former site of the 1976 Summer Games, the park includes Olympic Stadium with its inclined tower and panoramic views, the Aquatic Centre, Maurice Richard Arena, Olympic Village and the former Vélodrome, now being converted into the new Montreal Biodome. The Biodome, scheduled to open in 1992, will display various ecosystems and house the former Montreal Aquarium exhibits.

Lafontaine Park
Sherbrooke est between St-Hubert and Papineau
872-2644
About 40 ha (100 acres) of pleasantly treed, gently rolling terrain, divided into two distinct sections. The western part is in the English landscape tradition; paths gently follow the natural landscape and circle past two pretty man-made ponds. To the east, the park displays classical French garden design with its tidy geometric paths and plantings.

For outdoor enthusiasts, Lafontaine Park has 17 public tennis courts, two outdoor pools, boat rentals, playing fields, bicycle paths and picnic benches. During the summer, there are open-air theatre performances and concerts, including special presentations for children. The park also has a wealth of public monuments, the most recent dedicated to Quebec poet and songwriter Félix Leclerc.

Angrignon Park
3400 des Trinitaires
872-2815 (summer)
872-3066 (winter)
During the summer, this 107-ha (264-acre) park is an ideal spot for family picnics. The park is equally popular during the winter, for cross-country skiing, snowshoeing and beautifully illuminated night skating.

Maisonneuve Park
Sherbrooke at Pie IX
872-6555
Next to the Montreal Botanical Garden and opposite Olympic Park, this is an excellent place for jogging, cycling, cross-country skiing or snowshoeing.

Lafontaine Park. (City of Montreal)

WATERFRONT PARKS

Île Notre-Dame and Île Ste-Hélène
These two small islands in the St. Lawrence River lie directly east of the main island of Montreal. Together, they represent one of the city's largest green spaces. Easily accessible by car, bicycle or *métro*, the islands offer a variety of recreational facilities and several major attractions.

Île Ste-Hélène has open fields and treed parkland well suited to quiet walks and picnics. The Old Fort and its powder magazine (La Poudrière) are of historic interest. The fort houses the David M. Stewart Museum (see Museums/Art Galleries) and the Festin des Gouverneurs restaurant (see Nightlife under Dinner Theatres). La Poudrière is used as a French-language theatre during the summer (check the newspapers for show information). Two modern installations on the western tip of the island date from 1967: sculptor Alexander Calder's *Stabile Man*, and architect Buckminster Fuller's geodesic dome (which served as the U.S. pavilion at Expo '67). The dome, badly damaged in a subsequent fire, is currently being transformed into a museum complex dedicated to the St. Lawrence River and the environment, expected to open in 1993. The island's principal attractions for children are the Aqua-Parc and La Ronde amusement park (see With the Kids).

Part of Île Ste-Hélène was artificially extended with landfill to accommodate Expo '67, and neighboring Île Notre-Dame was created at the same time. Île Notre-Dame is still home to the Palais de Civilization, which served as the French pavilion at Expo '67, and is now used to host annual international exhibitions. Check the newspapers for details.

Île Notre-Dame offers some excellent and innovative sports and recreational facilities. The most recent development has been a 600-metre (1970-foot) sandy beach. For information on boating, windsurfing, swimming and skating, see Sports/Recreation.

The magnificent floral park on Île Notre-Dame is a legacy of the Floralies Internationales. In 1980, this was the site of the first world horticultural exhibition held in North America, and flowers from all over the world are still exhibited every summer. The park includes a rare taiga flower display, the only one of its kind to exist in a formal garden. The floral park is open mid-June to mid-Sept 8:30 AM-9 PM. Admission is free.

The two islands figure prominently in Montreal's annual calendar of events. During the winter, the frozen Olympic Rowing Basin becomes the main site for the annual Fête des Neiges. The Benson & Hedges International Fireworks competition draws large crowds every June, while Île Notre-Dame's technically challenging Circuit Gilles-Villeneuve hosts the exciting Canadian Grand Prix Formula 1 race every summer.

To reach the islands by car or bicycle, take the de la Concorde or Jacques-Cartier bridge. If you take the *métro*, simply get off at the Île Ste-Hélène station. During the summer, there is a free shuttle service linking the *métro* with the island's major sights, and bus service between the Papineau *métro* station and La Ronde. The Montreal-Longueuil ferry also stops in summer at La Ronde (see Sightseeing for information on the ferry).

REGIONAL PARKS

Montreal's regional parks provide ready access to largely unspoiled countryside. They are especially popular for nature walks and cross-country skiing. (Note: dogs and other domestic animals are not permitted in these parks.) Two of the best:

Cap-St-Jacques Park
Chemin du Cap-St-Jacques
Pierrefonds
280-6715
This park has the longest cross-country

ski trails of any of the regional parks, as well as a maple-sugar cabin, ecology farm, bird-watching centre, beach, snack bars and washrooms. Open daily 9-4.

Île-de-la-Visitation
2425 Gouin est
280-6715

Excellent cross-country ski circuit and hiking trail, lookouts over Rivière des Prairies, and a restaurant and washrooms. Open daily 8 AM-sundown.

GARDENS

Montreal Botanical Garden
4101 Sherbrooke est at Pie IX
872-1400

The garden was founded in 1931 by an illustrious Canadian botanist, Father Marie-Victorin. The exhibition conservatories, open to the public since 1958, and 81 ha (200 acres) of outdoor garden provide a fascinating look at more than 26,000 plant specimens, including a prestigious collection of orchids, one of the best non-Asian col-

lections of bonsai and numerous crowd-pleasers such as the curious-looking *Welwitschia mirabilis* with its pair of 2-m (6½-foot) long leaves.

Two superb Oriental gardens complement the formal French and traditional English styles represented elsewhere in the garden. The 2.5-ha (6-acre) Chinese Garden was a joint project of the botanical garden and the City of Shanghai; the Japanese Garden, also 2.5-ha, includes traditional lanterns and pavilions among the tailored growth and provides exhibitions on Japanese culture and the traditional tea ceremony.

Guided tours of the conservatories are available to small groups by reservation. Audio guides can be rented any time the gardens are open for $2. Hours: 8-8 daily.

Also here is the **Insectarium**, one of Montreal's newest attractions. Designed to resemble a giant bug, the museum houses a number of thought-provoking and entertaining entomological displays. Through interactive exhibits and A/V presentations, visi-

The Chinese Garden in the Montreal Botanical Garden. (City of Montreal)

tors can test their knowledge of the various species' history, role in human literature and mythology and contribution to the environment. Displays include insect products, such as honey, silk and medications, and a superb necklace from Ecuador fashioned from jewel beetles. A special children's activity area provides fun and educational hands-on experiences such as the identification of insect shapes.

By far the most interesting features here are the live insect displays. Butterfly aviaries and vivariums enable visitors to admire such graceful creatures as Quebec's monarch butterfly (the Insectarium's symbol), the stunning iridescent-blue morphos butterflies, golden scarabs, giant (and noisy) Malaysian cicadas and hissing cockroaches from Madagascar. There are also arachnids (spiders and scorpions) and a few myriapods (millipedes)—not true insects, but interesting nonetheless.

Even the most squeamish will find it hard not to share at least some of the enthusiasm of the founders, Brother Firmin Laliberté, a self-taught entomologist, and Georges Brossard, a former notary who travelled the world in search of fascinating insects. Largely due to their generous donations, the Insectarium's collection is considered one of the best in the world. Open from 9-6 daily.

Admission to the Botanical Garden (includes admission to Insectarium): adults $5 Oct to May, $7 June to Sept; discounts for youths and seniors; children under 5 free. Admission to Insectarium only: adults $4; discounts for youths, seniors and the handicapped; children under 5 free. Between May and Sept a miniature train ride is available on the garden grounds for $1.50. A free shuttle bus links the gardens with Olympic Park across the street from mid-May to mid-Sept.

The Discovery Room in the Insectarium. (City of Montreal)

MUSEUMS/
ART GALLERIES

MAJOR MUSEUMS

Musée des Beaux-Arts/ Montreal Museum of Fine Arts
1379 Sherbrooke ouest at du Musée
285-1600

Founded in 1860, the Montreal Museum of Fine Arts is Canada's oldest public art gallery. Its extensive holdings (currently only about five per cent are on display) encompass a number of important collections, including a sampling of the works of Canada's highly regarded Group of Seven and of James Wilson Morrice, Canada's best-known neo-impressionist artist. The museum also has a fine collection of early Quebec furniture and decorative arts and hosts travelling exhibitions from around the world.

The main building, designed by Montreal architects Edward and William Maxwell, was completed in 1912 and substantially enlarged in 1976. The front entrance was remodelled several years ago to once again allow visitors the opportunity to enter via its grand staircase—a treat not to be missed! The museum recently undertook a major building campaign. A new pavilion on the south side of Sherbrooke, designed by well-known Montreal architect Moshe Safdie, opened in late 1991 adding some 22,874 m² (about 246,000 sq. ft.) of exhibition space. The pavilion incorporates the façade of a 1905 apartment house and is connected to the main building by a series of underground galleries.

Admission: adults $4, discounts for students, free to senior citizens and children under 12. Open Tues to Sun 10-5, with extended hours during special exhibitions.

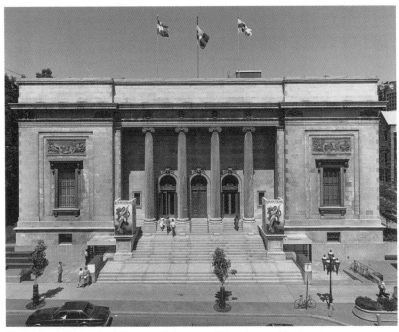

The main building of the Montreal Museum of Fine Arts on Sherbrooke.

THE MONTREAL MUSEUM OF FINE ARTS

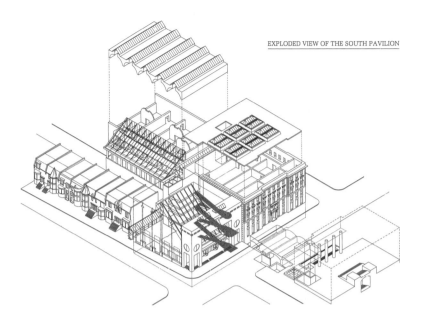

EXPLODED VIEW OF THE SOUTH PAVILION

10 MFA Bests
Pierre Théberge, director,
Montreal Museum of Fine Arts

1. **Paul Émile Borduas**, *The Black Star*.
2. **Ozias Leduc**, *Still Life with Open Book*.
3. **Honoré Daumier**, *Nymphs Pursued by Satyrs*.
4. **Emanuel de Witte**, *Interior with a Woman at the Clavichord*.
5. **Nicolas Poussin**, *Man Pursued by a Snake*.
6. **Henry Moore**, *Seated Torso*.
7. **Giuseppe Penone**, *Grand geste végétal*.
8. **Artist unknown**, *Large hemispherical basin*, Syria, Ayyubid period.
9. **Artist unknown**, *Famille rose vase*, China, Qing dynasty. Brass.
10. **Artist unknown**, *Head of a king*, Benin Kingdom, 19th century. Bronze.

Château Dufresne, home of the Montreal Museum of Decorative Arts. (Montreal Museum of Decorative Arts)

Musée d'art contemporain de Montréal/Montreal Museum of Contemporary Art
Cité du Havre
873-2878

This museum houses a superb collection of Canadian and international works from the past 50 years and an extensive reference library dealing with contemporary art. The museum is scheduled to move to a new building at the corner of Ste-Catherine ouest and Jeanne-Mance in early 1992. Admission is free (donations encouraged). Open Tues to Sun 10-6. Guided group tours available.

Montreal Museum of Decorative Arts
2929 Jeanne-d'Arc near Pierre-de-Coubertin
259-2575

The museum is housed in the Château Dufresne, a private residence built by two brothers in 1918 in the beaux-arts style and recently restored to its original splendour. The museum is home to a first-rate collection of international post-1935 design objects assembled by Montrealers David and Lilianne Stewart and hosts regular temporary exhibitions of glassware, textiles and furniture. Admission: adults $3, discounts for students and seniors, children under 13 free. Open Wed to Sun 11-5.

McCord Museum
690 Sherbrooke ouest near University
398-7100

This small gem houses superb collections of paintings, period costumes, furniture and Quebec folk art. It is also home to the Notman Archive, an extensive collection of 19th-century photographs of Montreal and its citizenry. The museum is currently closed for renovations and is scheduled to reopen in 1992. Call for hours and admission prices.

The Château Ramezay in Old Montreal. (MUC)

Château Ramezay Museum
280 Notre-Dame est near St-Alexis
861-3708

This former residence of Claude de Ramezay, 11th governor of New France, dates from 1705. In Old Montreal, it's a well-preserved example of early 18th-century architecture. Constructed of rough stone with cut-stone trim, the attractive façade is detailed with S-shaped iron bars. These bars, seen on many buildings of the same period, are the ends of rods used to anchor the main beams.

The château was bought by a fur-trading company following de Ramezay's death. During the 1775 occupation of Montreal by the Americans it became the invading army's headquarters. Benjamin Franklin is said to have stayed here. Later, the building was used successively as a courthouse and school. Today it's owned by the city of Montreal and houses a small but exquisite collection of early Amerindian and Canadian artifacts. Admission: adults $2, children under 6 free. Open daily 10-5. Closed Mon from mid-Sept to mid-June.

David M. Stewart Museum
Old Fort
Île Ste-Hélène
861-6701

The museum is devoted to Canadian history and contains extensive collections of early firearms, old maps and scientific and navigational instruments. During the summer months, 18th-century French and English military drills are performed daily. Admission: adults $4, discounts for families and groups. Open Wed to Mon 10-5 (until 6 PM in summer).

Canadian Centre for Architecture
1920 Baille at du Fort
939-7000

The CCA was founded in 1979 by

architect Phyllis Lambert, an heir to the Seagram liquor fortune. It features a study centre and museum devoted to the art and history of architecture and contains one of the world's largest archives of architecture books, drawings and photographs.

Designed by Montreal architect Peter Rose, the building is integrated with Shaughnessy House, an impressive period mansion built for a member of Montreal's late 19th-century commercial elite. The CCA sculpture garden, designed by Melvin Charney, is across from the centre on the south side of René-Lévesque and is itself well worth a visit.

The CCA library currently has some 130,000 volumes. Among the special collections are significant holdings of 15th- to 19th-century books on Italian cities, early architectural treatises, 18th- and 19th-century guides to British houses and trade catalogues from various eras. The periodicals collection is also extensive, numbering more than 700 current titles. The print and drawing collection comprises 20,000 works dating from the late 15th century to the present, and its photographic archive contains close to 45,000 images.

Exhibits are changed regularly. Admission: adults $5, discounts for seniors and students, children under 12 free. Open Wed to Sun 11-5 (until 8 PM on Thurs).

OTHER MONTREAL MUSEUMS

Bank of Montreal Museum
129 St-Jacques at Place d'Armes
877-7373
This museum, in the same 1847 building as one of Montreal's oldest (and arguably most spectacular) bank branches, contains interesting displays of banking memorabilia, including a collection of mechanical savings banks. Admission is free. Open Mon to Fri 10-4.

Marc-Aurèle Fortin Museum
118 St-Pierre near Place d'Youville
845-6108
A permanent collection of the works of artist Marc-Aurèle Fortin (1880-1970) well known for his oils and watercolours of Quebec landscapes. The museum also hosts exhibitions of works by other leading Canadian artists. Admission: adults $2.50, discounts for students and seniors, children free. Open Tues to Sun 11-5.

Montreal History Centre
335 Place d'Youville at McGill
872-3207
Housed in an old firehall, the centre's exhibits detail the history of Montreal from its founding 350 years ago to the present. Plan to spend an hour or so here before you start your tour of Old Montreal. Admission: adults $2, discounts for students, seniors and young children. Open daily May to Sept 10-6, Sept to May 11-4:30.

The Redpath Museum on the campus of McGill University. (MUC)

Marguerite d'Youville Museum
1185 St-Mathieu at Sherbrooke ouest
937-9501

Named after the founder of the Congregation of the Sisters of Charity (commonly known as the Grey Nuns), the museum contains d'Youville's tomb and various religious objects and furniture dating from the early 18th century. Admission is free. Open Wed to Sun 1:30-4:30.

Redpath Museum
McGill University Campus
859 Sherbrooke ouest at McGill College
398-4086

The Redpath was the first building in Canada designed specifically as a museum. Its principal exhibits are of rare fossils, shells and minerals collected by the university's staff during the past century. The leading natural history museum in Quebec, the Redpath has

what is regarded as the second most important collection of ancient Egyptian artifacts in Canada. Admission is free. Open Mon to Fri 9-5; closed Fri between Sept and June.

Post Office Museum
640 Ste-Catherine ouest near University
283-4185

This is where Santa Claus's mail from Canada's children ends up! Many stamp displays, together with films and rotating exhibitions. Free guided tours can be arranged in advance. Admission is free. Open Mon to Fri 8-5:45, Sat 8:30-4:45.

Marguerite Bourgeoys Museum
Notre-Dame-de-Bonsecours Church
400 St-Paul est at Bonsecours
845-9991

Marguerite Bourgeoys, Montreal's first teacher and the founder of a major

Quebec religious order, was canonized in 1982. The museum tells her story in a series of doll-size tableaux.

A museum ticket also entitles the holder to visit the rooftop observatory, which affords a good view of the harbour area. Admission: adults $2, discounts for children. Open daily May to Oct 9-4:30; 10:30-4:30 in the off season.

Maison St-Gabriel
2146 Favard near Dublin
935-8136

The museum, first opened in 1966, is in a large three-storey mansard-roofed house that dates from 1668. Operated by the nuns of the Congregation of Notre-Dame, it offers a re-creation of daily life in the 17th and 18th centuries. Admission is free. Guided tours offered Tues to Sun from Apr to Dec. Call for hours.

Clock Tower
Quai Victoria
Vieux Port

The tower was erected in 1921 as a war memorial honouring Canada's naval fleet. Beneath it stand two cannons, gifts of the British Admiralty. The Tower mounts regular exhibitions on the Old Port's history. Good views of the port area and Old Montreal from the three observation points. Admission is free. Open daily July and Aug 10-5.

REGIONAL MUSEUMS

Canadian Railway Museum
122A St-Pierre
St-Constant
632-2410

Heaven for railway buffs! This is Canada's most extensive collection of old rolling stock, trams and steam loco-motives. A train or tram normally operates on Sunday. Open daily 9-5 May to Sept; 9-5 on weekends until the end of Oct. Admission: adults $3.50, children $1.75.

St-Laurent Art Museum
615 Ste-Croix near du Collège
St-Laurent
747-7367

Housed in the neo-Gothic former chapel of College St-Laurent, this museum's permanent collection celebrates early Quebec arts and crafts. Periodic exhibitions of contemporary work with an emphasis on the decorative arts. Admission is free. Open Tues to Fri and Sun 11-5.

Musée Régionale de Vaudreuil
431 St-Roche
Vaudreuil
(514) 455-2092

Another small museum devoted to aspects of pioneer life. Admission: adults $2, discount for students. Open Mon to Fri 11-5, Sun 1-5.

MAJOR PRIVATE ART GALLERIES

Montreal has one of the most dynamic arts communities in Canada. While the emphasis in the galleries is on Quebec talent, usually you can find examples of works by other major Canadian and international artists.

At last count there were some 90 commercial galleries in the city, carrying everything from the staid to the avant-garde. Many of the more established are on Sherbrooke ouest in the several blocks flanking the Montreal Museum of Fine Arts. In recent years, several good galleries specializing in contemporary works have sprung up on Ste-Catherine ouest near Place des Arts.

Several pockets of "parallel" galleries can also be found on St-Laurent between Sherbrooke and Rachel.

Galleries are normally open Tues to Sat, 10-5. The weekend edition of the *Gazette* usually contains comprehensive listings of current exhibitions as does the free English-language weekly *Montreal Mirror*. The better galleries distribute free copies of *Slate*, a magazine devoted solely to art gallery listings. Several good monthly and quarterly magazines that will be of interest to serious art aficionados are *Vie des Arts*, *Guide Parcours*, *Parachute* and *etc*. Check one of these publications for current shows and hours.

Galerie Walter Klinkoff Inc.
1200 Sherbrooke ouest near Drummond
288-7306

The "establishment" gallery of Montreal where one goes to buy the work of the Group of Seven, Adrien Hébèrt, James Wilson Morrice, and the like, as well as more conservative contemporary works. The day-to-day operation is now in the hands of Walter Klinkoff's sons, Eric and Alan, both extremely knowledgeable and willing to share their expertise with visitors.

Galerie Barbara Silverberg
2148 Mackay near Sherbrooke ouest
932-3987

The only gallery in Montreal devoted exclusively to contemporary ceramics, with everything from bizarre garden furniture to exquisite vases. Ask to see what's on the shelves in the back storeroom.

Galerie Elca London
1616 Sherbrooke ouest at Guy
931-3646

An excellent selection of first-rate Inuit soapstone sculpture, plus work by a number of U.S.-based artists.

Waddington & Gorce Inc.
2155 Mackay at Sherbrooke ouest
847-1112

Consistently interesting—and expensive—work by some of Canada's better artists, including Dorothy Knowles, Ulysees Comtois and Ron Martin. Some international artists. A recent show featured works on paper by Milton Avery, Robert Motherwell and David Hockney.

Galerie Jean-Pierre Valentin
1434 Sherbrooke ouest near Mackay
849-3637

One of our favourites. Good work by some of Quebec's better present-day artists (Henry Jones, Élène Gamache and Danielle Rochon) and other Quebec masters (Pellan, Bellefleur, Roberts, Masson, Lemieux, Cosgrove, Borduas and Riopelle). The gallery represents the estate of Quebec landscape painter Marc-Aurèle Fortin and deals extensively in works by Montreal's most enigmatic painter, Louise Scott.

Galerie Elena Lee Verre d'Art
1518 Sherbrooke ouest near Simpson
932-3896

Devoted exclusively to works of glass.

Galerie d'Art Esquimau
1434 Sherbrooke ouest ner Mackay
844-4080

An excellent selection of Inuit soapstone and whalebone carvings.

Galerie Bernard Desroches
1444 Sherbrooke ouest near Redpath
842-8648

This gallery usually has a good selection of '50s and mid-'60s paintings by Quebec masters such as Toupin, Borduas and Riopelle. The contemporary work it carries is less exciting.

Galerie Kastel
1366 Greene near Sherbrooke ouest
933-8735

A large gallery that represents dozens of Quebec and Canadian contemporary artists, including Jori Smith, Henry Jones, Leonard Brooks, Claude Le Sauteur and Antoine Bittar. One of the preferred galleries of the wealthy Westmount crowd, Kastel also carries works by Canada's Group of Seven and other lesser-known but acknowledged masters such as Kathleen Morris, Fredrick Coburn, Fritz Brandtner and René Richard. The gallery's owners are knowledgeable and pleasant to deal with.

Galerie Trois Points
Fifth floor
307 Ste-Catherine ouest near de Bleury
845-5555

One of the newer contemporary galleries, Trois Points is tucked away on an upper floor of a nondescript office building. Don't let the location fool you—this gallery carries good work at reasonable prices and represents up-and-coming artists such as Marc Garneau, Yves-Louis Seize and Paul Beliveau. And there's a bonus out the window—an outstanding view of the new Musée d'art contemporain.

Galerie Frédéric Palardy
Fifth floor
307 Ste-Catherine ouest near de Bleury
844-4464

The staff here are among the most pleasant we have encountered. The gallery carries the work of such artists as Caroline Bussières, Léon Bellefleur and sculptor Jean-Louis Émond. Good value for money.

Galerie Brenda Wallace
372 Ste-Catherine ouest near de Bleury
393-4066

This two-year-old gallery, in a building still largely devoted to the garment trade, consistently takes risks. It shows tough but outstanding pieces by such artists as Tadashi Kawamata, Liliana Berezowsky and Holly King. The imaginative sculptor Micah Lexier shows here, as does painter Regan Morris.

Galerie René Blouin
372 Ste-Catherine ouest near de Bleury
393-9969

Owner Blouin, well connected to Canada's public art gallery establishment, represents one of Canada's senior artists, Betty Goodwin, as well as rising stars such as Genevieve Cadieux.

Michel Tétreault Art Contemporain
1192 Beaudry near René-Lévesque ouest
521-2141

This gallery is somewhat off the beaten track but still merits a visit. Artists represented include Kitty Bruneau, Pierre Blanchette, Jacques Hurtubise and Jennifer Macklem.

Galerie Graff
963 Rachel est near Mentana
526-2616

When it opened a quarter-century ago, this gallery/print-making cooperative was *the* alternative gallery. While it's no longer consistently on the cutting edge, it's still well worth a visit.

Canal Complex
4710 St-Ambroise near de Courcelle
935-1291

Next to the Lachine Canal in Pointe-St-Charles, this former mattress factory has been very successfully converted into a massive studio complex. A number of interior spaces are used to exhibit resident artists' work from time to time.

Stephen Landau Fine Arts
1456 Sherbrooke ouest at Crescent
849-3311

This gallery specializes in expensive works by 20th-century European and American masters. By appointment only.

Galerie Art & Style
4875-A Sherbrooke ouest near Prince Albert
484-1384

On the main Westmount shopping strip, this gallery favours contemporary works in traditional Quebec style and carries work by Colette Boivin, St-Gilles, David Brown and Bruno Côté. Extremely knowledgeable owner Raphael Shano deals extensively in the work of René Richard and P.V. Beaulieu, among others. A good

---

The Best of Montreal

Best music venue: Club Soda, 5270 du Parc near Fairmount

Best Montreal author: Mordecai Richler

Best Montreal artist: Betty Goodwin

Best radio station: CKUT Radio McGill

Best street to satisfy a whim: St-Laurent

Best restaurant for eavesdropping: Beauty's, 93 Mont-Royal est at St-Urbain

Best hotdog: Montreal Pool Room, 1200 St-Laurent at Ste-Catherine

Best hamburger: La Paryse, 302 Ontario est at St-Denis

Best ice-cream: Ben & Jerry's (various locations)

Best coffee: A.L. Van Houtte (various locations)

Best bagel: Real Bagel, 4940 de la Reine-Marie near Lemieux

Best late-night drinking spot: Lola's Paradise, 3604 St-Laurent at Prince Arthur

Best souvenir: Mountie doll with plastic horse

Best bike shop: ABC Cycle & Sports, 5584 du Parc near St-Viateur

Best pool room: Bar Saint-Laurent, 3874 St-Laurent near St-Cuthbert

Source: *Montreal Mirror*, 1990 reader poll

The Worst of Montreal

Worst public art: *The Illuminate Crowd*, McGill College Ave.

Best place to break your neck: Anywhere in winter

Most uncomfortable seats: Centaur Theatre

Most obscene use of taxpayers' money: Olympic Stadium

Worst pub clientele: Peel Pub

Worst intersection: du Parc and des Pins

Worst pothole: Peel, from des Pins to Sherbrooke

Worst *métro* station: Lucien-l'Allier

Source: *Montreal Mirror*, 1990 reader poll

bet if you want to take home a reasonably priced souvenir of Quebec to hang on your wall.

Guilde canadienne des Métiers d'Art/Canadian Guild of Crafts
2025 Peel near de Maisonneuve ouest
849-6091
A high-quality crafts store. A great place to find that small, last-moment gift.

Artexte
3575 St-Laurent near Sherbrooke
845-2759
Montreal's premier art bookstore, Artexte offers a vast selection of art books, magazines and posters. The store also maintains an international documentation centre specializing in post-1965 art, which houses 4,500 exhibition catalogues and 3,000 artist dossiers.

ENTERTAINMENT/ CULTURE

WHERE TO BUY TICKETS

Tickets for theatre, concerts, dance performances and special film screenings are normally available from the box office of the particular performance hall. Most box offices are open from about 10 AM until show time. Tickets for many—but not all—performances can also be obtained through the following ticket agencies. Smaller theatres usually don't sell tickets through the agencies since this further reduces their already limited revenues.

Ticketron
300 Leo-Pariseau near Jeanne-Mance
288-3651

Admission Inc.
1217 Notre-Dame est near Montcalm
522-1245, 1-800-361-4595 (outside Montreal)

Dupont & Dupond
2021 Union near de Maisonneuve ouest
845-3535

AT THE MOVIES

FILM FESTIVALS

Montreal is extremely active on the Canadian and international film festival circuits and hosts a remarkable variety each year, including festivals of women's films, videos and Chinese films. Two of the biggest are the Montreal World Film Festival and the Festival of New Cinema and Video.

Montreal World Film Festival
848-3883

From its modest beginning in 1977, this event has grown into the largest publicly attended film festival in the western world. Features and shorts are juried. The best feature receives the Grand Prix of the Americas; other awards include Best Actor, Best Artistic Contribution, and several viewers'-choice awards. Entries in the Canadian Student Film Festival (part of the larger festival) vie for the National Film Board of Canada's Norman McLaren Award. Watch for international stars at the screenings, held at several downtown locations including the Port-Royal theatre at Place des Arts.

The World Film Festival usually runs from late Aug to early Sept. In 1991, individual tickets cost $6.50; booklets of 10, $45; an open pass (to view any film shown between 9 and 5), $160.

Montreal International Festival of New Cinema and Video
843-4725

Since it began in 1971, this festival has become perhaps the most important showcase of independent film and video in Canada, the only one expressly devoted to the cutting edge in filmmaking. Over the years, it has helped introduce North American audiences to the work of such directors as Britain's Peter Greenaway and Germany's Wim Wenders. Films are screened at Cinémathèque Québécoise (842-9763) and Parallèle (843-6001). Phone for ticket information. The festival takes place in Oct.

FIRST-RUN FILMS

Montreal has lots of commercial movie theatres, many concentrated on Ste-Catherine in the downtown core.

See the daily newspapers for listings of recent commercial releases, or check the *Mirror* or *Voir* (free entertainment weeklies available in many shops and restaurants).

REPERTORY CINEMA

Montreal has a number of good repertory cinemas. Most change their films daily. For schedules, check the *Mirror* or *Voir*, or phone the theatres.

Cinéma ONF/National Film Board
Complexe Guy-Favreau
200 René-Lévesque ouest near
Jeanne-Mance
283-8229
Films can also be rented here.

Cinéma de Paris
896 Ste-Catherine ouest near
St-André
875-7284

Cinémathèque Québécoise
355 de Maisonneuve est near
St-Denis
842-9763
Cinémathèque is dedicated to the preservation of Quebec's cinematic heritage and hosts a number of movie festivals every year. The lobby museum houses a collection of filmmaking equipment dating back to 1879. Cinémathèque also has one of North America's largest cinema-related libraries. For a rare treat, go for the Friday-night show at 6:30, when old silent movies are screened to piano accompaniment. Admission to the lobby museum and library is free. Tickets are $2.50.

Conservatoire
1455 de Maisonneuve ouest at
Bishop
848-3878

Goethe-Institut
418 Sherbrooke est near St-Denis
499-0159
Occasional showings of films by Germany's best directors. Call for details.

Ouimetoscope
1204 Ste-Catherine est at
Montcalm
525-8600
Ouimetoscope also screens children's movies on Sunday afternoons.

Outremont
1248 Bernard ouest near
Champagner
273-0437

Parallèle
3682 St-Laurent at Guilbault
843-6001
A major player in the International Festival of New Cinema and Video.

Rialto
5723 du Parc near Bernard ouest
274-3550

READINGS

The Double Hook Bookstore
1235A Greene near Sherbrooke
ouest
932-5093
The Double Hook often invites Canadian authors to read their poetry, fiction and children's literature. For other children's readings, see With the Kids under Entertainment (Library Programs) and Shopping (Books).

Saidye Bronfman Centre
5170 Côte-Ste-Catherine near
Mountain Sights
739-2301
Occasional readings of prose and poetry. Call for details.

A scene from *Les trous dans le ciel*, presented by Quebec's Compagnie Marie Chouinard at the Festival of the Americas. (Ornsby Ford)

THEATRE

Montreal offers a wide selection of French and English theatre and hosts a major international festival. Check the newspapers for current productions or call the theatres directly.

Festival of the Americas
842-0704

For two adventurous weeks in spring every other year, the Festival of the Americas showcases works from North, Central and South America. Started in 1985, the festival recently extended its mandate to include European and international productions. For information call the number above, or write to: Festival of the Americas, C.P. 7, Succursale E, Montreal H2T 3A5.

ENGLISH-LANGUAGE THEATRE

English Theatre Hotline
843-8698 (T-H-E-A-T-R-E)

The Quebec Drama Federation has just announced this new theatre hotline and an upcoming bimonthly calendar of events in the anglophone theatre community. Phone for details.

Centaur Theatre
The Old Exchange Arts Centre
453 St-François-Xavier at Hôpital
288-1229

The theatre is in the Old Stock Exchange building in Old Montreal. It was started in 1968 by artistic director Maurice Podbrey. The annual seven-play season runs Oct to May and features productions by many Canadian playwrights, including David Fennario of *Balconville* fame. Centaur 1 seats 240; Centaur 2 seats 400. All seating is general admission. Box office: 288-3161.

A scene from the Centaur Theatre production of David Fennario's *Balconville*, a prize-winning play about Montreal tenement life. (Centaur Theatre)

Le Stage and Le Cabaret
7385 Decarie
731-7771
These two popular dinner theatres present musicals and light comedies. Recent productions have included *Nunsense, Ain't Misbehavin'* and *Anglo* (a comedy about life as an anglophone in today's Quebec). Le Stage is a rectangular theatre/dining room; Le Cabaret presents shows on a raised stage. In 1991 dinner and show cost was $48.30, including taxes and tip. Tickets for the show only are also available, space permitting.

Saidye Bronfman Centre
5170 Côte-Ste-Catherine near Mountain Sights
739-2301
A permanent Jewish theatre company offers plays in Yiddish twice annually (in June and Nov) and several English productions each year. At other times, the 300-seat hall is used for theatre, music, dance and film. Ticket prices vary. Box office: 739-7944, 739-4816.

FRENCH-LANGUAGE THEATRE
These are the city's major French-language theatres.

 théâtre du nouveau monde

Théâtre du Nouveau Monde
84 Ste-Catherine ouest near St-Urbain
861-0563
Repertory, contemporary, classics.

Théâtre du Rideau Vert
4664 St-Denis near Bienville
844-1793
Founded in 1948, this is Montreal's premier French-language theatre. It offers performances of French classics as well as modern works by Quebec playwrights.

Théâtre St-Denis
1594 St-Denis near de Maisonneuve est
849-4211
The theatre is used for all sorts of performances, including concerts and comedy acts during the annual Just for Laughs festival.

Théâtre le Biscuit
221 St-Paul est near Place Jacques-Cartier
845-7306
This new marionette theatre in Old Montreal is especially appealing to children.

Cirque du Soleil
522-2324
A circus without animals that captivates audiences with a mix of theatrical gymnastics, original live music, extravagant costumes and numerous special effects. Since it began in 1985, Quebec's Cirque du Soleil has achieved cult status on its American tours. If you are lucky, you might catch it in Montreal.

OPEN-AIR THEATRE
During the past few summers, the Repercussion Theatre has toured Montreal's parks (including Westmount Park) staging free open-air Shakespearean productions. Call 695-1545 or 485-8875 for details. Another open-air theatre group is the Mount Royal Shakespeare Company. Performances are usually held in July at 7 PM in Mount Royal Park near the Cartier monument. Watch the *Gazette* or the *Mirror* for details, or call 284-3074. Read the ads carefully—you may even find Shakespeare being performed in a parking lot. In 1991, a small French troupe performed *Macbeth* in Old Montreal, rain or shine, starting at 2 AM (yes, 2 in the morning!). Summer theatre productions take place at Lafontaine Park (872-2644) and on Île Ste-Hélène at the Old Fort (861-6701) and Théâtre de la Poudrière (954-1344; productions here take place indoors).

CLASSICAL MUSIC

Montreal International Music Festival
866-2662
This annual festival, held in Sept, includes classes, concerts, conferences and recitals. Performances take place at Place des Arts, Chapelle Historique du Bon Pasteur and many other sites.

Charles Dutoit, artistic director and conductor of the Montreal Symphony Orchestra. (Eric Mahoudeau)

Montreal International Piano Festival
866-2662

Formerly the Montreal International Music Festival. The name change reflects the festival's emphasis on the piano; its main goal is to promote Montreal as the international meeting place of the instrument. Recent performers have included the great Soviet pianist Evgeny Mogilevsky in recital and the Salzburg Chamber Orchestra under the direction of Italian maestro Rodolfo Bonucci. Various venues.

Montreal Symphony Orchestra
842-3402

Under conductor Charles Dutoit, the Montreal Symphony Orchestra has achieved an excellent international reputation through its extremely successful recordings and international tours. Regular concerts at Place des Arts and Notre-Dame Basilica, with occasional performances at other venues, including free concerts in city parks during the summer.

Metropolitan Orchestra of Montreal
598-0870

Conducted by Agnes Grossmann, this assembly of young musicians performs regularly at Place des Arts.

McGill Chamber Orchestra
487-5190

This is one of Montreal's oldest chamber orchestras, founded in 1940 by Alexander Brott, patriarch of the famous Canadian musical family. Performances are given at Place des Arts and in Notre-Dame Basilica.

Pollack Concert Hall
555 Sherbrooke ouest at Aylmer
398-4547

The concert hall was designed by architect Bruce Price and built in 1899. Frequent evening concerts are given here by student ensembles and soloists from McGill's Faculty of

Conductor Alexander Brott with the McGill Chamber Orchestra, which he founded in 1940. (McGill Chamber Orchestra)

Music. The hall also serves as a venue for concerts and recitals by professional musicians. Call for details.

St. Joseph's Oratory
3800 de la Reine Marie
733-8211
The oratory has carillon concerts Wed to Sat during the year and organ recitals Wed evenings during the summer featuring guest artists from Canada and abroad. Admission is free.

Basilique Notre-Dame/ Notre-Dame Basilica
116 Notre-Dame ouest at Place d'Armes
849-1070

Tosca, presented by L'Opéra de Montréal. (L'Opéra de Montréal)

Various concerts are offered throughout the year, the most popular being Handel's *Messiah* at Christmas and the annual Mozart Plus festival held in the summer with the Montreal Symphony Orchestra (the "plus" includes other religiously inspired artists like Brahms, Schubert and Beethoven). The summer concerts are popular, and the reserved seating in the nave of the church frequently sells out, so buy your tickets ahead of time. Notre-Dame's resident musical star, the massive pipe organ, is one of the largest in North America. Tickets are available from Place des Arts and Ticketron.

Christ Church Cathedral
1444 Union at Ste-Catherine ouest
843-6577
The cathedral has organ and choral recitals in addition to performances by instrumental ensembles. Performances are at noon and in the evening. Check the daily newspapers. Admission is by voluntary donation.

Atrium at Maison Alcan
1188 Sherbrooke ouest at Stanley
848-8469
Maison Alcan offers frequent free informal concerts from noon to 1:30 PM in its pleasant atrium. Past concerts have featured a varied program of classical guitarists, pianists, orchestras and choirs. For the current month's schedule, check the daily newspapers or call Maison Alcan.

St. James United Church
463 Ste-Catherine ouest near St-Alexandre
288-9245
Frequent organ recitals. Phone for details.

L'OPÉRA ☐ MONTRÉAL
DE

L'Opéra de Montréal
Place des Arts
260 de Maisonneuve ouest at
Jeanne-Mance
985-2222

Established in 1979, the Montreal Opera ranks among North America's top 10 opera companies. It takes considerable pride in promoting local Canadian talent, but international stars are also regularly featured. Under the general and artistic direction of Bernard Uzan, the company has broadened its horizons, offering inexpensive Friday night operas in concert (without sets or costume), public lectures in collaboration with Place des Arts and an expanded program of staged operatic productions. The 1991 program included *Rigoletto*, *Eugene Onegin* and *La Belle Hélène* sung in the original languages with French and English surtitles.

The Montreal Opera performs at the Salle Wilfred Pelletier of Place des Arts, mid-Sept to mid-May. Tickets range from $18 to $72.50.

Festival Orford
Centre d'Arts Orford
Autoroute des Cantons de l'est,
exit 118
Parc Provinciale Mont-Orford
Route 141 Nord
Orford
(819) 843-3981, 1-800-567-6155
(Montreal)

This popular annual summer festival in the beautiful setting of the Eastern Townships features mostly classical concerts by professionals and students. In 1991, performers included Anton Kuerti, various quartets and a Trinidadian steel band. Artistic director Agnes Grossmann also conducts the Metropolitan Orchestra of Montreal. Festival tickets are available in Montreal from the Admission Inc. ticket service at 522-1245.

Festival International de Lanaudière

Every July, musicians from around the world descend on Joliette—an hour's drive from Montreal—to take part in the Mozart piano competition and a number of indoor and outdoor classical concerts. Express buses to the festival grounds are available from Montreal. For information, call Admission Inc. at 522-1245.

Impromptu jazz in Place d'Armes.

POPULAR MUSIC

Check the *Mirror* or *Voir* for current club bookings and concerts. See also Nightlife.

Montreal International Jazz Festival
871-1881

There's no doubt about it: Montreal has the biggest and by far the best-organized jazz festival in the world. The festival has also become one of Montreal's most prestigious cultural events. For 10 days beginning in late June, much of downtown Montreal is transformed into the *village du jazz* as festival performances utilize virtually every major theatre and concert hall. Many free shows can be enjoyed in the city's streets and parks. Tickets for the big-name performers usually sell out quickly. If you're lucky, you might catch a jazz virtuoso or two in an impromptu performance at one of Montreal's jazz clubs. During the festival, the always popular Biddle's becomes a jazz mecca. The festival spreads to Club Soda, Cinémathèque Québécoise, Maison Alcan and several of the larger bars along St-Denis. Tickets for performances are available from the individual venues or (usually) through Admission Inc.

Nuits d'Afrique
Club Balattou
4372 St-Laurent near Marie-Anne
845-5447, 499-9239

Currently in its fifth year, this is a 14-day celebration of traditional and contemporary African and West Indian rhythms. In addition to the featured performances at Club Balattou, there is a daily street festival on St-Laurent involving shows, stands and contests from 10-10. Festival passes range from $65 for five shows to $119.50 for 10 shows. Tickets are available from Club Balattou or through Admission Inc.

One of the many outdoor concerts held during the annual Montreal Jazz Festival. (City of Montreal)

DANCE

Montreal is unquestionably the most important city for dance in Canada. Two of the oldest companies, Les Grandes Ballets Canadiens and Les Ballets Jazz, have enjoyed considerable international success. Montreal has also developed a reputation for producing some of the world's most exciting and innovative contemporary dance; the city's extremely active dance scene is second only to that of New York.

International Festival of New Dance
287-1423
This two-week festival features some of the world's most interesting contemporary dance. Held every second year. Call for information.

L'Agora de la Danse
840 Cherrier est near St-Hubert
525-7575, 525-1500
This new beaux-arts-style facility is dedicated to modern dance as an art form. L'Agora houses three different performance spaces, the largest seating approximately 300. It is the permanent home of Tangente, a local presenter of independent choreographers, and of the University of Quebec at Montreal dance department.

DANCE COMPANIES
Montreal has developed an excellent reputation for the quality of its solo dance artists. Names to watch for include **Marie Chouinard, Margie Gillis** and **Paul-André Fortier**. For more information on these artists, other independent choreographers and smaller dance companies, check the current listings in the *Mirror, Voir* or the *Gazette*.

Les Grands Ballets Canadiens
849-8681
A mixture of classical and modern repertory has attracted enthusiastic audiences for over 30 years. Les Grandes

The Montanaro Dance production of Zman Doe's *Lost in Time*. (Chris Randle)

Ballets has featured the works of many new Canadian composers and choreographers over the years. Its December production of *The Nutcracker Suite* is a perennial favourite with Montreal's children.

Les Ballets Jazz de Montréal
982-6771
Contemporary ballet and jazz dance.

Montanaro Dance Integrated Media
281-6510
Montanaro Dance is one of the most innovative dance companies in Canada, crossing traditional boundaries to incorporate other art forms. The use of 16mm film, original music and computer-controlled special effects results in uniquely styled performances. The artistic director is Michael Montanaro.

La La La Human Steps
288-8266
Under the artistic direction of Edouard Lock, this has become one of the most successful dance companies in the world. The company has just six dancers. Lock choreographed David Bowie's recent Sound and Vision concert tour.

Fondation Jean-Pierre Perrault
525-2464
Perrault is well-known for blending large groups of dancers with visual art.

Montreal Dance
845-2031
This repertory company works with many independent choreographers, both Canadian and international.

O'Vertigo Danse
251-9177
Known for its vigorous style, O'Vertigo has achieved considerable international success.

Ensemble national de Folklore les Sortilèges
274-5655
Les Sortilèges, Canada's only professional folk-dancing company, has a repertoire representing 15 countries.

NIGHTLIFE

Nobody comes to Montreal for a good night's sleep. Not according to the Quebec Tourist Office, anyway, which proudly claimed in a recent ad campaign that there is more to do in Montreal, around the clock and year-round, than in any other city in Canada. You can enjoy a late dinner, catch a comedy act, bar-hop, dance and breakfast at a trendy all-night eatery, all before dawn. And you'll be in good company. Montreal is home to a great number of irrepressible *bons vivants* who seem to like nothing better than partying and cruising till the wee hours. We recommend that you spend at least one Friday or Saturday night (the two busiest) experiencing the incredible energy of the city after dark. After all, you can always sleep when you get home.

There are three major districts to choose from. Downtown, there are the pubs, dance clubs and *brasseries* (restaurant/bars) near Crescent and de Maisonneuve. To the east, St-Denis has lots of bistros and bars; to the north, St-Laurent (the Main) is the place to go for fashionable snooker, the latest dance crazes and alternative music. Jazz, pop, and rock are played in all three areas but you will have to head up St-Laurent for Latin or African rhythms. There are also a number of good clubs and bars in the major hotels.

Your mother would probably advise you to be careful when you go out at night. She's right. If you stick to the well-lit, crowded streets you should be okay, but never forget that you are in a big city. Watch your purse or wallet, and take cabs rather than venture into quiet neighbourhoods on foot. All in all, it's still a pretty safe city to wander around in at night.

Dress comfortably if you like, but don't wear denim jeans. Some bars prohibit them, even if they're the expensive kind. Casual sophistication is the unofficial dress code for most of the clubs. On the other hand, if you feel like wearing something stunning by shock-designer Jean-Paul Gaultier, no one will bat an eye.

Many bars offer a happy hour with reduced prices starting at about 5 PM, but the action doesn't usually heat up until well after 10. Long lineups are common at the popular spots, so dress warmly in winter.

The recommendations here are based on current trends at the time of printing. Since nightclubs and their patrons are a fickle lot, we suggest that you check current entertainment listings in the *Gazette, Devoir* or *Mirror*. You can also refer to *Montreal Scope*, a magazine distributed free at most major hotels. When in doubt, simply join the longest lineup and follow the crowd.

RESERVATIONS

Dupont & Dupond
2021 Union near de Maisonneuve ouest
845-3535
If you are pressed for time, this agency will arrange excellent dinner-theatre or restaurant reservations for a small fee. They can offer suggestions for any cultural or entertainment events in town.

JAZZ

Biddle's
2060 Aylmer near de Maisonneuve ouest
842-8656
This well-established chicken-and-ribs restaurant is by far the most popular place for jazz in Montreal. Prime time comes during the annual Mon-

treal International Jazz Festival, when big-name performers often drop in for impromptu sets. During the rest of the year, amateurs are invited to play along on Mon nights, while Tues to Sun is reserved for the pros. With "Charlie Biddle on the fiddle" and Johnny Scott and the rest of the gang, the beat starts up at 6 PM and continues until sometime between midnight and 2:30 AM. Reservations strongly recommended. Cover charge on weekends.

L'Air du temps
191 St-Paul ouest near Square Victoria
842-2003
A small, smoky club in the heart of Old Montreal that offers an intimate jazz-club atmosphere. Happy hour with two-for-the-price-of-one drinks is 5-8 daily. Live music 8:30 PM-3 AM. Cover charge Wed to Sun. Open daily.

Le Bijou
300 Lemoyne near Square Victoria
288-5508
Jazz Mon to Wed, followed by rhythm and blues Thurs to Sat. Live bands with at least four musicians on stage. From 10 PM. Cover charge.

Le Grand Café
1720 St-Denis near Ontario est
849-6955
Principally a blues bar, with occasional jazz. *Fin du siècle* decor. Thur to Sat after 10 PM.

Claudio's
124 St-Paul est near Place Royale
866-0845
Toe-tapping live jazz in earthy surroundings.

Club Jazz
2080 Clark near Evans
285-0007

Jazz and blues are the standard fare.

Holiday Inn Crowne Plaza
420 Sherbrooke ouest at Hutchison
842-6111
A very popular downtown bar, featuring jazz piano and ensembles.

Upstairs
1421 Bishop near Ste-Catherine ouest
845-8585
Jazz it up, Mon to Sat night. If you just can't get enough of a good thing, Upstairs serves a jazz brunch every Sun.

See also Entertainment and Culture (Popular Music) for the **Montreal International Jazz Festival**.

NICE QUIET BARS

Bar le Grand Prix
Ritz-Carlton Hotel
1228 Sherbrooke ouest at Drummond
842-4212
A civilized rendezvous for the well-heeled, this mellow jazz piano bar is also frequented by members of Montreal's corporate elite. Share the fantasy. Daily except Sun, 8:30 PM-2 AM.

Bar Chez Antoine
Hôtel Le Grand
777 University at St-Antoine ouest
879-1370
Nightly easy-listening jazz and views of the glittering skyline. 8 PM-12:30 AM.

C'est la Vie
Hôtel La Citadelle
410 Sherbrooke ouest at Hutchison
844-8851
Art-deco chairs, glass walls, pink mar-

ble floors and lush greenery. Relaxing piano bar Mon to Fri, 4:30-7. Vocal artists at the piano from 9 PM.

Les Voyageurs
Le Reine Elizabeth/Queen Elizabeth Hotel
900 René-Lévesque ouest at Mansfield
861-3511
Piano from 5-10 PM, Mon to Fri.

Belvedere
Bonaventure Hilton
1 Place Bonaventure (de la Gauchetière ouest at University)
878-2332
A low-key lobby piano bar by the garden terrace. Fabulous city views.

Bar du Foyer
Le Meridien
4 Complexe Desjardins (Ste-Catherine ouest at Jeanne-Mance)
285-1450
Jazz and people-watching 11 PM-3 AM daily.

DINNER THEATRES, CABARETS AND NIGHTCLUBS

Le Caf' Conc
Château Champlain
1 Place du Canada (Peel and St-Antoine)
878-9000
Dinner with lively music and dance acts, Las Vegas style. Tues to Thur 9 PM, Fri and Sat 9 and 11 PM. Cover charge for the 11 PM show.

Le Castillon
Hôtel Bonaventure
1 Place Bonaventure (de la Gauchetière ouest at University)
878-2332
A cabaret featuring top local and international acts, Thurs to Sun.

Arthur's Café Baroque
Le Reine Elizabeth/Queen Elizabeth Hotel
900 René-Lévesque ouest at Mansfield
861-3511, ext. 2361
Can-can style dancing with colourful costumes. Good, old-fashioned entertainment.

Le Festin des Gouverneurs
Vieux-Fort
Île Ste-Hélène
879-1141
Held in the cavernous stone-walled hall of the Old Fort, this two-hour, four-course feast re-creates a 17th-century atmosphere. Guests are seated at long wooden tables and served by period-costumed entertainers. Corny fun with lots of boffo humour and bilingual sing-alongs. Limited cutlery provided, in keeping with the times, so be prepared to dig in with your fingers.

Le Phenecien
7000 du Parc near Beaumont
271-1851
Middle-eastern delights on and off the menu. Enjoy Lebanese cooking while being entertained by live performances of traditional music. Belly-dances performed Thurs to Sun at 8:45 PM. The show is free with dinner, at about $25 per person including drinks.

Club Soda
5270 du Parc near Fairmount
270-7848
One of Montreal's most dynamic clubs, featuring shows by top performing artists.

LIVELY PUBS AND BARS

Le Swimming
3642 St-Laurent near Prince Arthur
282-7665
An ultramodern maze of pool tables with a high-tech industrial look. Designed by award-winning local architect Jacques Rousseau, this place attracts some pouty, well-dressed singles. Billiards, Montreal's latest hot activity, isn't the only game played here.

Le Belmont
4483 St-Laurent at Mont-Royal
845-8443
Another opportunity to test your skills at pool after mingling at the bar or hanging out on the terrace. Quite trendy.

Bar St-Sulpice
1682 St-Denis near Emery
844-9458
Rated one of the most popular bars on the St-Denis strip.

Lola's Paradise
3604 St-Laurent at Prince Arthur
282-9944
The favourite late-night drinking spot of young anglo Montrealers, according to a recent poll.

Bar Salon St-Laurent
3874 St-Laurent near St-Cuthbert
844-4717
A real, live, kind-of-raunchy pool hall for guys (mostly) who actually want to play. An unpretentious slice of life.

La Nausée
1405 St-Laurent at Ste-Catherine
281-8058
Alternative and underground music, perhaps just what you'd expect from a club named "Nausea." Camus fans who like to shoot pool can presumably experience the ennui of eight-ball. Pool tables and a roof terrace bar. Open—"very open," according to their ads in the *Mirror*—from 3 PM-3 AM daily, except Sundays.

Business
3510 St-Laurent near Milton
849-3988
A highly successful bar from the day it opened in 1986. Part of the same Jacques Rousseau empire that brought us L'Oeuf and Le Swimming.

Boulevards
3435 St-Laurent near Milton
499-9944
One of the slickest, most popular night spots on the strip.

Quiet by day, the cafes, bistros and bars of St-Denis come alive at night.

The Sir Winston Churchill on Crescent bustles at night—expect a lineup if you go late.

Shado Bar
3711 St-Laurent near des Pins
845-2881
A sing-along *karaoke* club with a dance floor. Your big chance to make your Montreal debut.

L'Envol Discothèque
5369 St-Laurent near St-Viateur
276-7952
A non-smoking dance club featuring top-of-the-charts recorded music.

In "Kahootz"
1445A Bishop near Ste-Catherine ouest
284-1702
An eclectic mix of comedy acts, rock music, jazz, pool tables and TV.

Sir Winston Churchill
1459 Crescent near de Maisonneuve ouest
288-0616
A popular downtown pub in the authentic English style. Very popular

with anglophones. Expect a long lineup if you go late.

Thursdays
1449 Crescent near Ste-Catherine ouest
849-5634
Frequented by a youngish, good-looking and mostly anglo crowd. Also a popular hangout for some of the Habs (Montreal Canadiens hockey players). Drinks, mingling and dancing.

La Cage aux Sports
2250 Guy at Lincoln
931-8588
Chicken and ribs by day, a lively sports bar by night. Large-screen TVs and lots of draft beer. Sports equipment all over the walls.

Peel Pub
1107 Ste-Catherine ouest at Peel
844-6769
A huge straight-ahead bar with lots of beer and cheap food. Don't have too much fun—the Peel's reputed to have the worst bouncers in town.

Foufounes Electriques
87 Ste-Catherine est near Berger
845-5484
Billing itself as "Montreal's cultural and musical mosaic," this alternative music bar features gigs by such local bands as the Legendary Polka Dots, All/Left Insane and Malevolent Creation. A generally wild place that works to stay on the edge.

LATIN AND AFRICAN RHYTHMS

Salsathèque
1220 Peel at Ste-Catherine ouest
875-0016

Head up the illuminated staircase and get down.

La Playa
4459 St-Laurent near Mont-Royal
843-6595
Popular with Montreal's various Latin communities. Salsa, lambada and African rhythms. Wed to Sat from 9 PM.

Alexandre
1454 Peel near de Maisonneuve ouest
288-5105
Lambada, disco and good food, served up seven days a week from 9 PM.

Le Coconut Club
1417 St-Laurent at Ste-Catherine
499-0967
Tropical music and a fun beach atmosphere. Thurs to Sun from 9 PM.

Keur Samba
5408 du Parc near Fairmount
278-5409
Afro-tropical rhythms. Tues to Sun from 9 PM until dawn.

Balattou
4372 St-Laurent near Marie-Anne
845-5447
This club hosts the annual Nuits d'Afrique festival; see Entertainment and Culture (Popular Music). A popular dance club year-round.

Rising Sun
5380 St-Laurent near St-Viateur
278-5320
Reggae, with live bands on the weekend.

CAFÉS AND CAFÉ-BARS

During the summer, many bars and restaurants set up European-style sidewalk terraces. Many of the livelier ones are clustered in Place Jacques-Cartier, on Crescent, de la Montagne, St-Denis, Laurier, St-Laurent and du Parc. The following indoor cafés are popular year-round.

Lux
5220 St-Laurent at Laurier
271-9272
This trend-setting, all-night eatery-cum-newsstand gained immediate cult status when it opened in 1986. Architect Luc Laporte of L'Express restaurant fame gutted an old factory

to make way for this dramatic, predominantly black, pseudo-industrial zone. A 16-m (54-foot) mirrored dome looms like an inflated ego over the steep central staircase. It may look like the stairway to heaven, but it actually leads to the loo. *Très amusant*. Lux serves great burgers and breakfasts, but angst-filled dévotés often drop in late at night just to flip through exotic magazines, check out the crowd and sigh over a cappuccino. A terminally hip joint. Wear lots of black, and try not to look too impressed.

L'Oeuf
3618 St-Laurent near Prince Arthur
842-6383
In the Lux mould, this narrow 1991 industrial-look café-bar is decorated in colours supposed to "echo today's anxieties." The crowd here is cool but surprisingly cheerful. Designed by hot Montreal architect Jacques Rousseau.

ROCK AND ROLL

American Rock Café
2080 Aylmer near Rouen
288-9272
Exclusively R&R with live bands on Fri and Sat nights. Party animal contests. Sounds exciting, eh?

Whiskey's Rock Bar
8921 Pie IX near 39th
328-1976
Three live bands every night. Happy hour Thurs to Sat 5-9.

Station 10
2071 Ste-Catherine ouest near du Fort
934-1419
New bands every night. Also Sat and Sun afternoon jam sessions.

Rock-away Café
3745 St-Laurent near des Pins
987-ROCK
The phone number says it all: for R&R diehards.

BOÎTES À CHANSON

These are friendly, unpretentious nightclubs where traditional songs are belted out to the clapping, foot-stomping crowd. Expect to be encouraged to sing along. Don't worry—sometimes there are a few English songs, or at least some easy French refrains. The *Québécois de Souche* (descendants of the original founding families) around you will know most of the lyrics.

La Boîte à Lily—Le Bistro d'autrefois
1229 St-Hubert near René-Lévesque est
842-2808
Live music Tues to Sat from 10:30 PM. Piaf, Brel and other sing-along French bistro fare.

Aux Deux Pierrots
104 St-Paul ouest at St-Sulpice
861-1270
A popular spot in historic old Montreal. There are performances on the outside terrace in warm weather. Tues to Sat.

Le Vieux Munich
1170 St-Denis at René-Lévesque est
288-8011
Bavarian bands and real yodellers. Open seven days a week.

Old Dublin
1219A University near Ste-Catherine ouest
861-4448
Irish folk songs, seven days a week. Top-rated by the locals.

One of the venues of the annual Just for Laughs comedy festival. (Image Actuelle)

COMEDY CLUBS

Club Soda
5240 du Parc near Fairmount
270-7848
When the annual summer comedy festival, Just for Laughs, comes to an end, it's back to business as usual at Club Soda. This means a return to the popular Le Lundi de Ha Ha amateur stand-up comedian nights. From Sept to Jan. See the *Gazette* or the *Mirror* for information, or call Club Soda. Usually in French.

The Comedy Nest
1234 Bishop near Sherbrooke ouest
395-8118
English stand-up comedy. Cover charge. Tues to Sat. Phone for times.

GAY CLUBS

Café Bloc
1355 Ste-Catherine est at Panet
522-2989
Espresso, pastries, a menu that changes daily and an opportunity to meet with other gays until 6 AM, Thurs to Sat.

For up-to-date listings of popular gay venues, including bars and dinner clubs, consult *Montreal Scope* or the *Mirror*.

SPORTS/ RECREATION

Montreal offers a wide variety of sports and recreational activities for both spectators and participants. The city boasts major league teams in hockey (the Canadiens) and baseball (the Expos) and hosts a number of key annual sporting events, including Formula One racing, tennis, cycling and horse racing.

If sightseeing and shopping don't satisfy your exercise requirements, you can enjoy numerous public facilities either free or for a nominal fee. For more information on public recreational facilities, call the City of Montreal sports and leisure department at 872-6211.

AUTO RACING

Circuit Gilles-Villeneuve
Île Notre-Dame
392-0000 or 871-1421

The Molson Grand Prix Formula One race takes place every June on Île Notre-Dame. The modern track, named after a former Canadian champion who died in competition, is considered one of the most difficult courses in Formula One racing.

BOATING

There are several private boating clubs in Montreal, including the posh Royal St. Lawrence Yacht Club. Public access to small pleasure craft is possible through a variety of public organizations and sailing schools.

BOAT RENTALS

École de Voile Terre des Hommes/Man and His World Sailing School
Regatta Lake
Île Notre-Dame, near
Île-Ste-Hélène *métro* station
872-6093

Rentals of small sailboats and sailboards. A short *métro* ride from downtown. Parking available. Open mid-May to Labour Day 10-9.

École de Voile de Lachine/Lachine Sailing School
2105 St-Joseph near Lionel-Groulx *métro* station
Lachine
634-4326

Light sailboats and windsurfers for rent with or without lessons. Approved by the Quebec Sailing Federation. Call for times.

Parc Lafontaine
Rachel est at Calixa-Lavallée
872-2644

For parents with young children or homesick Venetians, there are rowboats and pedal-boats for hire at Lafontaine Park to circumnavigate the two pretty man-made lakes (see also Parks/Gardens).

JET-BOATING
See Sightseeing (Touring Montreal).

BOWLING

When was the last time you went bowling? There are 34 bowling alleys in the Montreal area. Check the *Yellow Pages* under "Salles de Quilles" for a nearby location, or head straight to:

Rose Bowl Lanes
6510 St-Jacques at Cavendish
482-7200

Its 72 lanes (24 10-pins and 48 duck-pins) are open for business 24 hours a day, seven days a week. The lanes are often busy with children's birthday parties on Saturdays.

CYCLING

Riding a bicycle in Montreal can be almost as thrilling—and life threatening—as running with the bulls at Pamplona. Montreal's drivers are a frenzied lot and take little notice of cyclists. Unless you are a seasoned road warrior/bicycle courier, you'd be well-advised to confine your cycling to quiet streets and designated bicycle paths. Even so, several serious accidents have occurred on bikeways in the past few years—watch out, wear a helmet and pay attention to the road signs.

The first thing you should do is pick up a free bike-path map published by the MUC planning department, usually available from tourist information centres and bicycle shops (or call the department at 872-6980). The map outlines the more than 180 km of designated routes in and around Montreal.

There are three types of bikeways in the city. *Bike routes* share roads with car traffic so are the most hazardous. *Marked bicycle lanes* are corridors of asphalt separated from the rest of the street by painted lines, narrow poles or planters. *Bicycle paths* are completely separated from other vehicles and allow for scenic, virtually uninterrupted cycling. The MUC map clearly indicates routes of each type, and will give you a good idea of some of the more popular routes. These include the 12-km (7$\frac{1}{2}$-mi.) Lachine Canal

Montrealers take to their bikes for an annual tour through the streets. (City of Montreal)

and the 4.2-km (2$\frac{1}{2}$-mi.) Montreal Aqueduct paths.

More caveats: use a good bicycle lock, always secure your bike in a safe area, and, once again, watch out for road signs. (One gallery owner we know was actually issued a parking ticket for locking his bike in a "no parking" zone.)

The **Grand Prix Cycliste des Amérique (World Cup)** takes place every year in Oct. Roads throughout the city are closed for the day as professional cyclists complete the 224-km course. For information call 879-1027, or contact the city's sports and leisure department at 872-6211.

BICYCLE TOURS

Parks Canada organizes free guided bicycle tours of the Lachine Canal during the summer. English tours are given on Saturdays, French tours on Sundays. Phone 283-6054 for starting points and times. There is also a bicycle club, called Le Monde à Bicyclette, which sets off early every Sunday morning from the corner of Sherbrooke and Lafontaine Park. The routes change every week, and anyone with a bike is welcome to tag along. Free. Call 844-2713 or 849-9700.

BIKE RENTALS

Cycle Peel
6665 St-Jacques ouest near Cavendish
486-1148
Rentals of three-, five- and 10-speed bikes for around $15 a day. Some kids' bikes also available. Phone ahead to check availability. Hotel delivery and pick-up can be arranged. Open year-round, seven days a week.

Cyclo-Touriste
Centre Infotouriste
1001 Square Dorchester
393-1528
Bike rentals mid-May to mid-Oct. Rates vary; phone ahead. Open 9-7:30.

Acces Cible
Vieux-Port (immediately south of Place Jacques-Cartier)
525-8888
Bike rentals from mid-May to Labour Day. Phone for rates and availability. Open 11-8 daily.

Quadricycle International
Vieux-Port (immediately south of Place Jacques-Cartier)
768-9282

Rentals of bicycles and quadricycles, the latter being somewhat cumbersome but fun—especially for families with energetic kids. The quadricycles are for use in the Vieux-Port area only. Open June to Aug 10-midnight; Sept and Oct on weekends only, 10-midnight.

FISHING

Fishermen must obtain a provincial licence (around $6, available at most sporting-goods stores). Fishing day-trips can be recommended by the Ministère du Loisir, de la Chasse et de la Pêche (the ministry of recreation, hunting and fishing). The ministry can be reached toll free at 1-800-462-5349.

ICE FISHING

Chez Aumais
1400 Perrot
Île Perrot
453-6253
Imagine yourself huddled around a wood stove with your buddies inside a traditional Québécois ice-fishing shack. This small family-run business drills holes in the ice, sells permits and bait and rents tackles and colourful *cabanes*. The rest is up to you. If you don't have any luck with the muskie, perch and pike below, you can catch a bite at the snack bar. Shack rental costs vary, but are usually around $25 to $40 per day. Open 6-6 daily, all winter. Reservations accepted.

GOLF

An increasingly popular sport everywhere, golf has long been a popular pastime for Montrealers. There are many public courses to choose from in the Montreal area. We have listed the best of those are easily accessible from downtown. Hours of operation are generally from 6:30 AM to sunset but it's always a good idea to phone ahead. Reservations can usually be made and are especially advisable on weekends.

Golf Municipale de Montréal
Viau, north of Sherbrooke
872-1143
The only course easily accessible by *métro* (get off at the Viau station), this is a nine-hole par 3 perfect for a half-day outing.

Fresh Meadows Golf Club
505 du Golf
Beaconsfield
697-4036
Another nine-holer, 20 minutes west of downtown off Autoroute 20.

Golf Dorval
2000 Reverchon (Autoroute 20 west, exit at des Sources nord)
Dorval
631-6624
Thirty-six holes about 15 minutes west of downtown by car. Occasional jet noise from the nearby airport doesn't seem to deter golfers from using this popular course. Reservations advisable for Fri, Sat and Sun morning starts. Call 631-4653.

Club de Golf de LaPrairie
75 Taschereau
LaPrairie
659-1908
An 18-hole course about 20 minutes' drive from downtown.

Club de Golf Vaudreuil
1126 St-Antoine
Vaudreuil
455-2731
Another good 18-hole course, approximately 30 minutes west of downtown.

HIKING/
BIRD-WATCHING
While Montreal's major parks all offer many kilometres of scenic walks, Mount Royal is by far the preferred venue of those seeking an invigorating climb. Begin your ascent from either the Mont-Royal *métro* stop or the central parking lot. You can cut through the woods or follow well-marked trails to reach the two lookouts. Especially popular with lovers and young families, the views from the main chalet and the Camillien-Houde Parkway are outstanding.

Bird-watchers and other nature-lovers can pick up an interpretive guide to local flora and fauna for $1 at the main chalet. Bird-watchers often flock to Westmount's adjacent Summit Park, where over 150 species of birds have been sighted. The easiest access to Summit Park is from the Westmount Lookout parking lot.

HORSE RACING

Blue Bonnets Hippodrome
7440 Décarie near Jean-Talon ouest
739-2741
Mostly harness racing. Open Mon, Wed, Fri and Sat at 7:30 PM, Sun at 1:30 PM. Admission: $2-4, depending on your choice of seat.

HORSEBACK RIDING
For information on private stables in the Montreal region, call Québec à Cheval ([514] 252-3002) or the Fédération (Équestre du Québec ([514] 252-3053).

Trotting action at Hippodrome Blue Bonnets. (Hippodrome Blue Bonnets)

PROFESSIONAL SPORTS

BASEBALL

Expos
Olympic Stadium
4141 Pierre-de-Coubertin at Pie IX
253-3434 (information)
522-1245 (tickets)
1-800-361-4595 (outside Montreal)
The Expos meet their National League
rivals from Apr to Sept at the Big O. Attending a baseball game is a relaxing way
to end a tour of the Olympic site (see also
Sightseeing). Afternoon games usually
start at 1:35 PM, night games at 7:35.

HOCKEY

Montreal Canadiens
The Forum
2313 Ste-Catherine ouest at
Atwater
932-2582
The red-and-blue sweatered Montreal
Canadiens have won the Stanley Cup,
awarded to the best team in North
America, 23 times since 1916. They
win the hearts of Montrealers every
hockey season. Montrealers are passionate about their home team, which
is known across Canada as *Les Habitants*. To catch the Habs and their fans
in action, head to the Forum. The
hockey season starts in Oct and can
end as late as May. Call for ticket and
schedule information.

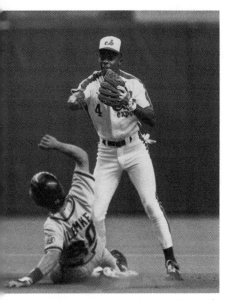

Expos in action at the Big O. (Montreal Expos)

SKATING

You can bet that a city this passionate about hockey has lots of places to skate. If you suddenly crave ice time during the winter, you will never have to go far. Montreal has over 150 public outdoor rinks, most of them in neighbourhood parks. Some of the biggest and most popular are in Mount Royal, Lafontaine and Maisonneuve parks—great places to skate and people-watch. A pretty place to skate at night is Angrignon Park, which is lit up like a winter fairyland. The park also has an ice slide and an ice labyrinth, which the kids will enjoy.

Montreal's largest skating rink is on Île Notre-Dame. The rink, nearly 2 km (over a mile) long, is actually the former Olympic rowing basin. Dress warmly—the winds here can be fierce.

A pleasant place to skate downtown is in carré St-Louis, west of St-Denis and just north of Sherbrooke est. This tree-lined square is bordered by handsome (and for the most part restored) Victorian buildings. You can warm up afterwards at a charming local café or *brasserie* on nearby St-Denis.

SKIING/ SNOWSHOEING

Cross-country enthusiasts have easy access to excellent ski trails right on Mount Royal. It is also possible to ski in the larger city parks. The ecology trail at the Montreal Botanical Garden is also open to skiers and snowshoers.

For alpine skiers, the city has a few runs with lifts, but these are strictly for beginners. Mount Royal, Ignace-Bourget and des Hirondelles parks all have short runs and are very popular with young families. Call the city's sports and leisure department at 872-6211 for details.

Montreal is so close to the fabulous runs in the Laurentians and the Eastern Townships that serious skiers should consider a side trip. It's an easy drive to any one of the many ski areas within 90 minutes of Montreal. The Murray Hill bus line runs daily ski express buses to popular ski areas such as Station Mont-Tremblant. See also Out of Town Excursions.

SWIMMING

The City of Montreal operates a great number of community pools, both indoor and outdoor. For a complete list, check the "Blue Pages" at the back of the *White Pages*, or call the city's sports and leisure department at 872-6211. Several privately run pools are also open to the public.

Île Ste-Hélène
872-6093

A very popular place to cool off in summer, a stone's throw from the Île Ste-Hélène *métro* station. Three outdoor pools, change rooms, showers, lockers and a nearby snack bar. Call for times and rates.

Le Lac de l'Île Notre-Dame
Île Notre-Dame
872-6093

If you use your imagination you could be in Miami or Acapulco—but no: this 600-m (1970-foot) sand beach is just a short *métro*-ride from downtown Montreal. The lake water is extremely clear, thanks to a special filtration system. A popular spot on hot summer days, the beach can accommodate up

to 5,000 sun-worshippers. There is a bus from the Île Ste-Hélène *métro* stop; take the de la Concorde bridge if you are travelling by car or bicycle. Open daily 10-7, July to Sept. Admission is $5.

Olympic Park Aquatic Centre
4141 Pierre-de-Coubertin near Viau *métro* stop
252-4622

With its five modern indoor pools, this is a world-class facility. Admission is $2.50. Phone for times.

Université de Montréal
2900 Edouard-Montpetit near Louis Colin
343-6150

A modern indoor pool good for lane swims. Admission is $2.50. Phone for times.

Cégep de Vieux Montréal
255 Ontario est near Hôtel-de-Ville
872-2644

Free admission. Phone for times.

TENNIS

There are public tennis courts in a number of community parks throughout the city, including Jeanne-Mance, Kent, Lafontaine and Somerled. For details call the city's sports and leisure department at 872-6211.

The **Player's Limited International Tennis Tournament** takes place every July at Jarry Park. Top-seeded male players from around the world compete in singles and doubles play. For tickets and information call Jarry Park at 273-1515.

John McEnroe at the Player's International, held every July at the Jarry Park Tennis Centre. (Don Vickery/ Player's Limited Tennis Library)

SHOPPING

SHOPPING AREAS

Montreal, like Paris, is a city of countless local shopping districts. Some of the best are concentrated along the following streets:

STE-CATHERINE OUEST

This is the traditional downtown shopping street, with the best shopping found between Guy and Carré Phillips. You will find branches of many popular Canadian and U.S. chains as well as the large department stores Ogilvy, Eaton and La Baie (known outside Quebec as Ogilvy's, Eaton's and the Bay). Ogilvy is by far the most impressive, having undergone a recent and spectacular renovation. It also houses a number of independent high-fashion boutiques. From Ste-Catherine you can get to a number of chic shopping malls, both above and below ground, many of which are connected by the passageways of the underground city. Underground shopping is fine when the weather is poor, but most Montrealers are loath to abandon the daily fashion parade above. A reasonable balance of mall-hopping and schlepping along Ste-Catherine should help you satiate your consumer urges. Take the *métro* and walk, as parking in the area is usually hopeless.

LAURIER OUEST

A tiny strip of shops between Côte-Ste-Catherine and du Parc offers high fashion, specialty foods, gorgeous children's wear and fabulous housewares. A very civilized place to shop. Unlike downtown, it's usually easy to find parking here.

GREENE

A selection of tasteful shops similar in price and quality to those found on Laurier. Greene is a smaller and quieter street, though, less frequently visited by tourists. The Old Post Office building at de Maisonneuve is a good place to stop for refreshment. It's also easy to find parking near here. Close to Greene are two shopping centres, Westmount Square and Alexis Nihon Plaza.

SHERBROOKE OUEST

The section of Sherbrooke between Peel and Guy has a number of art galleries, antique stores, famous-name boutiques including Ralph Lauren and Yves St. Laurent and the expensive Holt Renfrew department store (which also has a small branch in the Ritz-Carlton Hotel). Running south from Sherbrooke are two extremely popular streets for shopping and nightlife, Crescent and de la Montagne. Their charm is largely due to the fact that businesses here are housed in attractive Victorian-style townhouses.

ST-LAURENT

Trendy stores are springing up among the traditional Old World family bakeries and grocery stores. A lively place to explore. Don't miss great side streets like Fairmount, where you will find Fairmount Bagel and Willensky's Light Lunch.

NOTRE-DAME OUEST

Mostly for antiques. See Antiques, later in this chapter.

CHABANEL

For adventurous shoppers only. This is where you will find many of Montreal's garment factories and fashion wholesalers, concentrated mostly in the 400 to 600 blocks. Some showrooms are open to the public only on Sat mornings; it's best to call ahead. See the *Yellow Pages* under "Women's Apparel—Wholesale & Manufacturers" for businesses on Chabanel and the surrounding area.

SHOPPING MALLS

Les Cours Mont-Royal
1550 Metcalfe at Ste-Catherine ouest
842-7777

Place Montreal Trust
1600 McGill College at Ste-Catherine ouest
843-8000

Place Ville-Marie
René-Lévesque ouest at University
861-9393

Les promenades de la Cathédrale
625 Ste-Catherine ouest near University
849-9925

Le Centre Eaton de Montréal
705 Ste-Catherine ouest near McGill College
288-3708

Complexe Desjardins
Ste-Catherine ouest at Jeanne-Mance
281-1870

Le Faubourg Ste-Catherine
1616 Ste-Catherine ouest near Guy
939-3663
Food shopping only.

Place Alexis Nihon
1500 Atwater at Ste-Catherine ouest
931-2591

Place Bonaventure
1000 de la Gauchetière ouest at University
397-2233

Westmount Square
1 Westmount Square at Ste-Catherine ouest
932-0211

DEPARTMENT STORES

Eaton
677 Ste-Catherine ouest near Mansfield
284-8484

Holt Renfrew
1300 Sherbrooke ouest at de la Montagne
842-5111

Ogilvy
1307 Ste-Catherine ouest at de la Montagne
842-7711

La Baie
Carré Phillips at Union
281-4422

ANTIQUES

Most of Montreal's better *antiquaires* are in three areas: Notre-Dame ouest between Guy and Atwater, and Sherbrooke ouest in the downtown area and in Westmount. Bargain-

La Baie, one of Montreal's biggest department stores

DOWNTOWN SHOPPING

1. Complexe Desjardins (S)
2. La Baie (D)
3. Les promenades de la cathédrale (S)
4. Eaton (D)
5. Le Centre Eaton de Montréal (S)
6. Place Ville-Marie (S)
7. Place Bonaventure (S)
8. Place Montréal Trust (S)
9. Les Cours Mont-Royal (S)
10. Holt Renfrew (D)
11. Ogilvy (D)
12. Le Faubourg Ste-Catherine (S)
13. Place Alexis Nihon (S)
14. Westmount Square (S)

■ subway station

D   department store
S   shopping centre

hunters favour Notre-Dame. While several shops here are decidedly up-scale, the majority offer an eclectic jumble of decent to good-quality furniture, collectable memorabilia and fascinating junque. Shopping along Notre-Dame requires time, patience and comfortable shoes. It also helps to be a good conversationalist as prices are generally negotiable.

Discriminating collectors with less time on their hands may prefer to confine their search to Sherbrooke ouest in the downtown area and Westmount. If your pulse quickens at the sight of exquisite mahogany or Royal Crown Derby china, shopping in these areas will be a delight. Fine

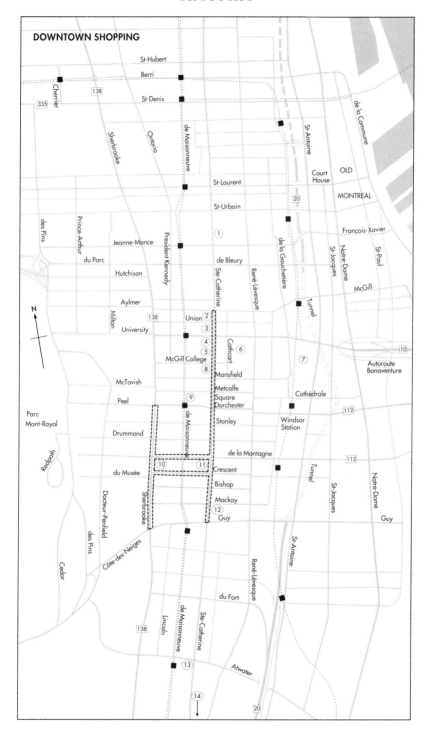

DOWNTOWN SHOPPING

OLD

MONTREAL

Court
House

François-Xavier

N

Parc
Mont-Royal

Autoroute
Bonaventure

Windsor
Station

Cathédrale

European, English, Canadian and Oriental pieces can be had at a price. Popular old silver and china patterns, culled from Montreal auction houses and estate sales, are usually in good supply. Prices here are rarely negotiable, but, as they say, you'll never regret buying quality.

If you happen to visit Montreal during the first two weeks of July, you can catch the annual antique show, with more than 200 dealers, at the Place Bonaventure convention centre.

NOTRE-DAME OUEST

Moving west along Notre-Dame from just east of Guy you will find several clusters of antique shops. Most are open Mon to Sat 11-5 and some are open Sun as well. If you are keen to visit a particular store, it's best to phone ahead.

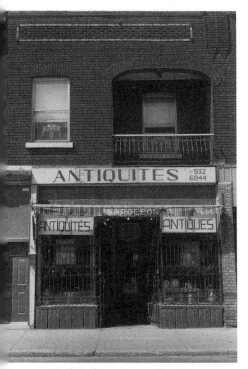

Antique-lovers can easily while away a day along Notre-Dame ouest.

Doing all the stores on Notre-Dame is a good way to spend the better part of a day. Although the quality of stock inevitably varies, the following stores are usually worth a visit.

Les Portes & Vitraux Anciens Du Grand Montréal
1500 Notre-Dame ouest at Lusignan
932-8869
This shop contains hundreds of original and reproduction building details. Rows of leaded glass windows and ornate doors are suspended from the ceiling and provide a spectacular display of Montreal's architectural heritage. Mantelpieces and mouldings are in good supply, as are chandeliers, light fixtures and bathroom fixtures.

Dynasties
1610 Notre-Dame ouest near Guy
932-9992
A huge sprawling store with back rooms and a cellar loaded with oak and pine wardrobes, English and European furniture, wall sconces, English and French china and crystal, silverware and silver dresser sets. The store also has a small stock of vintage clothing.

Marc Lareau Antiques
1638 Notre-Dame ouest near Guy
932-5950
The proprietor, an "estate furnishings liquidator," offers vintage bric-a-brac and costume jewellery at reasonable prices. Lots of quirky souvenirs.

Daniel J. Malynowsky Inc.
1642 Notre-Dame ouest near Guy
937-3727
A good place to look for better quality antiques, including large dining-room tables, games tables, benches, crystal decanters and silver serving pieces and bowls.

Heritage Antique Métropolitaine
1646 Notre-Dame ouest near Guy
931-5517
This shop specializes in ornate furnishings and decorative accessories, including Chinese, rococo and French Provincial styles.

Parent Moquin Antiquités
1650 Notre-Dame ouest near Richmond
933-9435
Lots of small sterling and silverplate, including serving pieces, napkin rings and dresser sets, in addition to Moorcroft, Royal Crown Derby, Limoges and other china. Odd tables and chairs of assorted styles. On our last visit, we found a number of interesting custom-made lamps.

Antiquités Landry
1726 Notre-Dame ouest near Richmond
937-7040
Two large rooms of pine and oak furniture, much of it stripped and refinished. A small assortment of china and silver. There are piles of old picture frames in the basement.

Tendres Souvenances Antiquités
1808 Notre-Dame ouest at St-Martin
482-7500
This store specializes in English blue-and-white pottery and porcelain, including romantic and typographic transferware and Oriental flow blue.

Deuxièmement
1880 Notre-Dame ouest near des Seigneurs
933-8560
Enter if you dare. A spine-tingling collection of theatrical props, including stuffed birds and skulls lurking among stacks of eccentric vintage appliances, headgear, bizarre lamps, marionettes and other curiosities.

Martin Antiques
1964 Notre-Dame ouest near Chatham
932-6213
For lovers of Canadiana, this shop specializes in good pine furniture. Armoires, chests, blanket boxes and *huche pains* (dough boxes) galore!

Roland Sirois Jr.
1970 Notre-Dame ouest near Chatham
931-2059
Old toy collectors might spot something here as the owner carries some train sets, cars and lead soldiers.

Antiquitou
2475 Notre-Dame ouest near Vinet
932-3256
Model cars and other toys, along with duck decoys and pine and oak furniture of middling quality.

Cascade
2488 Notre-Dame ouest near Vinet
932-3713
Lots of Lionel and other old HO gauge model trains, as well as Dinky, Corgi, Matchbox and other collectable model cars and toys.

Grand Central
2448 Notre-Dame ouest near Vinet
935-1467
A huge store filled with light fixtures, stained glass, decorative mirrors and good-quality oak and mahogany furniture.

Retro-ville
**2652 Notre-Dame ouest near
Charlevoix
989-1307**

This shop specializes in neon beer signs, soft-drink memorabilia, old signage and magazines.

DOWNTOWN

Michel Taschereau Antiquités
**1227 Sherbrooke ouest near
Drummond
286-4630**

Fine 18th- and 19th-century English, French and Canadian antiques. By appointment only.

Antiquités Guy
**2325 Guy at Sherbrooke ouest
935-3600**

A small, unpretentious shop that offers popular Birks patterns and other estate silverware at reasonable prices. Some carpets, paintings, vases and jewellery.

Petit Musée
**1494 Sherbrooke ouest near
Simpson
937-6161**

Hundreds of superb museum-quality artifacts spanning the centuries. Exquisite and very expensive. Definitely worth a visit.

Galerie Mazarine
**1524 Sherbrooke ouest near
Simpson
931-8182**

A select assortment of prints, including botanicals, and rare maps. Excellent (and expensive) framing is also available.

David Brown Antiques
**Top floor, Ogilvy
1307 Ste-Catherine ouest at de la
Montagne
844-9866**

A modest but delightful display of choice, mostly English, antiques, along with high-quality Canadiana. Prices aren't cheap, but quality of this sort is hard to find.

WESTMOUNT

Connaisseur Antiques
**1312 Greene near Sherbrooke
ouest
931-6830**

An excellent selection of beautiful china, including 19th-century and other decorative pieces.

Coach House Antiques
1325 Greene near Sherbrooke ouest
937-6191
A fine selection of quality furniture, china, silverware, etc.

La France Antique
1350 Greene near Sherbrooke ouest
935-7504
Gorgeous mahogany and walnut furniture, some of it rather ornate. Watch out for the parrot!

Henrietta Anthony Inc.
4192 Ste-Catherine ouest at Greene
935-9116
Superb antiques from various periods spread over four floors. A member of the prestigious Canadian Antique Dealers Association.

Antiquités Westmount
4932 Sherbrooke ouest near Prince Albert
484-9393
A five-minute bus ride from Greene, this shop has a terrific selection of estate furniture, carpets, china and a huge stock of silver (many Birks patterns) in plate and sterling.

Antiquités Phyllis Freedman
5012 Sherbrooke ouest near Claremont
483-6185
Good-quality European and Canadian antiques, with a wide selection of china. Less than friendly staff (judging by recent visits). Member of the Canadian Antique Dealers Association.

OTHER AREAS
Numerous other antique stores can be found throughout Montreal if you have the time. Some of our other favourites:

Antique Puces Libres
4240 St-Denis near Rachel ouest
842-5931
Lots of good-quality pine Canadiana to be had here. Go to the second-floor showroom, push your way into the back, and you'll find another two floors to browse through.

Galerie Leport Tremblay
3979 St-Denis near Duluth
849-8563
This is a neat little shop specializing in 20th-century decorative arts, including art nouveau items and Arts and Crafts Movement-inspired furniture. This is the place to find the stuff you wish your parents hadn't thrown out 20 years ago!

AUCTION HOUSES

Hôtel des Encans de Montréal
2825 Bates near Darlington
344-4081
Regular catalogue sales of furniture, antiques and paintings. Several auctions each year are devoted entirely to Canadian paintings.

Empire Auctions Inc.
5500 Paré near Devonshire
737-6586
Regular sales of fine antiques, paintings and jewellery.

Fraser Auctions
8290 Devonshire near Royalmount
345-0571
Several catalogued fine-art and antique sales each year.

BOOKSTORES

Book-lovers will find a wide selection of bookstores in Montreal—English and French, general and specialist.

BOOKS IN ENGLISH

Academic and General Bookshop
385 Sherbrooke ouest near
Hutchison
849-3833
Good selection of used books.

Argo Book Shop
1915 Ste-Catherine ouest at
St-Marc
931-3442
Used books. Specializes in literature.

Avenue Bookshop Inc.
1368 Greene near Sherbrooke
ouest
Westmount
933-4201
English literature, children's books
and a good selection of cookbooks.

Bibliomania Book Shoppe
4685 du Parc near Bérubé
849-3175
Specializes in used books.

Book Center
5006 de la Reine-Marie near
Decarie
731-2677
A wide selection of general titles.

Bookseller S.W. Welch
5673 Sherbrooke ouest near
Oxford
488-5943
Used and rare books.

Cheap Thrills
1433 Bishop near Ste-Catherine
ouest
844-7604

2044 Metcalfe near de
Maisonneuve ouest
844-8988
Mostly used paperbacks.

Coles—The Book People
1171 Ste-Catherine ouest at
Stanley
849-8825
The largest bookstore in the city for
English titles. Smaller stores at other
locations.

Diamond Book Store
5035 Sherbrooke ouest near
Claremont
481-3000
Used books, out-of-print titles and
publishers' overstocks.

Double Hook Canadian Books
1235 Greene near Ste-Catherine
ouest
932-5093
Excellent for Canadian literature and
children's books.

Librairie Lexis
2055 Peel near Sherbrooke ouest
848-9763
A good selection of current titles.

Librairie Nicholas Hoare Ltd.
1307 Ste-Catherine ouest at de la
Montagne
499-2005
Located in the Ogilvy department
store. General titles.

McGill University
Main Bookstore
985 Sherbrooke ouest at McTavish
398-3654
The best university bookstore in Montreal and well worth a visit.

Paragraph Book Store & Café Inc.
2065 Mansfield at Sherbrooke ouest
845-5811
A very civilized store. Great for browsing.

Prospero Books
1455 Peel at Ste-Catherine ouest
844-5557
Located in Les Cours Mont-Royal. General titles.

Russell Books
275 St-Antoine ouest near Jeanne-Mance
934-5957
Out-of-print titles, used books and publishers' clearances.

Stage Book Shop/Librairie de théâtre
1207 Crescent near René-Lévesque ouest
954-0783
Specializes in theatre and dance books.

W.H. Smith
625 Ste-Catherine ouest near Union
289-8737
This outlet of the popular chain carries general titles and some children's books.

BOOKS IN FRENCH

Librairie Bertrand
3456 St-Denis near Sherbrooke est
861-5808
General titles, some English books, CDs and cassettes.

Librairie Champigny Inc.
4380 St-Denis near Marie-Anne
844-2587
General titles. Open seven days a week.

Librairie Flammarion
Place Montreal Trust
1600 McGill College at Ste-Catherine ouest
499-9675
General titles and reference works. Several other locations.

Librairie Gallimard Inc.
3700 St-Laurent near des Pins
499-2012
General titles.

Librairie Renaud-Bray Inc.
5219 Côte-des-Neiges near Swail
342-1515
Books, records, magazines and stationery. Several other locations.

Librairie scientifique et technique de Montréal Inc.
425 de Maisonneuve ouest near de Bleury
849-3569
Specializing in reference works and government publications, as well as management, administration and architecture texts. Some English titles.

Ulysse la librairie du voyage
560 du Président-Kennedy near Union
289-0993
1307 Ste-Catherine ouest at de la Montagne (in Ogilvy)
Specializes in travel-related books. Some English titles.

Comexfor Inc.
Complexe Desjardins
Ste-Catherine ouest at Jeanne-Mance
Good for travel guides, road maps, and street directories.

CAMERA STORES/ PHOTO DEVELOPING

Place Victoria Cameras
Square Victoria, St-Jacques at McGill College (*métro* level)
861-0826
Fast, good-quality film processing at a reasonable price. Highly recommended in a recent informal *Gazette* poll.

N.D.G. Photo
1108 de Maisonneuve ouest at Girouard
844-1766
A well-known supplier of new and used cameras at fair prices. Camera repairs and some rentals. Other branches at 5488 Sherbrooke ouest and in carré Phillips.

Simon's Cameras
11 St-Antoine ouest near St-Laurent
861-5401
Sales, rentals and repairs for all leading makes. In business for almost 60 years.

Japan Camera Centre
Le Centre Eaton
Ste-Catherine ouest near Mansfield
842-5133
One-hour photo processing. Five other locations.

Astral Photo
Complexe Desjardins
Ste-Catherine ouest at Jeanne-Mance
843-8219
Speedy film processing at reasonable prices. Sixteen other locations throughout the city.

CHINA AND SILVERWARE

Birks
1240 carré Phillips
397-2511
In addition to its own stately silver patterns—always popular for bridal registries—this prominent jeweller carries silver serving pieces, crystal (including Waterford), fine china (mostly Eng-

A detail from the Birks Building on Ste-Catherine.

lish) and assorted good-quality giftware. Birks tends to be marginally more expensive than its competitors for china and crystal, but its exclusive silver place-settings are good value for the money. Besides, everything comes in those great blue boxes. Ten other locations.

Linen Chest
2305 Rockland at L'Acadie (in Rockland Centre)
341-7810
A bustling, high-volume sales machine for fine china, crystal, dinnerware, cutlery and linens at guaranteed low prices. If you are contemplating a major purchase, it might be worthwhile to make the trip to Rockland Centre.

Caplan-Duval
5800 Cavendish near Kildare
483-4040, 1-800-361-6432
This place does a roaring business with both bridal registries and the tourist trade. Big discounts on famous brands keep them coming. It's wise, though, to check prices of specific items by phone before you make the trip.

CLOTHING

WOMEN'S WEAR

Au Coton
1352 Ste-Catherine ouest at Panet
875-2805
Stylish but totally casual clothes in natural fibres, moderately priced. Also in Ogilvy.

Aquascutum Pour Dames
1 Place Ville-Marie
René-Lévesque ouest at University
875-7010
Quality classics from this British chain,

including their world-famous raincoats. Expensive. Also in Ogilvy.

Goodman Manteau
5 Place Ville-Marie
University at René-Lévesque ouest
861-3977
Excellent quality, stylish Canadian-made coats, dresses and suits. Moderate to expensive.

Jaeger
1307 Ste-Catherine ouest at de la Montagne (in Ogilvy)
845-5834
Suits, coats and dresses from this famous British maker. Not too exciting, but always in good taste. Expensive.

Lily Simon
1 Westmount Square at Ste-Catherine ouest
935-9775
Gorgeous silk dresses and generally glamorous garb for all occasions. With a store like this, it's no wonder Montreal women of all ages stop traffic in rush hour. Expensive. Two other locations.

Marks and Spencer
1500 McGill College near Ste-Catherine ouest
499-8558
Part of the wildly successful and dependable English chain. A good source of basic woollens, conservative clothes and accessories, and pretty knickers that wear like iron. Inexpensive to moderately priced.

Parachute
3526 St-Laurent near Milton
845-7865
For the sartorially adventurous. Great designs that are always on the leading edge of fashion. Expensive.

Tall Shop (Boutique Son Altesse)
5131 Sherbrooke ouest near Vendôme
486-6461
Clothes and shoes for tall women. Moderate prices.

Tripp
21 Notre-Dame ouest near Place d'Armes
842-7361
Rummage through the racks and cardboard boxes for great deals on seconds, cancelled orders and manufacturers' overstocks. Top name-brand clothes can be picked up inexpensively if you happen by on a good day. Three other locations.

Tweedy
4209 Ste-Catherine ouest near Greene
937-7072
Before Bill 101 obliged this reliable Westmount store to change its name, it was called Tweedy Clothes. Today, Tweedy still sells quality classics, in the moderate to expensive range.

Le Château
1310 Ste-Catherine ouest at de la Montagne
866-2481
High fashion, low prices. The clothes tend to survive only a couple of washings but, hey, they'll be out of style by then anyway. Popular with fearless teens and younger women. Inexpensive.

Marie Saint-Pierre
4455 St-Denis near St-Pierre
281-5547
Saint-Pierre is one of Canada's absolutely hottest new women's-wear designers. In fact, her brand-new boutique has received financial backing

from both the federal and Quebec governments. Check out Saint-Pierre's innovative styles and the stunning sculptural chaise longue in her shop. Expensive.

Création Elles-Toiles
3971 St-Denis near Duluth
845-5674
A modest showcase for the work of several fabulous local designers. Anything you find on the racks can be altered or custom-made to your liking in a couple of days. A great place to buy a *très Montréal* outfit that you'll never see at home.

Formes
92 Laurier ouest near St-Urbain
273-4543
A branch of a well-known French chain that specializes in form-fitting maternity wear.

Maternité Monic
3920 St-Denis near Duluth
847-0746

A relaxed collection of maternity wear, moderately priced and largely Canadian-made.

Paradis Maternité
1110 Sherbrooke ouest near Peel
845-4350
A fine selection of maternity wear for business, social and casual settings including some fabulous flattering designs by Ran. Mostly Canadian-made, some imports. Moderately priced.

La Cache
1353 Greene near Sherbrooke ouest
935-4361
This is the flagship store of a successful women's wear/gift-shop chain with branches in other major Canadian cities. Their private-label garments, made of pretty Indian cottons, are similar to the Monsoon clothing line available in England. Also lovely woven table linens and decorative countryware. Moderately priced.

Alexandor
2015 de la Montagne near de Maisonneuve ouest
288-1119
A well-known local furrier.

Holt Renfrew
1300 Sherbrooke ouest at de la Montagne
842-5111
Fur garments in everything from basic raccoon and beaver to exotic famous-label designs. Holt's customer service is excellent. Also a wide selection of hats.

Ogilvy Fur Salon
1307 Ste-Catherine ouest at de la Montagne
842-7711
An elegant and reputable source of fur coats and jackets, including some high-fashion wear.

MENSWEAR

Aquascutum Pour Hommes
1 Place Ville-Marie
875-7010
Famous maker of British classics. Especially good for tweedy sports coats, overcoats and conservative suits. Expensive. Also at Ogilvy.

L'Uomo
1452 Peel at Ste-Catherine ouest
844-1008
Italian men's *haute couture*. Great ties and accessories. Expensive.

Holt Renfrew
1300 Sherbrooke ouest at de la Montagne
842-5111
A great source of quality clothes for that well-put-together look. Two other locations, including Rockland Centre.

Ogilvy Monsieur
1307 Ste-Catherine ouest at de la Montagne
845-4742
One of the best places to go for classic but stylish men's clothing. Particularly good for sports jackets, shirts and ties. Men who normally hate shopping tend to relax in Ogilvy's clubby surroundings.

Roots
1223 Ste-Catherine ouest at Drummond
845-7559
A Canadian success story. Roots' casual wear is distinctive, well made and always in style. The famous Roots Canada sweatshirt with its trademark beaver logo makes a great souvenir, much sought-after by kids. Also women's and children's clothing. Three other locations.

Old River
1115 Ste-Catherine ouest near Peel
843-5520
The Franco-Québécois version of the American preppy look. Lots of button-down shirts, cotton sweaters, chinos and penny loafers in classic and slightly off-beat colours and patterns. Moderate to expensive. Also at Rockland Centre.

West Coast
Rockland Centre
345-8670
Clothes to hang out in from NewMan, Britches, Gant, and the like. Moderate. Five other locations.

Dagenais et Fils
1172 Carré Phillips near René-Lévesque ouest
866-6031
Good men's custom tailoring at a reasonable price. Lots of Montreal men have their complete business wardrobes made here. Also good for tuxedos and other formal wear.

Charles Johnson & Son Inc.
1184 Carré Phillips near René-Lévesque ouest
878-1931
Another long-established custom tailor that has served Montreal's business community for generations. A great place to order that custom-made kilt you've always wanted. Moderate to expensive.

VINTAGE AND CONSIGNMENT

Drags
367 St-Paul est at Bonsecours
866-0631
Great vintage clothing and oodles of mid-century fashions you may have tried to forget. A fabulous resource for nostalgia buffs and total non-conformists.

La Ligue Turnabout Shop
386 Victoria at Sherbrooke ouest
488-8262
Great Westmount cast-offs, including secondhand school uniforms. Closed July and Aug.

La Boutique Fantasque
2080 Crescent near de Maisonneuve ouest
288-3655
Gorgeous women's clothes, gently used.

SHOES

Brown Chaussures
1 Place Ville-Marie
University at René-Lévesque ouest
861-8925
Good-quality leather shoes and boots

for men and women. Expensive. Five other locations.

French Shoes
1 Place Ville-Marie
University at René-Lévesque ouest
871-8142
Good-quality leather shoes and boots for women. Moderate to expensive. Eight other locations.

Roots
1223 Ste-Catherine ouest at Drummond
845-7559
Men's and women's cool or preppy casual leathers. Also great handbags, briefcases and the city's best leather jackets. Moderate to expensive. Three other locations.

Tony
1346 Greene near Sherbrooke ouest
935-2993
Is there any woman in Westmount who doesn't buy shoes at Tony's? The selection is so extensive, it's hard to imagine otherwise. On Saturdays the

shoes move out the door like fresh buns from a bakery. Moderate to expensive.

Karl's Chaussures
4259 St-Laurent near Rachel
849-3839
This is our favourite men's casual shoe store. If you have the patience to find two matching shoes amidst the vast jumble of boxes, you'll probably get a great deal.

CRAFTS

Galerie Elena Lee Verre d'art
1518 Sherbrooke ouest near Simpson
932-3892
A unique selection of custom-designed and affordable jewellery, as well as handblown glass sculptures and paperweights. A showcase for the work of about a dozen local artisans.

Guilde canadienne des Métiers d'Art/Canadian Guild of Crafts
2025 Peel near de Maisonneuve ouest
849-6091

A showcase for Canadian craftsmen, especially Québécois, working in a variety of media. Ceramics, handmade jewellery, textiles, prints, carvings and more. Excellent alternatives to the usual kitschy souvenirs.

O Kwa Ri
Route 138
Kanawake
632-5848

Handmade Mohawk souvenirs, including leather moccasins, miniature birch-bark canoes, snowshoes, prints and carvings.

FABRIC

Marshall Silks
1195 Ste-Catherine ouest near Stanley
844-2555

In business since the 1920s, Montreal's best-known fabric store has a selection of fine fabrics, including silks, cottons and pure woollens by famous makers like Liberty and Viyella. Marshall's staff are extremely helpful regarding yardage and notions. Moderate to expensive.

Minks
1383 Greene near Sherbrooke ouest
937-0642

Haute couture fabrics from Italy, Switzerland and France at *haute* prices. For serious sewers.

By the Yard
1357 Greene near Sherbrooke ouest

939-0013

Great discounts on brand-name drapery and upholstery fabrics, sometimes as low as $8 a metre. Part of a nationally franchised chain.

FURNITURE

Boutique Confort
201 Laurier ouest near du Parc

One of the best sources of antique reproduction Quebec pine furniture we have found. Well-constructed and thoughtfully finished armoires, blanket boxes, tables and chests in natural wood or traditional hues.

Eaton
677 Ste-Catherine ouest near McGill College
284-8411

From serviceable contemporary furnishings for the budget-minded to fine furniture in a variety of styles, Eaton has it all on the seventh floor. The vast furniture department here has both modern and traditional groupings and stocks a wide range of beds, sofa beds, occasional chairs, dining room suites, coffee tables and so on in addition to lamps and some decorative accessories. Prices are usually competitive and the quality is guaranteed. The best of the Eaton collection is tastefully presented in a special section on the seventh floor called La Gallerie. While at Eaton, remember to have a look at the unusual art-deco cafeteria on the ninth floor.

Mariette Clermont
2020 University at de Maisonneuve ouest
845-7296

The sleek, sophisticated, modern Italian look for those who think floral chintz is, well, chintzy. Expensive. Several other locations.

Struc-Tube
2081 Ste-Catherine ouest near Chomedy
934-5488
Inexpensive, modern, functional laminated furniture and lighting fixtures. Several other locations.

JEWELLERY

Birks
1240 carré Phillips
397-2511
The flagship store of the long-established Canadian chain, this branch merits a visit if only to admire its splendid interior. The mouldings are exquisite, and the wall-mounted plaques to the right of the entranceway provide some interesting family history. Gifts from Birks—whether Swiss watches, rare diamonds or good-quality costume jewellery—never fail to impress. Everything comes beautifully wrapped in Birks' trademark blue box. See also China and Silverware, this chapter. Ten other locations.

Turcott Joailliers
Hôtel Château Champlain
1 Place Champlain
Peel at St-Antoine
861-7823
A small shop specializing in fine jewellery and Les must de Cartier.

Yu
625 Ste-Catherine ouest near University
848-0518
Moderately priced high-fashion earrings and baubles to coordinate with everything that's new. Two other locations.

PUBLIC MARKETS

The city has four main public markets, where local farmers and permanent vendors sell fresh produce, meat, poultry, bread and cheese. The Maisonneuve and St-Jacques markets are open daily between May and Oct; the Atwater and Jean-Talon markets are open daily year-round. Hours for the markets are the same: Mon to Wed 7-6, Thurs and Fri 7-9, Sat and Sun 7-5.

Atwater Market
Atwater south of Notre-Dame ouest
872-2491
Over 60 vendors. Good for meat, vegetables and fruit. Au Paridis du Fromage has an excellent supply of cheeses from around the world. Fresh trout pond during the summer. The Lachine Canal cycle path touches the market's southern edge.

Jean-Talon Market
Between Henri-Julien and Casgrain, south of Jean-Talon
872-2491
With 100 seasonal and 20 permanent vendors, this is the largest of the city's markets. In the heart of Montreal's Little Italy.

Maisonneuve Market
Ontario est at Morgan
872-2491
Housed in a 70-year-old heritage building, this seasonal market is particularly strong in fruit and vegetables.

St-Jacques Market
Amherst at Ontario
872-2491
Another seasonal market. Emphasis on flowers and plants.

One of the many vibrant flower stalls at the Atwater Market.

RECORDS, TAPES AND CDs

Dutchy's Record Cave
1587 St-Laurent near de Maisonneuve
844-6208
A catholic selection, including all the new alternative releases. Lots of bargains upstairs.

A&A Records and Tapes
1621 Ste-Catherine ouest near Guy
937-3613
Part of a large chain. Broad selection and weekly specials.

Maison du Disque
4000 Hochelaga at Pie IX
255-0312

A choice collection of old 45s from the '40s to the '60s. These make wacky birthday presents.

Archambault Musique
500 Ste-Catherine est at Berri
849-6201
One of Montreal's largest record stores. Great selection in all areas.

SPECIALTY FOOD STORES

By George Catering
1343 Greene near Sherbrooke ouest
931-8814
This upper-crust Westmount caterer can supply you with a sumptuous assortment of gourmet foods, either packaged or freshly prepared. Gift baskets and picnic lunches can be arranged.

La Tulipe Noire
2100 Stanley at Peel
285-1225
Despite its French name, this popular café stocks many hard-to-find imported foods from Great Britain, including such esoteric items as Isle of Arran wild-bramble jelly. Also very good for fresh pastry.

Roger Colas—Traiteur
98 Laurier ouest near du Parc
271-1777
Colas is one of Montreal's foremost caterers. He has served the Pope, the Queen Mother and many of Montreal's elite families. His shop provides extraordinary ready-to-serve meals as well as attractively packaged private-label chutneys, sauces and preserves.

The Cheese Shoppe
505 President Kennedy near Aylmer
849-1232

This 80-year-old Montreal institution recently left its original premises on René-Lévesque and is now conveniently located near the Maison des Vins (see Specialty Shops, this chapter). The helpful staff can help you make your selection from an astonishing variety of cheeses. The shop ships gift baskets of cheese throughout the world. Be sure to have a look at the 18th-century brass scale, still in use.

Chocolats Andrée
4144 Ste-Catherine ouest
937-1814

Hand-dipped, mostly dark-chocolate candies, including rich truffles, are available from this famous Montreal chocolatier. Exquisite gift boxes from Europe ensure an elegant presentation. Two other locations.

Le Chocolat Belge Heyez
Place Bonaventure—Passage CN
1000 de la Gauchetière ouest at University
392-1480

Seventy types of fresh candies made from imported Belgian chocolate. Exquisite and delicious. Careful not to miss your train.

Le Commensal Cuisine Végétarienne
680 Ste-Catherine ouest near University
871-1480

Vegetarian take-out meals, breads, muffins, and more. Good, wholesome food at reasonable prices.

Bilboquet
1311 Bernard ouest near Outremont
276-0414

This popular Outremont hangout makes wonderful preservative-free ice cream and sorbets.

Fairmount Bagel
74 Fairmount ouest near Clarke

Montrealers are always ready to argue about where to get the best bagels in the city. While we don't pretend to have the definitive answer, this is one of our favourite shops. It makes both the traditional-style bagel and other specialty types, including a cinnamon variety that scores high on our list.

SPECIALTY SHOPS

Peel Pen Shop
1212 Union near Carré Phillips
866-1340

All sorts of beautiful pens and pen sets for those who still enjoy writing longhand.

Davidoff Tabac
2140 Crescent at Sherbrooke ouest
289-9118

Cigars (including Cuban), pipes and tobacco from all over the world.

Henri Poupart
1331 Ste-Catherine ouest at Crescent
842-5794

Montreal's largest selection of tobacco products, from all over the world. In the same location since 1905.

Montreal Lightning Rods
7950 Bombardier
Anjou
352-5740

Over 100 different types of weather vanes, starting from about $50.

L'Objet Voyage
1616 Ste-Catherine ouest at Guy
989-2964
A handy store for travel books, maps, electrical current converters and so on.

La Maison des Vins
505 President-Kennedy near Aylmer
873-2274
Operated by the provincial liquor board, this store has one of Montreal's best selections of fine and vintage wines.

Ma Maison
1170 Place du Frère André near René-Lévesque ouest
875-0511
One of Montreal's better kitchen-goods stores. Lots of cleverly designed and colour-coordinated tableware and kitchen utensils.

SPORTS EQUIPMENT

For bicycle rentals, see Sports/Recreation (Cycling).

Boutique Souvenirs des Canadiens
Complexe Desjardins
Ste-Catherine ouest at Jeanne-Mance
843-9071
Hockey paraphernalia for die-hard fans of Montreal's beloved Habs.

Le Baron
8601 St-Laurent near Bellarmin
381-4231
Discount hunting, fishing and camping supplies.

Murray & Co.
1200 Peel at Ste-Catherine ouest
861-9636
One of Montreal's largest and best-known sporting goods shops. In business since 1923.

Oberson
1202 Ste-Catherine ouest at Montcalm
874-1824
Ski and sailboard specialists. Part of a province-wide chain,

Olde English Dart Supplies
1290 Notre-Dame near de la Montagne
Lachine
637-6111
Quality darts and dartboards, including Harrows and Falcon brands.

Siren Ski Shop
6131 Sherbrooke ouest near Beaconsfield
482-2734
Cross-country and roller-ski sales, rentals and repairs. Also a good selection of ski wear.

Ski Dump (Poubelle)
8366 St-Laurent near Guizot
384-1315
New ski clothing and new (surplus) and used skis and skates. Rentals and car racks also available.

WITH THE KIDS

KIDS AND ANIMALS

Ferme expérimentale du MacDonald College/ MacDonald College Farm
Autoroute 40, exit 41
398-7701
Yes, Old MacDonald had a farm—and it's in Montreal. This experimental farm has delighted little visitors for generations. You'll see dairy cows, piglets, lambs, ducks, goats and rabbits. Be sure not to miss the afternoon milking of the cows at 3:30. Open daily 2-5. Free

Centre de rapaces du MacDonald College/Raptor Centre
211-111 Lakeshore
Ste-Anne-de-Bellevue
398-7932
This research centre for birds of prey is affiliated with McGill University and adjoins the MacDonald College Farm. Eagles, falcons and even vultures can be seen at close range. Open mid-June to Labour Day 1-4. Free.

Écuries du Service de police de la CUM/Montreal Police Stables
Parc Mont-Royal
1515 Voie Camillien-Houde
An opportunity to observe police horses while they are groomed and fed. The stablehands are usually very friendly and happy to answer questions. Open daily 9-5. Free.

Hippodrome Blue Bonnets
7440 Decarie near Jean-Talon
739-2741
Children aren't permitted to place bets, but they are bound to cheer for their favourite standardbreds. Serious young riders will also enjoy the world-class equestrian events occasionally

hosted here. Admission is free for children under 16 when accompanied by an adult.

KIDS AND NATURE

Parc Mont-Royal
An excellent venue for bird-watching and general nature study. An interpretive guide is available at the Grand Chalet for $1. See Parks/Gardens.

Summit Park
Bird-watching, woodlands and great views. See Hiking/Bird-watching in Sports/Recreation.

Morgan Arboretum
Autoroute 40 ouest
398-7812
Over a thousand species of trees on 225 ha (556 acres). Can be combined with visits to the Raptor Centre and MacDonald College Farm. Open daily 9-5. Admission $2.

Insectarium
Montreal Botanical Garden
4101 Sherbrooke est at Pie IX
872-1400
Most children are fascinated by creepy-crawlers. Moreover, they are bound to find it absolutely hilarious if you inadvertently shudder. See Parks/Gardens.

DAY TRIPS

Zoo de Granby
347 Bourget
Granby
Autoroute 10 est, exit 68 or 74, then follow signs
(514) 372-9113
Founded in 1953, Granby is Quebec's most important zoological garden, with over 200 species from five conti-

The Montreal Insectarium, a great place to learn to love bugs.

nents, including elephants, snow leopards, yaks and gnus, on its 30 ha (75 acres). The zookeepers give daily presentations, and there are a number of well-designed educational exhibits in addition to a petting zoo for small children. About an hour's drive from Montreal. Hours: May, June and Sept 10-5, July and Aug 10-7. Closed Oct to Apr. Admission: children up to 4 years $3, ages 5 to 17 $6, adults $12.

Laurentian Wonderland
Route 117
Ste-Adèle
(514) 229-3141
Billed as the Laurentians' largest park for children, this will be of most interest to children under 10, who will have the chance to meet such storybook characters as Robin Hood, Sleeping Beauty, the Seven Dwarfs and Little Red Riding Hood.

Parc Safari Africain
Autoroute 15 south to exit 6, then follow Route 202 west
Hemmingford, Quebec
(514) 454-3668
A drive-through simulation of a game reserve, complete with lions, monkeys and giraffes. The petting zoo, midway, swimming pool and elephant rides will add to the day's enjoyment. Open mid-May to Labour Day. Hours: May to mid-June, Mon to Fri 10-4, Sat and Sun 1-5; mid-June to Sept open daily 10-5. Admission: children up to 4 years $6, ages 5 to 12 $13, adults $17.

Centre Èducatif forestier du Bois-de-Belle Rivière
9009 Route 148
Near Mirabel
1-800-363-2589
The best time to visit this nature centre is during sugaring off. In early spring you can visit the two maple sugar cabins—one old, one modern—and learn all about the making of this

traditional sweet. The best part, of course, is tasting it. Phone ahead for times. Free.

Le Village québècois d'antan/Lower Canada Village
Autoroute 20, exit 181
RR3, Montplaisir
Drummondville
(819) 478-1441, (819) 478-1228
A reconstructed 19th-century village with buildings and artifacts collected from across Canada. As you wander through the homes, stores and farm buildings, period-costumed staff demonstrate how things were done in the old days and answer questions. A fascinating hands-on experience for children (and fun for parents who love real antiques). Open June 2 to Labour Day 10-5. Admission: children $4, family pass (two adults and two children) $18.

Le Musée Village de Seraphin
Autoroute des Laurentides, exit 72, or Route 117
Ste-Adèle
(514) 229-4777
Another recent reconstruction of a 19th-century village, on a more modest scale. While in Ste-Adèle, you might also want to take the kids to the Super Splash water slide.

Musée ferroviaire canadien/ Canadian Railway Museum
122A St-Pierre
St-Constant
(514) 632-2410
For kids of all ages who love trains. It's best to go on Sunday, when a train or tram is usually running. See also Museums.

La Ronde amusement park on Île Ste-Hélène. (City of Montreal)

Parc Aquatique Mont-St-Sauveur
Autoroute des Laurentides (15 nord), exit 58 or 60
(514) 871-0101

Leap into the wave pool, then splash your way down the various spiralling slides. The grande finale, billed as Canada's largest water slide, is a gas. The park also offers scenic views of the Laurentians. Once you've towelled off, head into the charming village of St-Sauveur to check out its many good restaurants and upscale boutiques. Open June 17 to Sept 4 until 7 PM (11 PM July and Aug). Admission: children aged four to 11 $12.

Super Splash
1791 Ste-Adèle
Ste-Adèle
Autoroute des Laurentides, exit 67
(514) 229-2909

During the summer months, the park features a wave pool and water slides. When temperatures drop, it adopts a winter theme more suited to the surrounding ski resorts. The ice slides here are lots of fun for kids and adult non-skiers. A summer trip can be combined with a visit to the Museum Village in Seraphin. The ice slides are open daily Dec 15 to (roughly) Apr, 9 AM-10 PM. The water slides are open daily June 24 to Labour Day 10-7. Admission: children under 12 $9.

See Out-of-Town Excursions for other ideas.

MUSEUMS

Many local museums organize special interpretive programs and tours for children throughout the year. Phone for information, or check the newspaper. Our personal favourites for children are the Château Ramezay, the David M. Stewart Museum, Dow Planetarium and the Montreal Museum of Fine Arts. See Museums/Art Galleries.

The Old Port, a great place for a family stroll.

ENTERTAINMENT

THEATRE AND CINEMA

Centre Saidye-Bronfman
5170 Côte-Ste-Catherine near Mountain Sights
739-7944

English-language productions for young children and teens. Phone for current information.

Théâtre le Biscuit
221 St-Paul est near Place Jacques-Cartier
845-7306

Let the kids loose at the Big Bean Toss at the Old Port.

This marionette theatre in Old Montreal produces children's plays, usually in French. Phone for information, or check the newspapers.

Cinéma ONF/National Film Board
200 René-Lévesque ouest near Jeanne-Mance
283-8229

Regular screenings of films from the NFB's vast collection provide excellent entertainment at little cost. Most films are suitable for family viewing, and many are in English. Phone ahead for schedule. Open daily except Mon until 8 PM. Admission is $2.

IMAX Theatre
Vieux-Port (immediately south of Place Jacques-Cartier)

496-4629
Spectacular films on a seven-storey-high screen. Suitable for family viewing. See Sightseeing (Attractions).

AMUSEMENT PARKS

La Ronde
Île Ste-Hélène
872-6222

An amusement park built for Expo '67, La Ronde continues to offer thrilling rides, games, a children's village and a petting zoo. The kids will beg to come back; unless you want to spend your whole vacation at La Ronde, save your visit here for the end of the trip. Also on site is the Aqua-Parc de la Ronde. Open weekends May and early June, daily mid-June to Labour Day, Sun to Thurs 11 AM-midnight, Fri and Sat 11 AM-1 AM. Admission costs vary. A day pass with rides for a family of four (without admission to the Aqua-Parc) costs about $45.

Festival du Vieux-Port
Vieux-Port (immediately south of Place Jacques-Cartier)
844-3301

Crafts and other activities are offered all summer long, usually at no charge. Phone for details.

PARKS AND PLAYGROUNDS

There are hundreds of small parks and playgrounds run by the city and surrounding municipalities. For descriptions of some of Montreal's major parks, see Parks/Gardens. If you are looking for a gorgeous, old-fashioned family park without any crowds or ice-cream stands, it's hard to beat Westmount Park, definitely our top choice for kids. Whichever park you choose, remember to keep an eye on your children.

LIBRARY PROGRAMS

Many public libraries offer free story-book readings in English. Most require no pre-registration. Phone for times.

Fraser-Hickson Free Library
4855 Kensington near Somerled
489-5301

Westmount Public Library
4754 Sherbrooke ouest near
Roslyn
935-8697

Montreal Children's Library
1200 Atwater below
René-Lévesque est
931-2304

Norman Berman Children's Library
5151 Côte-Ste-Catherine near
Westbury
345-2628

SPECIAL EVENTS

Many of Montreal's annual entertainment extravaganzas attract thousands of kids to special performances. The **Just for Laughs Festival** and the **Montreal International Jazz Festival** usually feature something for children. Celebrations such as **Chinese New Year** and **St. Jean Baptiste Day** occasion colourful parades through downtown streets. The **Benson & Hedges International Fireworks Competition**, held in May each year, is a real kid-pleaser. See Sightseeing (Calendar of Events).

SPORTS

SKATEBOARDING

Kids should definitely stick to quiet neighbourhood streets to do their stunts until the city completes its planned skateboard terrain at Jarry Park. In the meantime, there are two relatively safe places where keen boarders often gather to strut their stuff: behind the Olympia Pool in Longueuil and behind the Outremont Arena.

Piscine Olympia/Olympia Pool
670 Dorveau
Longueuil
646-8659

Arena Outremont
999 McEachran near Ducharme
495-6231

On guard at the Old Fort on Île Ste-Hélène. (City of Montreal)

TOBOGGANING AND ICE SLIDES

Some of the best tobogganing runs are in Mount Royal Park. Two ideal and very popular hills are by Beaver Lake and at the intersection of du Parc and Mont-Royal. George V Park in Westmount also draws local speed demons on Sunday afternoons. Ice slides are erected every winter at Place Jacques-Cartier and Angrignon Park. See Sports/Recreation.

SWIMMING

See Sports/Recreation.

RESTAURANTS

La Cage aux Sports
2250 Guy at Lincoln
931-8588
395 Lemoyne near St-Pierre
288-1115
8405 St-Laurent near Liege
382-2203

Lots of fun for kids who like sports. The walls of these restaurants are covered with an eclectic assortment of athletic paraphernalia. When the Guy St. location opened in 1986, the owners ran full-page ads in the daily newspapers offering free meals in exchange for used sporting goods. The decorating campaign was a wild success, and most of the 7,000 items received are on display—somewhere. The Lemoyne outlet is the most whimsical. The menu features barbecued chicken and ribs with fries and better-than-usual coleslaw. Children's menu available. Inexpensive. L Mon to Sat, D daily. Licensed. Major cards.

Barb-B-Barn
1201 Guy near René-Lévesque ouest
931-3811

The barnyard decor is appealing to young children, and the food won't cause any complaints. Barbecued chicken, ribs, French fries and coleslaw are dished out at high speed to the crammed tables. This place is always stampeded at lunchtime, so it's best to arrive early or late. Inexpensive. L and D daily. Licensed. Take-out. Major cards.

Encore Une Fois
351 Prince Albert near Sherbrooke ouest
488-3390

When we were young, this place was a greasy spoon frequented by factory workers from the huge Wonder (as in

Wonder Bread) bakery across the street. The bakery has long since been replaced by townhouses, and the corner hangout correspondingly upgraded to a trendy neighbourhood eatery. The old soft-drink signs and coolers now look pleasantly retro alongside new lace café curtains. Comforting, homemade fare at reasonable prices. The chocolate mousse cake will encourage kids to finish their vegetables. Go early: seating is very limited, and no reservations are accepted. Inexpensive to moderate. Not licensed, but adults can bring their own wine. L and D daily, brunch on weekends. No cards.

La Binerie Mont-Royal
367 Mont-Royal est at St-Denis
285-9078

The musical fruit has been the house specialty for more than 50 years at this Montreal institution—a real live greasy spoon. The menu lists typically working-class dishes like pork and beans, *tortière* (spiced pork pie) and *cretons* (spiced lard) on toast. Perfect for kids who rave about the food at summer camps and boarding schools. Inexpensive. Open Mon to Fri for B, L and D; Sat for B and L. Not licensed. No cards.

Pizzafiore
1624 Lincoln near Guy
937-7474
3518 Lacombe near Gatineau
735-1556
3467 du Parc near Sherbrooke ouest
499-9964

Some of the best pizza and calzone in the city—homemade pizza dough and sauces make all the difference. Customers are encouraged to watch orders being prepared and slipped into the wood-burning brick ovens. Special pizzas from the 22 listed include the Four Seasons with four topping sections,

and the Pizzafiore "pizzalad" (an unusual pizza-salad combo). Inexpensive to moderate. L and D daily. Fully licensed. Major cards.

Gérard Van Houtte
1042 Laurier ouest near Durocher
274-5601

This well-known coffee-shop chain, with numerous locations throughout the city, will entice you with buttery croissants, light meals, refreshing juices and huge, steaming bowls of hot chocolate in the European style. A terrific place to take kids to warm up in winter. Parents will also appreciate the superb selection of coffees. The Laurier outlet (the original shop) has the best gourmet decor and is close to some of the better Outremont stores. Inexpensive to moderate.

SHOPPING

CLOTHING

Boutique Les Gamineries
1458 Sherbrooke ouest at Mackay
834-4614

Gorgeous layette items and every thing from sleepers to snowsuits for children's sizes 1-16. Mostly excellent quality imports. *The* store for indulgent grandparents. Expensive.

Jeunes d'ici
Plaza Alexis Nihon
1500 Atwater at Ste-Catherine ouest
933-6504

One-stop shopping for all your baby's needs. Everything from nursery furniture to toddlers' clothing and toys is available through this small chain. Many fine imports. Moderate to expensive. Three other locations on Laurier.

Pom' Canelle
4860 Sherbrooke ouest at Victoria
Westmount
483-1787
The store's name means Candy Apple and the clothes are definitely sweet. Adorable party dresses, baby clothes and excellent quality garments for small boys (free of all those annoying sports logos). Expensive.

Lapin Collection
400 Laurier ouest at Hutchison
271-5512
Fun knits for kids in bright colours at moderate prices, all designed and manufactured under the store's own label. Moderately priced.

Noisette et Chocolat
316 Duluth near St-Denis
844-0394
Kids' clothes with pizazz! Finally, clothes your children will be eager to try on. Mostly knits and natural fabrics in bright colours and prints, all designed under the boutique's own label. A good spot to buy unique made-in-Montreal gifts for children up to six years. Inexpensive to moderate.

Ogilvy
1307 Ste-Catherine ouest at de la Montagne
849-8011
The children's department of this venerable Montreal institution offers many exquisite clothes for babies and children, including adorable smocked party dresses by Canada's Elen Henderson. Many meticulously sewn imports, especially from France and Italy where children's attire is taken very seriously. Ask for their distinctive gift wrapping. Expensive.

Roots
1223 Ste-Catherine ouest at Drummond
845-7559
Rockland Centre
2305 Rockland at l'Acadie
737-2211
Child-size versions of Roots' adult preppie lines, including their well-known logo T-shirts, button-down Oxford-cloth shirts, shoes and even leather jackets. There are also logo sleepers and sweatsuits for trendy babies. Not all locations carry children's wear, so phone ahead to check.

Piétine Chaussures
111 Querbes at Laurier ouest
Outremont
277-9838
Everything about this shop is delightful, including the business card in the shape of a footprint. Tiny hiking boots, sneakers, sandals and party shoes for well-heeled babies and youngsters. Mostly French and Italian imports. Expensive.

TOYS

Le Cerf-Volant
30 St-Paul est at St-Laurent
861-0177
The place to go for kites, balloons and flying toys. More than 30 types of kites are for sale, some made on the premises. Kits and supplies for hobbyists are also available.

Boutique Gabriel Filon Inc.
1127 Laurier ouest near de L'Epée
274-0697
This well-stocked emporium advertises that it provides "toys and games for children of 0 to 77 years." Take the grandparents and buy them something fun!

BOOKS

Livres Babar
Suite 6
46 Ste-Anne at Bord du Lac
Pointe Claire
694-0380

A little out of the way if you are downtown, but definitely worth the trip if you are choosy about what your kids do and read. If only every neighbourhood had a children's store like this! Extensive book collection, story cassettes, children's music and educational toys. If you go on a Saturday, you can attend one of the weekly storybook readings (English at 11 AM, French 11:30 AM).

Alibi
5962 Monkland at Hampton
481-6287

Much smaller than Babar, this store welcomes weary young browsers with wee tables and chairs. The selection is quite good.

Tintin
4419 St-Denis near Mont-Royal est
843-9852

Billions of blistering barnacles! Tintin-o-maniacs would gladly voyage to the moon to find this Hergé-inspired haven. You'll discover the beloved Belgian cartoon character Tintin, his fluffy mutt Snowy, the irascible Captain Haddock and all the other marvellous characters. The complete collection of Hergé's books as well as Tintin pens, erasers, watches and even puppets. Moderate to expensive.

USEFUL INFORMATION FOR PARENTS

See also the Essential Information chapter.

BABYSITTING/DAYCARE

You can never be too careful when selecting a sitter for your children. If you are staying in a major hotel, you can entrust the making of arrangements to the concierge. If you are planning an extended stay in Montreal, you may wish to consider a day-care centre that provides short-term or emergency care (note that most centres operate exclusively in French). A list of licensed centres can be obtained from the following regulatory bureau:

Office des Service de garde à l'enfance
100 Sherbrooke est near Colonial
873-2323

The bureau publishes the guide "Who cares for our children?" which is also available at most Montreal libraries. Keep in mind that the law requires you to do a certain amount of paperwork before you can book your child into a day-care centre. Allow plenty of time.

OUT-OF-TOWN EXCURSIONS

THE EASTERN TOWNSHIPS

To the southeast of Montreal lies the picturesque Appalachian foothills region known as the Eastern Townships or L'Estrie. Unlike the Laurentians, which were first settled by the French, this area was originally an anglophone preserve, created for Loyalists to the British Crown fleeing persecution during the American Revolution. French settlement began almost a century later with the development of the railroad and the local forest industry.

Today the Townships are a crazy quilt of English and French communities. Well-serviced urban centres like Sherbrooke and Drummondville are predominantly francophone, while bucolic towns like Sutton and North Hatley are quintessentially English. As well, generations of summer cottagers from neighbouring New England have influenced the character of both tourist towns and the waterfronts of lakes Brome, Magog and Memphrémagog.

With their rolling green hills, covered bridges and quaint little villages, the Townships are often said to be Quebec's own version of New England. While the Anglo-American heritage is obvious in the Townships' many fine examples of colonial and Victorian architecture, the French community can be credited with such salutary contributions as the development of a renowned local gastronomy and the establishment of several successful vineyards.

The Townships offer skiing at four major resorts, water sports on lakes Brome, Massawippi, Magog and Memphrémagog, and many other outdoor activities. Popular attractions include Granby Zoo, the summer

theatre festival at North Hatley and the music festival at Orford. The slightly warmer climate of the Townships (compared to the Laurentians) favours the local maple trees, and there are a great many places to choose from in spring for "sugaring off." Touring the local wineries will be of interest to oenophiles, while the whole family can enjoy a drive or stroll through delightful villages like Sutton and Ayer's Cliff.

To get to the Townships from Montreal, cross the Champlain Bridge, then follow Autoroute 10 est. The autoroute leads directly to the major centres. For a more scenic drive, leave the autoroute at exit 37 and follow Route 112. If you don't have a car, don't worry—good bus service is available. There is no longer any passenger rail service to the region.

We've focused on the areas of the Townships closest to Montreal, since these are most easily accessible for day trips and many of the major attractions are found here. For very detailed information on the Townships, be sure to pick up the excellent free government tourist guide available at Infotourist offices in Montreal or from the Association touristique de l'Estrie (ATE) at 25 Bocage, Sherbrooke J1L 2J4. The guide can also be picked up on Autoroute 10 at the Maison de Tourisme de l'Estrie at exit 68. The tourism booth is open daily 9-8 June to Sept, 8:30-4:30 Oct to May.

WHERE TO GO

As you enter the Townships, watch for the following cities and towns.

Granby (pop. 38,508)

Magnificent Loyalist-style houses, annual gastronomic and song festivals, the Granby Zoo and nearby Yamaska Park with its excellent recreational

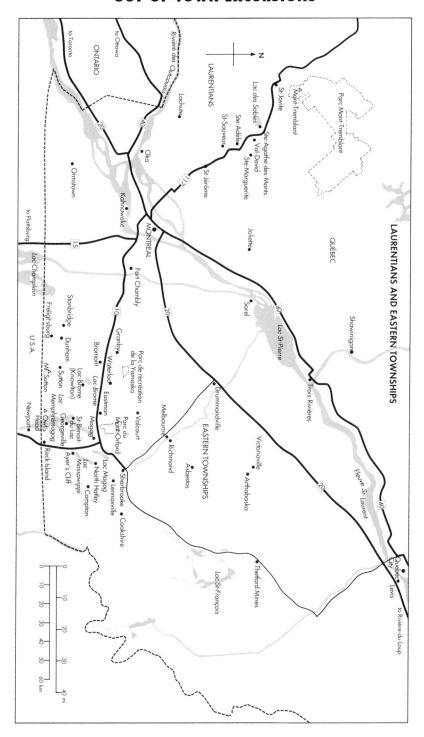

LAURENTIANS AND EASTERN TOWNSHIPS

facilities (including the area's longest beach).

Dunham (pop. 3108)
Gorgeous century houses along the main street. Notable mostly for its nearby vineyards.

Bromont (pop. 2838)
Home to a major tourist resort of the same name that features water slides and skiing. Bromont was the Canadian site for the 1986 World Cup skiing competition. Also here: golf, a recognized spa, a huge flea market and the Olympic Equestian Centre (where the Bromont International is held each June). Tours of the nearby Hyundai auto works also available to small groups.

Lac-Brome (Knowlton)
(pop. 4466)
Founded in 1971, Lac-Brome is an amalgamation of seven communities, including the delightful village of Knowlton with its many fine century houses. Also here: downhill skiing on Mount Glen, ice fishing on Lac Brome, the Brome County Museum.

Sutton (pop. 1602)
A mountain resort town with exceptional alpine slopes, golfing, cross-country skiing and organized bicycle tours. Sutton is home to Quebec's only communications museum.

Ayer's Cliff (pop. 799)
A quaint village on the shore of Lac Massiwippi, with the best public access to the lake. The Victorian architecture here is beautifully illuminated at Christmastime. Ayer's Cliff is also the site of one of Quebec's last remaining gazebo-style bandstands.

Asbestos (pop. 6961)
Mostly of interest to geologists for the famous local mine (one of the world's top producers of the fibrous mineral) and the related museum. There is also

Skiing at Mont Sutton. (Denis Boulanger)

a summer food festival, golf and cross-country skiing.

Georgeville (pop. 812)

A beautiful 19th-century village on the shores of Lac Memphrémagog, this was one of the locations for the shooting of Denis Arcand's award-winning film *The Decline of the American Empire.*

Magog-Orford (pop. 13,530)

A very popular tourist destination featuring a local spa, alpine skiing at Mount Orford, ice fishing, snowmobiling, golf, horseback riding and cruises and water sports on Lac Memphrémagog. The Orford Arts Centre offers excellent popular and classical music concerts during the summer.

North Hatley (pop. 715)

The town prospered during Prohibition, when wealthy Americans opted to summer across the border where they could entertain in style. Some of their magnificent houses have been converted into hotels. Many artists and writers have taken up residence here. There are several commercial art galleries and good shopping. Summer English-language theatre at the Piggery Theatre. Try the locally made beer, on tap at Canada's first micro-brewery.

Sherbrooke (pop. 74,438)

A dynamic, well-serviced urban centre with a large university and museums of local history, natural science and fine art. Sherbrooke also offers skiing, numerous cultural events and an annual international water-skiing competition on Lac des Nations. The city has many beautiful buildings, particularly the 19th-century houses of the Old North Ward.

OUTDOOR ACTIVITIES

ALPINE SKIING

There are several good small ski centres in the townships, but the four major ski resorts are Bromont, Orford, Owl's Head and Sutton. Known collectively as Ski East, the resorts offer an interchangeable ticket for a set fee. The pass allows you access to 130 km (80 mi.) of runs with Quebec's highest average vertical drop. For rates and further information, call Ski East at (819) 564-8989.

Station de Ski Bromont
150 Champlain
Bromont
(514) 534-2200 (in Que. and outside Canada), 1-800-363-8920 (elsewhere in Canada)

Mont Sutton
Chemin Maple
Sutton
(514) 538-2339, 866-5156 (in Montreal)

Mont Orford
Parc de récréation du Mont-Orford
(819) 843-6548, 878-1411 (in Montreal)

Ski Owl's Head
Chemin de la Station
Mansonville
(514) 878-1453

BIRD-WATCHING

For tips on local vantage points, contact one of the following groups:

Société ornithologique de L'Estrie
C.P. 2363, Succ. Jacques-Cartier
Sherbrooke J1J 3Y3
(819) 563-6603

L'Île du Marais
C.P. 21
Kateville JOB 1W0
(819) 565-1256

BOAT CRUISES
Phone for seasonal schedules and rates
for trips on the following lakes.

Lac Lister
(514) 849-2674

Lac Mégantic
(819) 583-2171

Lac Memphrémagog
(819) 843-8068

CROSS-COUNTRY SKIING
In all, there are more than 900 km (560
mi.) of trails at 20 centres, including
the Yamaska and Mont-Orford recreation parks. Cross-country and tele-
mark enthusiasts will also enjoy
Skiwippi. Three choice country inns in
the Lac Massawippi region offer this
European-style holiday package,
which enables guests to ski from inn to
inn during the day while their luggage
and car are transported for them. For
information on Skiwippi, call one of
the participating inns:

Le Manoir Hovey
Chemin Hovey
North Hatley
(819) 842-2421

Auberge Hatley Inn
Route Magog
North Hatley
(819) 842-2451

Ripplecove Inn
700 Ripplecove
Ayer's Cliff
(819) 838-4296

CYCLING
Bicycle rentals are available in most of
the major tourist towns and outdoor
recreation centres.

Vélotour de l'Estrie
Sutton
(514) 538-2361
Organizes two- to three-day excursions.

Cyclo-guide de l'Estrie
(514) 252-3152
Phone for free cycling information.

HIKING
Les Sentiers de l'Estrie
C.P. 93
Sherbrooke J1H 5H5
(819) 563-6200
The Eastern Townships are a hiker's
paradise. Write or call this organization for information. Be sure to ask for
the useful trail guide called "Topo-
guide des Sentiers de l'Estrie."
    For more information on hiking in
the townships, call the Fédération
Québécoise de la Marche at 252-3157.

HORSEBACK RIDING AND
SLEIGH RIDES
Centre Équestre Omerville
639 St-Michel
Frelighsburg
(819) 843-4559
Summer and winter horseback riding,
including lessons and short excursions.
Sleigh rides during the winter. Call for
rates.

ICE-FISHING
A fishing permit is required (see
Sports/Recreation under Fishing).
Tackle, bait and cabin rentals available
at the following locations:

The sharply peaked roofs characteristic of the Townships help shed snow. (Jurgen Vogt)

Domaine des Érables
688 Bondville
Lac-Brome
(514) 243-0618

Domaine Martin (Lac Magog)
Route 216
Katevale
(819) 843-7435

Village de Pêche sur glace du lac Memphrémagog
Route 112 (Rue Principale)
Magog
(819) 843-8550

SCUBA DIVING
Lussier Marine
Magog
(514) 378-7927 (Granby office)

Plongée Jonas
Magog
(819) 847-1369

Centre de Plongée Memphré
Georgeville
(514) 594-5866, (819) 564-7980

SNOWMOBILING

Joseph-Armand Bombardier, inventor of the snowmobile, was born in the Eastern Townships in the small town of Valcourt (which now calls itself the Snowmobile Capital of the World). Two annual international competitions are held here in Jan and Feb on nearby trails. For complete information on snowmobiling in the Townships and a free *motoneige* guide, call the ATE in Sherbrooke at (819) 565-5469.

Note: Quebec law requires that all snowmobile trail users hold a special membership card ($60) or pass ($25). For more information, call the Fédération des Clubs de Motoneige du Québec at (514) 252-3076.

SNOWSHOEING

There are trails and snowshoe rentals at several ski centres and parks. Two popular places:

Parc de récréation du Mont-Orford
Acceuil le Cerisier (819) 843-9855

Parc de récréation de la Yamaska
8th Rang est near Granby
(514) 372-3202

WATER SPORTS

You don't have to stay at a resort or hotel to enjoy access to the Townships' many lakes. Canoeing, windsurfing, sailing, swimming, pedal-boats and fishing are all available on a daily basis at Yamaska and Mount Orford parks.

Parc de récréation de la Yamaska
(514) 373-3204

Parc de récréation du Mont-Orford
(819) 843-6233

OTHER ATTRACTIONS

ARCHITECTURE IN THE TOWNSHIPS

The Townships have many fine examples of colonial/Loyalist architecture, which was very popular between 1810 and 1930. A gabled roof with a small, round *oeil-de-boeuf* window is its most salient feature. The Victorian era ushered in a whimsical variety of multi-storied, romantic buildings evocative of medieval castles, Italian villas and Napoleonic châteaux. Outstanding houses of both periods can be admired in Sherbrooke's Old North Ward and in the towns of Cowansville, Coaticook, Danville, Lac-Brome, Lennoxville and Stanstead.

One of the region's remaining covered bridges. (Jurgen Vogt)

COVERED BRIDGES

A common sight in neighbouring New Hampshire, covered bridges can also be spotted in the townships. One of the oldest bridges, dating from 1837, is at Cookshire.

MUSEUMS

Musée de Missisquoi
Rue Principale
Stanbridge est
(514) 248-3153
More than 1200 articles of Canadiana housed in three rural buildings. Open daily late May to mid-Oct 10-5. Admission is $2.

Musée de la Société d'histoire du comté
Route 243
Melbourne
(819) 826-5879
A restored century-old farmhouse that highlights the daily life of the region's early settlers. Open June to Oct, Sun 2-5 (and other days in July and Aug). Call for precise times. Admission is $1.50.

Lieu historique national Louis St-Laurent
6 Principale sud
Compton
(819) 835-5448
A museum devoted to the life and times of one of Canada's best-known prime ministers (St. Laurent was born in Compton). Phone for times. Free admission.

Musée Héritage-Sutton
30A Principale sud
Sutton
(514) 538-2544
A communications museum in an old Sutton house. Open May to Sept Wed to Sun 10-5. Admission is $1.50.

Interesting Sights in L'Estrie

1. At **Haskell Opera House** in the border town of Rock Island, the audience is seated in the United States, and the stage is in Canada.
2. **Ayer's Cliff** gazebo-style bandstand.
3. **Round barns** can be spotted in Barnston, Ways Mills, Mansonville, West Brome and St-Jacques-le-Majeur. One of Canada's **longest barns** is on Morgan St. in Coaticook.
4. Two of Quebec's oldest **covered bridges** are the Cookshire (1837) and the St. Armand (1845).

Musée des sciences naturelles de Séminare de Sherbrooke
195 Morquette
Sherbrooke
(819) 563-2050
The seminary's museum focuses on ethnology, ornithology and fine arts. Open year-round, Tues, Wed, Thurs and Sun 12:30-4:30. Admission is $1.

Domaine Howard
1300 Portland
Sherbrooke
This museum, housed in the former estate of Senator Charles Howard, offers guided tours of its own local history displays and heritage tours of the city itself. Open year-round. Hours: June to Sept, weekdays 9-noon and 1-5, weekends 1-5; Oct to June, weekdays only 9-noon and 1-5.

Musée québécois de la chasse
45 de l'Horizon
Waterloo
(514) 539-0501
A hunting museum with an interesting antique gun collection and lots of stuffed animals and birds. Open May to Sept 10-5. Admission is $2.50.

Musée J.-A. Bombardier
1000 J.-A. Bombardier
Valcourt
(514) 532-2258
The museum is dedicated to the history of snowmobiling and highlights the life of its Valcourt-born inventor. Tours of the local Bombardier plant are also available to groups. Phone for times.

Mineralogical and Mining History Museum
104 Letendre
Asbestos
Local history, mineral displays and a film on asbestos production. Open

June 25 to Labour Day 10-5 (other times upon request). Admission is free.

SPAS
These health centres offer various combinations of hydrotherapy, massage, exercise, hiking and special diets. Phone for more information.

SpaConcept Bromont
Le Château Bromont
90 Stanstead
Bromont
(514) 534-2717

Clinicor, Domaine St-Laurent
40 Cochrane
Compton
(819) 835-5464

Centre de Santé d'Eastman
Chemin des Diligences
Eastman
(514) 297-3009

Calendar of Events

Contact the ATE in Sherbrooke ([819] 565-5469) for complete information.

Jan: Snowmobile Festival (Thetford Mines).

Feb: International Snowmobile Festival (Valcourt).

Mar: Sugaring-off at the maple syrup shacks.

May: Festival des harmonies brass band festival (Sherbrooke). Victorian Days Festival (Lac-Brome).

June-Aug: Festival Orford, popular and classical music concerts (Orford and Sherbrooke).

July: Granby National antique car contest and other events (Granby).

Aug: Ayer's Cliff County Fair.

Sept-Oct: Panoramaduodlacôte autumn colour festival (Sutton). Festival de la chanson (song festival) and Festival gastronomique (food festival) (Granby).

Institut Andréanne
2283 Chemin du Parc
Magog-Orford
(819) 843-4615

Centre Paulette Hiriart
Rue McCullough
Sutton
(514) 538-2903

SUGAR SHACKS

When the sap begins to flow in March, the *érablières* open for business. You can see how maple sugar is made and enjoy samples of this sticky sweet. Two popular choices are listed here, but there are several others.

Cabane à sucre Mégantic
10ᵉ Rang
Lac-Mégantic
(819) 583-1760

Ski Montjoye
Route 108
North Hatley
(819) 842-2411

THEATRES

There are 18 active theatres during the summer. At least three present works in English. We've also listed two outstanding French theatres.

Piggery Theatre (English)
Route 108
North Hatley
(819) 842-2431
The theatre also puts on a country supper for an additional $12.

Centennial Theatre (English)
Bishop's University
Lennoxville
(819) 822-9692, 822-9600

Theatre Lac-Brome (English)
Knowlton, Lac-Brome
(514) 243-0361

Théâtre de Marjolaine (French)
Chemin du Théâtre
Eastman
(514) 297-2860

Le Vieux Clocher (French)
64 Merry nord
Magog
(819) 847-0470

VINEYARDS

Wine production is a fairly recent development in the Townships, but four vineyards are successfully producing both red and white varietals under their own labels. All welcome visitors, but be sure to write or call ahead.

Domaine des Côtes d'Ardoise
889 Route 202
Dunham
(514) 295-2020

Vignoble de l'Orpailleur
1086 Route 202
Dunham
(514) 295-2763

Vignoble les Arpents de Neige
4042 Principale
Dunham
(514) 295-3383

Vignoble le Cep d'argent
1257 de la Rivière
Magog
(819) 864-4441

THE LAURENTIANS

In geological terms, the Laurentian Mountains are part of the Canadian Shield, an area of eroded Precambrian rock (the oldest rock on the continent). Mount Tremblant at 960 m (3150 feet) is the highest peak. The mountains are dotted with hundreds of small lakes and traversed by numerous rivers and streams. The vast forests combine coniferous and deciduous growth and provide a largely unspoiled habitat for an abundance of wildlife, including beaver, porcupine, deer and moose. This naturally perfect outdoor playground is easily accessible from Montreal and has become an internationally acclaimed tourist destination.

Most visitors come to ski. The resort towns are charming, and the runs are the most challenging east of Alberta. Deciding where to spend the day may be your most difficult task: the Laurentians offer the greatest concentration of alpine ski centres in North America. Cross-country trails are also excellent. Non-skiers can choose from a variety of other popular winter activities.

There are many other seasonal delights. Spring is ideal for river rafting, and is *le temps des sucres*, when the maple sap begins to flow. Traditional sugar shacks open their doors so that visitors can observe maple syrup production firsthand and sample the result. Tourism tends to slow down during the annual blackfly invasion in early June. The tiny pests are essentially harmless but can give you some rather itchy bites. Happily, they tend to steer clear of the developed town sites. Hiking, swimming, fishing and a full range of recreational activities are available during summer months, while Sept and Oct are especially memorable for their blaze of autumn colour.

Whatever season you choose, you can always be sure of spectacular scenery and a warm welcome. Museums and other local attractions can add interest to your trip, but a simple stroll through one of the resort towns can be an equally entertaining way to spend an afternoon. You will find handicraft shops, art galleries, cafés and clothing stores in every style and price range. The extensive selection of restaurants may surprise you. Some of Canada's best restaurants are tucked away in this rolling countryside no secret to many regular patrons, who think nothing of driving up from the city.

Access to the Laurentians from Montreal couldn't be easier. There are two routes to choose from. The modern Autoroute des Laurentides, No. 15, is the fastest. Route 117, the old highway, is a more time-consuming but prettier drive that takes you through the main (*principale*) street of several interesting towns along the way. Traffic jams on both highways most often occur on Friday nights northbound and Sunday nights southbound. With clear sailing at other times, count on 45 minutes to St. Sauveur and $1^{1}/_{2}$ to 2 hours to Mount Tremblant via the autoroute.

For non-drivers, buses depart Montreal for the Laurentians almost every hour from the Terminus Voyageur. (Schedules vary depending on the time of year.) Unless you're up for leisurely sightseeing, make sure that you board an express bus. Passenger train service, sadly, is a thing of the past.

Excellent free tourist information on the Laurentians can be obtained at the Montreal Infotourist offices (see Essential Information). There is also a Laurentian Tourist Information centre just off the autoroute; take exit 39 to Highway 58 and follow the signs.

WHERE TO GO

You will pass lots of small towns along the autoroute. Some of the most attractive:

St-Sauveur-des-Monts

(pop. 4110)
Excellent downhill skiing, boutiques, galleries, summer theatre, an aqua park, restaurants, resorts and nightlife. A most attractive, stylish town nestled between Mont-St-Sauveur and Mont-Habitant—Quebec's version of Banff.

Ste-Adèle (pop. 7000)

A larger, well-serviced town with more excellent ski slopes, restaurants, shops, local artisans and an active nightlife scene. Other attractions include the curious Village du Seraphin, the Pays des Merveilles and the Supersplash water slide. Chantecler, a well-known four-season luxury resort, is nearby.

Ste-Marguerite (pop. 1870)

The area around this town has some of the best-rated cross-country ski trails in Quebec. L'Esterel, a highly regarded resort with excellent sport and dining facilities, is a 15-minute drive away.

Val David (pop. 2500)

More great skiing and, believe it or not, a Santa's Village during the summer. Val David is home to La Sapinière, a resort known for its absolutely superb French cuisine.

Ste-Agathe-des-Monts

(pop. 8500)
The largest of the Laurentian towns, offering great skiing in winter and water sports and boat cruises on Lac des Sables during the summer.

St-Jovite (pop. 3690)

St. Jovite is on the edge of Mount

Tremblant Park, a provincial wildlife sanctuary and camping facility.
Nearby is popular Gray Rocks, the oldest ski resort in the Laurentians. Gray Rocks has 18 ski runs, most of which overlook Lac Ouimet. It's also known for its summer tennis facilities, including children's tennis camps. Nearby Station de Ski Mont-Tremblant, the largest ski resort in the Laurentians, has the longest vertical drop in the area. Its many challenging runs make it a favourite with serious skiers.

OUTDOOR ACTIVITIES

CROSS-COUNTRY SKIING

For complete information, contact the ATL at (514) 436-8532. A few recommended sites:

Centre de Ski de fond Ste-Agathe
Chemin du Tour-du-Lac
Ste-Agathe-des-Monts
(819) 326-5577

Winter's icy signature in rural Quebec.
(Jurgen Vogt)

Centre de Ski de fond Morin-Heights
612 du Village
Morin Heights
(514) 226-2417

Centre de Ski de fond Mont-Tremblant/St-Jovite
305 Brébeuf
St-Jovite
(819) 425-2434, 425-8997

Parc Regional de la Rivière-du-Nord
1051 International
St-Jerome
(514) 431-1676

DOGSLEDDING
L'Hotel Estérel
Chemin Fridolin-Simard
Ville d'Estérel
(514) 228-2571
Cost: $20 per person for a 20-minute excursion.

GOLF
There are 19 public golf courses in the Laurentian region. The following two will rent equipment and, unlike most clubs, they offer unrestricted access on weekends and holidays.

Club de golf Chantecler Ste-Adèle Ltée
2520 du Golf
Ste-Adèle
(514) 229-3742 (in Que.),
1-800-363-2587 (elsewhere in Canada)

Club de golf Bel-Air
7410 Industriel
Mirabel (Ste-Scholastique)
(514) 258-4444

HORSEBACK RIDING
Centre d'équitation Ste-Marguerite
75 Montée Gragnon
Ste-Marguerite-du-Lac-Masson
(514) 228-4141
This stable has it all—year-round horseback riding with or without lessons and seasonal excursions in charming sleighs or *calèches*.

HUNTING AND FISHING
Permits are required. Write to Le Ministère de la Chasse et de la Pêche, C.P. 22,000, Quebec G1K 7X2, or call (819) 688-2283.
The following fish and game reserves are open to permit-holders in season.

Papineau-Labelle
(819) 771-4870

Rouge-Matawin
(819) 275-1811

Parc du Mont-Tremblant
(819) 688-2281
Fishing only.

There are also many other places to fish in the Ste-Agathe, St-Adolphe-d'Howard and Blainville areas.

MOUNTAIN-BIKING
The best place to go is Morin Heights. Call one of the following organizations. Rentals available.

Centre de Ski alpine Morin-Heights
Chemin Bennett
(514) 226-1333

Centre de Ski de fond Morin-Heights
612 du Village
(514) 226-2417

PUBLIC BEACHES

Here are two of the nicest. They are well-serviced with picnic tables, public washrooms and snack bars. There is a small admission charge of $1 to 3, plus parking. Open June to Sept.

Parc Paul-Sauvé
Lac des Deux Montagnes
Oka
(514) 479-8337

Plage Major
Chemin du Tour-du-Lac
Lac des Sables
Ste-Agathe-des-Monts

RAFTING

On the Rouge River, Apr to Oct. Life jackets provided, but dress warmly and take a change of clothes. For details, call:

Aventures en eau vive
(819) 242-6084 (in Que.),
1-800-567-6881 (elsewhere in Canada)

Nouveau Monde
(514) 733-7166

SKIING

The following are some of the Laurentians' major ski centres. All offer rentals. Day passes range from $18 to $25 on weekends. For more complete information, contact the Association touristique des Laurentides (ATL) at (514) 436-8532.

A retired calèche. (Jurgen Vogt)

Station de Ski Gray Rocks
Route 327 at Lac Ouimet
Mont-Tremblant
(819) 425-2772 (in Que.),
1-800-567-6767 (elsewhere in
Canada)

Station de Ski Mont-Tremblant
Chemin de Lac-Tremblant
Mont-Tremblant
(819) 425-8711 (in Que.),
1-800-567-6761 (elsewhere in
Canada)

Station de Ski Morin Heights
Chemin Bonnett
Morin Heights
(514) 226-1333 (in Que.),
1-800-363-2527 (elsewhere in
Canada)

Station de Ski Mont-Christie
Côte St-Gabriel est
St-Sauveur-des-Monts
(514) 226-2412

Station de Ski Mont-Habitant
12 des Skiers
St-Sauveur-des-Monts
(514) 227-2637, 393-1821

Station de Ski Mont-St-Sauveur
350 St-Denis
St-Sauveur-des-Monts
(514) 227-4671, 871-0101

Station de Ski le Chantecler
Chemin Chantecler
Ste-Adèle
(514) 229-3555 (in Que.),
1-800-363-2420 (elsewhere in
Canada)

Station de Ski Mont-Alta
Route 117
Val David
(819) 322-3206

Station de Ski Vallée-Bleue
1418 Vallée-Bleue
Val David
(819) 322-3427

Station de Ski Belle-Neige
Route 117
Val Morin
(819) 322-3311, 430-8092

Station de Ski Mont-Sauvage
1167 2e (Deuxième) Avenue
Val Morin
(819) 322-2337

SNOWMOBILING

Rentals of snowmobiles and equipment are available at the following locations. Permits are required (see the Eastern Townships under Snowmobiling).

Hotel L'Estérel
Chemin Fridolin-Simard
Ville d'Estérel
(514) 866-3224, 228-2571

Location Page
1985 du Village
St-Adolphe-d'Howard
(819) 327-2433

WATER SLIDES

See With the Kids (Day Trips).

OTHER ATTRACTIONS

ART GALLERIES

There are a number of commercial art galleries in the Laurentians. Our favourite:

Galerie d'Art Michel Bigué
315 Principale
St-Sauveur-des-Monts
(514) 227-5409
The only gallery in the region that consistently carries works of quality by

Quebec and international artists. While owner Michel Bigué sells a great deal of historical Canadian art, he also consistently takes chances with new talent such as Catherine Henripin and Élène Gamache. Also some emphasis on up-and-coming young American artists.

FLEA MARKETS

Lachute Fairgrounds
Route 148, west of Lachute
Bric-a-brac and the occasional gem.

Also lots of brand-new clothes and household goods at amazingly cheap prices. Go very, very early for the best chance at antiques. Tues 6-4, unless rained out.

Terrain du ciné-parc
25ᵉ Avenue
St. Eustache
Absolutely huge, especially on weekends. If you find something you like, buy it before you get lost. Thurs and Fri 1-9, Sat and Sun 9-6.

Calendar of Events

Contact the ATL in St-Jérôme ([514] 436-8532) for complete information on annual festivals and other events in the Laurentians. Some highlights:

Jan: Traversée des Laurentides, 130-km cross-country skiing excursion.

Feb: Cross-country Skiing Marathon, from Lachute to Hull.

June: Festival mondial de la chanson de la vallée de St-Sauveur, 10-day international youth song festival. Canadian Race Car Championship (Mont-Tremblant).

July: Jim Russel Championship, Formula 2000 automobile race (Mont-Tremblant). Classique internationale de Blainville horse show (Blainville).

Aug: Laurentian Wine Festival, a celebration of wines and gourmet cuisine in some of the best restaurants of the region.

Sept: Symphony of colours (Mont-Tremblant), various fall-oriented activities in the village and at the Parc du Mont-Tremblant. Festival of colours (Mirabel, St-Adolphe-d'Howard, St-Sauveur-des-Monts, St- Faustin).

INDEX